OUTSIDER IN THE PROMISED LAND

Nissim Rejwan

OUTSIDER IN THE PROMISED LAND

An Iraqi Jew in Israel

UNIVERSITY OF TEXAS PRESS
Austin

Requests for permission to reproduce material from this
work should be sent to:
    Permissions
    University of Texas Press
    P.O. Box 7819
    Austin, TX 78713-7819
    www.utexas.edu/utpress/about/bpermission.html

⊗ The paper used in this book meets the minimum
requirements of ANSI/NISO Z39.48-1992 (R1997)
(Permanence of Paper).

LIBRARY OF CONGRESS
CATALOGING-IN-PUBLICATION DATA
Rejwan, Nissim.
Outsider in the promised land : an Iraqi Jew in Israel /
Nissim Rejwan. — 1st ed.
        p.   cm.
Includes index.

        ISBN: 0292722362.

1. Rejwan, Nissim.   2. Jews, Iraqi — Israel — Biography.
3. Journalists — Israel — Biography.   4. Israel — Social
conditions — 20th century.   5. Israel — Ethnic relations.
6. Israel — Intellecual life — 20th century.   I. Title.
DS113.8.I72R44   2006
956.94'0049240567092 — dc22

                                                    2005034308

A man lives not only his own personal life as an individual but also, consciously or unconsciously, the life of his epoch and his contemporaries.

THOMAS MANN

Contents

Author, August 1955.

Author, far right, *discussing* Al Yawm's *political line in Baqa al-Gharbiyya,* *1963.*

Author, second from left, *with Jacqueline Kahanoff,* second from right, *and* hosts in Acre, 1964.

Author with wife, Rachel, and their three sons: left to right, *Rony, Amir, and Elan, 1965.*

Author, third from right, *with reporters and hosts in Taiba, 1965.*

Left to right: *Elan, Amir, and Rony, 1966.*

OUTSIDER IN THE PROMISED LAND

Chapter 1 | ℱIRST IMPRESSIONS

ℐn an autobiographical fragment written in the early 1960s, Walter Zeev Laqueur, a Polish-born Israeli and formerly a *Jerusalem Post* contributing editor, writes of one autumn evening during an interval at a conference somewhere near Athens, when the conversation turned to the subject of "the need for roots." They were, Laqueur relates, eight around the table, and it emerged that none of them lived where he was born and that only one would be able to see again the parental home if he went back to his birthplace. In seven cases out of eight, the parental home — the house itself — was there no longer.

None of the eight, however, was physically or by law barred from going back to his birthplace had he wanted so to do — and I found myself wondering, on reading this, how these fellow emigrés would have felt had they lived with the knowledge that they were physically and permanently barred from visiting their hometowns, even if only for a brief look.

I am mentioning this because in recent years I have had reason to believe that one day I would be able to visit Baghdad, and possibly even to see some of my many non-Jewish friends of yore. As luck would have it, however, first came the long Iran-Iraq War, which lasted some eight years, then the war over Kuwait and, in its disastrous aftermath, the virtual third-worldization of Iraq.

I came to Israel together with my mother in February 1951. I was twenty-six. A twenty-year-old unmarried sister, who had arrived the previous year, was already at some kibbutz; my father had died four years earlier. We stayed for a few nights at the home of an aunt in Haifa. The husband said why, with the kind of experience you have and with your knowledge of English, you can easily find a job. He made me write four applications — to the oil refineries, the electric company, Discount Bank, and Bank Leumi. All four wrote back expressing an interest, and finally for some reason or other I chose Discount, was duly accepted, and started work immediately.

It was hell! All day long I dealt with checks signed illegibly, compared the signatures with the specimens on file at the bank, verified the account holder's balance and the identity of the person presenting the check, and ordered the cashier to pay. At the end of the day, after putting everything back in perfect order, I took the bus north to somewhere that looked like the middle of nowhere, somewhere not far from Afula, where, literally in the middle of a deserted grapefruit grove, the three of us were allotted a tent. This went on for two or three weeks until I decided I had had enough. One Friday, after asking to leave work early so I could reach Jerusalem at some reasonable hour — that was in the days when a trip from Haifa to Jerusalem took at least four hours — I took the bus to where Jacob, my friend from Baghdad, lived, miserably, at some ramshackle dorm in Musrara.

That was the last I was ever to see of the bank in Haifa; on Sunday I started the long procedure of enrolling at the Hebrew University (the whole of which, except for one largish lecture hall at the Ratisbonne compound, was housed in the Terra Sancta Building, where the excellent British Council Library was also to be found) and the even more complex procedure of finding a place in a *ma'bara* (transit camp) in Jerusalem. Finally we got a place in the Talpiot ma'bara, not a tent but a tin hut that was good for refrigeration in winter and baking in summer — almost.

At the university, on my friend Elie Kedourie's advice, I took courses in Islamic civilization and Arabic language and literature, and there were also quite a few other preliminary subjects grouped under the name *mekhinah* (preparatory year). By then I somehow managed to speak and hear Hebrew, and at the end of what must have been the second or third lecture in Islamic civilization, our teacher, the late professor Shmuel Dov Goitein, often let me accompany him to his home nearby, and we had a chat in his study — always in English.

One of the things Goitein told me was that, in case I didn't know, every one of the Iraqi students at the university was considered a communist. This being the case — and because I seemed to him so "different" (he also used the word "intelligent") — it would be sensible of me to change my family name. I don't think I responded to that, but I swear he made the suggestion. Be that as it may, he said I had better attend a Hebrew *ulpan* (Hebrew study center), and duly gave me a letter to the powers-that-be asking that I be admitted. That was the way it was with the Orientals (African and Asian Jews) — you had to be "intelligent," exceptional, and "clean," or whatever, to be taught the elements of the Hebrew language!

I enjoyed the ulpan because of the long-missed female company—mainly a number of "eligibles." Midway through the ulpan I managed to get a job at the *Jerusalem Post* as a proofreader. That was quite a break with tradition, letting a barbarian from Baghdad do proofreading for the great English-language paper, a job reserved exclusively for "Anglo-Saxons" (that was the appellation used at the paper at the time). After much agonizing, however, and a trial period, I was finally accepted. But I remained pretty hard to stomach, and the editor often referred to me as "that Egyptian Communist."

Shortly after providing conclusive proof that I could read and correct galley proofs, I approached the *Post*'s book-page editor Dr. Eugene Meyer—a gentle soul hailing from Czechoslovakia, diligent, meticulous, and highly well-organized—with the batch of cuttings of my book and movie reviews from the *Iraq Times,* which I had successfully "smuggled" via Elie in Oxford, since it was somewhat risky to send printed matter to Jews abroad. I left the bunch with him, and some time later he told me he found the stuff "interesting," especially a review article on the famed Egyptian writer Taha Hussein. I considered that an encouraging sign and decided to try my hand at writing for the book page. However I foolishly failed to take what later transpired as something of a hint—namely, that I had better concentrate on the things I was supposed to know about, such as Arab authors and Arabic literature.

This was made obvious to me following the publication of a long review I wrote of a book that dealt with cultural relations, or nonrelations, between Europe and the United States. It was the lead article in that Friday's book page. The following week, friends in the editorial department told me what had happened. Gershon Agron, founder and editor in chief, had remarked in an editorial meeting, "What business has Rejwan to write about America and Europe? He comes from Iraq, and he should write about the Arab world!"

Needless to say, I was not in the least amused. Not only did I know next to nothing about the Arab world, but I am never a guy to be pushed around. So what if Agron decided to confine me to my Arab ghetto? But then, what with the book-page editor gradually persuading me to review books on the Arab world and Islam and such—and especially after the Sinai war of 1956 made Israelis more aware of their surroundings and the need to communicate with their despised neighbors—I somehow found myself dragged into the Arab affairs field.

It was like this. As a reserve soldier—and once again because of where I hail from—I was mobilized during the war period as part of the intelligence branch, and after a week or so of doing nothing, I was "lent" to Israel Radio's Arabic service. It was terribly short of Arabic-literate journalists, and suddenly realized that Israel had Arabic-speaking neighbors who needed to be addressed in that language. To cut a long story short, I worked in the radio's news department, but after a few days the *Post*'s executive editor, Ted Lurie, who learned of my whereabouts, objected that it was irregular or illegal for the army just to donate me as a present to the radio, and that I had either to be demobbed or to actually serve in the army.

Well, Lurie had it his way, but, I no longer recall exactly how, he managed to maneuver me into accepting a job with the radio as news editor, provided the company agreed to my continuing to contribute — or starting to contribute — a weekly column and an occasional editorial for the paper. I should perhaps add that by that time I had moved to the editorial desk at the *Post,* but that there — though no one had any doubts about my being able to do the job — they thought I was "too slow" when the situations were hot and everyone was working against the deadline. I think that was why Lurie wanted to get rid of me as a regular employee but wanted so much to keep me as a slavelancer.

The 1951–1952 academic year went all to waste, since I had to cope with my studies as well as the following: being awakened in the very early hours of the morning by my neighbors in the maʿbara — manual laborers who had to report early to work; attending classes, which were scattered all over the day and early evening without any logic or consideration; reading, either in the British Council Library or at the YMCA reading room; having some terrible lunch at the students' *mensa* (dining hall) — and then either reporting to work at the *Post,* when I was doing the afternoon shift, or trying to rest or attending the few and far between classes that I had to attend.

Now, the afternoon shift ended on weekdays at perhaps seven or seven thirty in the evening, so I could be with one of my female friends and either go to the movies or to her room — and then finally come "home" and to bed. When I was doing the night shift I finished work always after one in the morning, sometimes two, and then waited for an editor friend who lived in Bakʿa to give me a lift to the maʿbara. His name was Jake Rykus, and he was doing this voluntarily, since the paper didn't provide transportation. Incidentally, it was a six-day workweek whether you were working afternoons or nights. Pure hell, it now sounds, and certainly no life fit for study.

That was the (1951–1952 academic) year that was! I spent nearly a year and a half in the ma'bara, at the end of which time I managed to rent a tiny room on the roof of an apartment building on Princess Mary Avenue. It was one of perhaps four or five rooms, each with a tiny kitchen, that were meant for the servants. Tiny but cozy—and mine anyway. All in all it was fun—so close to the *Post* and downtown. After my sister Simha married and moved to somewhere in the Sharon area, we managed to squeeze a bed in the kitchen for Mother, since there was no possibility whatsoever of crowding another bed in that room of mine.

Back to school. Living in such comparative luxury, I decided the time had come to enroll, this time choosing to study, believe it or not, medieval history and international relations. It went well with both, until I discovered that Latin—which went with medieval history—was not for me. Nor was the other subject much more appealing—I don't even remember what they taught us there. Medieval history, on the other hand, proved to be a fascinating subject—and topical into the bargain.

That year, Professor Yehoshua Prawer was giving a course on the Crusades, and his lectures very often contained hints, broad enough sometimes but never specific, of a possible analogy between the Crusaders and the Zionist colonizers. A number of students, who, by the way, were mostly rather older than they would be nowadays—no doubt as a result of the war and its accompanying difficulties—regularly pleaded for him to be more specific. But the professor never budged.

And so it came to pass that I stopped going to school. Not that I didn't learn anything; I learned a great deal. But this was due mainly to the fact that I took the so-called bibliographies, which was the name given by the teachers to the list of books they claimed to be "required reading," rather seriously. I read every one of the recommended books, of which I managed to purchase and keep quite a few, and from those books I learned about more and more related literature that I sought and read, taking notes and writing down some comments and so on.

However, because of my poor knowledge of Hebrew and also because I was naive enough to think that reading the recommended bibliographies (all in English) rendered the practice redundant, I didn't take notes during lectures, as all the other students were busy doing most of the time. (Some of them, I noticed with wonder, made carbon copies so that— as it transpired—they could give them to classmates who were unable to attend and who had asked them to do it for them.)

Though I don't think I sat for any of the end-of-year exams, by the end of the year I became convinced that to take those bibliographies seriously, as I did, was to court certain failure. It was then that I thought of coining a sort of dictum: In the university you have to choose between two alternatives: either learning or getting a degree. I am sure there is a great deal of exaggeration in this — also rationalization — but I began consoling myself with the thought that, after all, I had learned a lot and to hell with diplomas.

There is a kind of follow-up to all this — my university noneducation, I mean. Some thirteen or fourteen years later, at the ripe age of forty-two and out of a job, I enrolled as a first-year student at Tel Aviv University, taking this time around sociology and anthropology (I thought I would find the root causes of the problem then claiming my whole attention, i.e., the so-called communal or ethnic problem in Israel). This time, too — only much more so — I concentrated all my attention on the bibliographies and far beyond, and as a result I wrote quite a few articles on the subject and gave a few lectures. Later, during the miniwar I declared to right some of the wrongs I thought were being done to members of what came to be called the Second Israel, I think I made the best use of sociology and, especially, anthropology, of all the subjects I pretended to be learning during my fragmented university years.

As to academic degrees and such, in the case of my Tel Aviv University venture two factors made getting a degree impossible. In the first place, the sociology discipline included a course in statistics, which, as hard as I tried, I couldn't do, mainly because I didn't have the basic mathematical knowledge needed, either because I had not acquired it at school or because I had forgotten all about it.

The other factor was the Six-Day War of 1967, which broke out smack at the end of the academic year and just before the exams. Not only was I due to be mobilized by the army, but the war itself and the famous victory it brought to Israel depressed me to no end. Rather than wait for the defeated Arabs to telephone — as did General Moshe Dayan — I decided that the war had harmed the chances for peace.

PRODDINGS

Diary entries

25 April 1993

A few weeks ago I suddenly felt a need to recapitulate that distant chapter in my life. So I decided to organize a kind of get-together of people who had worked in the *Post* building during the years I toiled there, mostly as proofreader but also as frequent contributor to the book pages and finally making it briefly to the editorial desk. After quite some organizing we managed to get nine of them, whom we invited for lunch on Independence Day. Seven came with their wives, and two were no longer *with* wives, and, incredible as it may sound, we managed to seat them and feed them to satiation.

All in all it was fun, but the most curious thing was that everybody kept repeating how thoughtful it was of me to organise the meeting and what a wonderful, wonderful idea it all was. So Rachel kept wondering why, if the idea was so great, none of the participants had managed to air it, let alone actually organise the get-together.

And speaking of the *Post* these days, every time I open the paper and glance at the editorial page, I tell myself—and Rachel—I don't believe I go on writing for that paper. But then I recall the time when charges of "pro-Arab," "Leftist," and such were hurled at me by none other than the "old guard," itself now variously dubbed, ironically enough, pro-PLO, anti-Israel, and even anti-Jewish, and start thinking. Can it be that, now that the paper is finally and safely established as right-wing, pro-Likud, or whatever, the editor is no longer vulnerable and feels confident enough to have a pariah like myself participate? Or is it a question of "balance"? Or am I just being a good boy and refraining from mixing opinion with fact or writing "think pieces"?

The other day my good friend Helen made a query. Incredible as it may sound, the fact is that I have never even *thought* about the question she asked—relevant and fascinating as it is—namely, why in the world was I writing in English in Iraq. Come to think of it, in the normal course of events (as they say) I should've been writing in Arabic, since, unlike my very few friends—and I can think only of Elie and Jacob—I never had attended an English school; my English, in fact, was practically non-existent when I was all of sixteen years of age! (When I was 20 my Arabic teacher, Dawood el-Sayigh, a fellow Communist sympathizer who happened to be watching over us when we sat for the English exam, actually dictated to me the right answers and thus enabled me to pass . . .) Altogether the reason why I learned English enough to read it in the first place was sheer curiosity: I wanted to know more about what was going on in the world, then at war, and particularly what the Commies were saying about it. The first English periodicals I ever read were a weekly called *World News and Views* and the monthly *Labour Monthly*, both official, bona fide communist.

I was of course soon disenchanted, and my readings began to focus on literature and the like — not just literature but *avant-garde* literature — Eliot, Auden, Spender, Louis MacNeice and other contemporaries in poetry; and Kafka, Joyce, Thomas Mann, Virginia Woolf, and the more recent ones in prose. (I must have boasted to Helen more than once that I was the proud reviewer of Saul Bellow's first novel, *Dangling Man.*) And so on. So what was the question again? Who knows, maybe it had something to do with my being such an incurable snob . . .

16 June 1994

The publication recently of a fragment from my autobiographical work-in-progress ("Bookshop Days," *The Literary Review,* Winter 1994) has provoked the usual pleas and remonstrances from friends and acquaintances — in the line of "When are you going to finish that memoir of yours?" "Are you aware that it's now ten years and more since you first confided that you were actively working on your Baghdad memoirs?" And so on.

None of these reactions, however, has been as urgent, as pleading, as detailed, as heart-warming and — let's admit it! — as flattering as the one that has just come from my friend F of Philadelphia, an acknowledged Shakespeare scholar and the wife of a political science professor.

F's letter opens with these words: "Damn, why didn't I write you four days ago when the thoughts were racing around in my brain, when I knew just what I wanted to say, before we spent three days with an ex-Russian diplomat who thinks that what Russia needs now is a strong man, who asked Al if Stalin would not be remembered as Napoleon is, i.e., for all his good things and not for his 'murders.' Al tactfully ignored the fact that Napoleon's 'murders' were not in gulags, not of his own people, etc., and simply listed Nappie's accomplishments, lasting, whereas Stalin has not contributed one positive law, government, etc. Our gentle host could see this was one point of view . . ." The relevant passages from the letter, dated June 6, 1994, are:

So, you see, all this has added layers and layers between the wonderful ones I felt on reading your article, at which time I felt so strongly that if you would like to be one smart man you would throw overboard all those other projects alluded to in the bio. at the beginning, and you would bring to completion this *wonderful* book. That strictly political stuff is ephemeral, passing (go see the new Bertolucci film *Little Buddha,* visually beautiful and a seductive way to learn—or, for the learned like you, be reminded of—the beginnings of Buddhism. One point it makes is the impermanence of everything, telling us to look around at the hundreds of people we know or see with the realization they will all be gone in a hundred years. I could almost see the screen extending down to include the seated audience in front of me, up to and including us. I found it a very calming thought . . .).

I have the thought that so will all the governments in their present form, the institutions, even values, all will disappear. And that the main contribution one can make to others is oneself—books like Sterne's *Sentimental Journey,* Rejwan's *Passage from Baghdad*— they are the way we learn what it's all about down here . . .

Your first paragraphs reminded me of Walt Whitman's "When I Heard the Learned Astronomer":

> When the proofs, the figures, were ranged in columns
>   before me,
> When I was shown the charts and diagrams, to add,
>   divide, and measure them,
> When I sitting heard the astronomer where he lectured
>   with much applause in the lecture-room,
> How soon unaccountable I became tired and sick,
> Till rising and gliding out I wandered off by myself,
> In the mystical moist night air, and from time to time,
> Looked up in perfect silence at the stars.

And all those who read those pages of yours will be reminded or will realize that that's what they should do.

These doubtless worthless few lines which can only poorly serve you in that they kept you from what I propounded as your main task are my attempt to connect . . .

Now, though I have always enjoyed Sterne's *The Life and Opinions of Tristram Shandy* I had never read his *Sentimental Journey,* and, what I find even more shocking, I don't have it among the English classics I have stacked in various cupboards, most of them unread, I hasten to add. Now I intend to read it—if only to find out why F has singled it for mention in the context, trusting as I do her literary judgements.

Anyway, while in truth there was no lack of prodding and of encouragement concerning the completion of that memoir, F's remarks are so touching, so elegant, and so sincerely felt and expressed that as of today I've decided to devote much more thought and time to the completion of the work, knowing however that no work of this kind can ever be complete. How can it be, with so much to include, with the difficulty of picking and choosing, with a memory that's no longer entirely reliable, with only a few jottings from the past and with such a sea of documentary material—letters, diaries, cuttings from published articles and reviews, memoirs others wrote or spoke about the same period of change and upheaval. How?

Be that as it may, this is how I reacted to F's letter:

27 June 1994
Dear F:

Finally a whole letter—and what a letter! Well, I am flattered, and promise to take your advice-admonition, i.e., throw overboard everything—well, almost everything—and start putting the finishing touches to that part of the story that ends with February 10, 1951, when I and my late mother boarded that rickety plane at Baghdad Airport to land four hours or so later in Lydda Airport.

But this is child's play compared to another problem I now have with these memoirs—with the title this time. A good friend of mine says she is not happy with the title *Passage from Baghdad*, partly in that, she says, it's suggestive of something that I am the last person in the world to want to impart. It makes your years in Baghdad, she says, so rich in experience and so "formative" of your person—it makes them sound too transitory, something that can be dismissed so easily, passed by, passed over, passed up, as quite insignificant. And I tended to agree—and the title now is *The Last Jews in Baghdad: Remembering a Lost Homeland*.

And speaking of difficulties, one of the difficulties I have with this autobiographical work is the shape and scope of its sequel, which is to cover the 15–16 years which follow that "exit." The difficulty is that I cannot seem to find a way in which the sequel can in any way be similar to the first volume in either style or mood.

You see, almost as soon as I was able to find my way in this coun-

try, however partially, my life and work became enmeshed in controversy—hopelessly enmeshed in a hopeless and unwieldy controversy.
"The expense of spirit"—is that from Shakespeare?—that went into
those fights, the sacrifices, the material losses, the toil that it took just
to cope—that was what essentially comprises my autobiography since
1951. How to put all that in a readable, manageable form will be quite
a tricky business.

Apropos of this, a friend of mine—a fellow immigrant from
Iraq—said something the other day that set me brooding. The subject was the respective performances of the two of us in Israel. Our
two careers, he maintained, were diametrically different. "You, Nissim," he said, "had everything going for you, everything I wanted to
have—a standing, command of the language, talent, various publications to write for, some regularly; you became editor-in-chief of a
daily newspaper; you were fast becoming a celebrity. And then, at the
slightest provocation, you decided you didn't want any of it—or at
least that's the impression I had of the way you behaved."

And so on. And I must admit that, factually at least, that was
roughly what happened. *Factually*, I emphasize, because as far as
motive and aspiration and emotions are concerned I am not quite
sure—and that is what has been exercising my mind these past few
days. One of the things that come to mind is how a reasonable solution to this dilemma can affect in a meaningful sense the thrust of
my account of what happened to me and inside me these past four
decades.

One possible, though rather fanciful, explanation came to mind
the other day. Clive Fisher, George Orwell's latest biographer, writes
at one point that Orwell "exemplified" what he, Fisher, calls "that
most enduring of British qualities—the fascination of defeat, . . .
the glamour of failure." Fisher also speaks of "the British cult of
modesty."

Well, I couldn't be considered "British" by any stretch of the
imagination—unless of course such ingrained qualities can be acquired by a deep fascination with Orwell the person and an even
deeper identification with his general outlook.

Go figure.

QUESTS

Diary entries

21 June 1994

In a little less than six months I will be completing the 70th year of my life. Seventy years, of which the first 27 were lived in Baghdad, the remaining 43 in Israel, mostly in Jerusalem. In all honesty I cannot say it has been an uneventful life, and some sort of stock-taking has long been overdue, as friends never tire of telling me. Not that I haven't tried it myself. I've already sketched certain high points in my life, even venturing into print with certain fragments.

It was, in fact, one of these that has led a good friend of mine to volunteer the comment that provokes these reflections concerning "stock-taking." Referring to his project for an autobiographical work of his own (among other things, as professor of literature, he had taken a special interest in the genre) he marveled at what he saw as a contrast between our respective fortunes after immigrating to Israel in 1951.

He had always pondered on this "contrast," he confided to me for the first time during our long acquaintance. "I," he summed up, "worked my way in this country from the periphery into the center; you, in sharp contrast, managed somehow to work your way from the center to the periphery."

My friend didn't actually use the word, but I suspect he was saying that I virtually *maneuvered* myself out of the center and sideways to the margins. To be sure, I had never formulated the matter in that particular way or in those stark terms, although naturally I had given the matter a good deal of thought throughout the years.

Now, in the perspective of over three decades, I am beginning to wonder—and over the past few days I've become fairly convinced that what I had done throughout my years in "the center" was invariably if only partially consciously bound to ease me out from there and back to the periphery. I say "back" because, now that I look back at the whole matter with some measure of serenity, I had not only been "marginal" throughout—in childhood, in youth, in middle age; in Baghdad, in Tel Aviv, in Jerusalem—but had felt perfectly at home at "the margins." There is, in fact, a very valid sense in which I *did* work my way "out of the center and sideways to the margins," as my friend had put it.

The way this singular feat was accomplished becomes clear, I hope, as the story of my first fifteen years in Israel is told, however inadequately, in what will comprise the second volume of my autobiography—for which, for a change, I had no difficulty in choosing a title.

28 June 1994

Commenting on the acts of violence which swept some British cities in 1981, social history professor Eric Hobsbawm was quoted by *Time* magazine as saying that the phenomenon "might not seem altogether unhealthy." Hobsbawm had written extensively on what he calls "collective bargaining by riots"—social outbursts that were accepted as a legitimate way of putting pressure on society for change. One notable example was the countryside protests in 1688, led by Protestant parliamentarians, which helped to eject Catholic King James II in favour of Protestant William of Orange. Britain, Hobsbawm said, remembers these "riots" as the Glorious Revolution.

When my truckload of immigrants arrived in Shaʿar Haʿaliyya near Haifa, where newcomers were received, examined, supplied with the necessary papers, and sent to their various destinations, I found good examples of bargaining by riots—not quite the collective variety but something strikingly similar. Greeting the newcomers were always small crowds of fellow-immigrants who had preceded them by a few days or weeks and had already acquired some knowledge of the workings of the new bureaucracy. Some gathered there because they had nothing more useful to do, some in the hope of finding relatives or friends among the arrivals.

However, even on those rare occasions where no relative or acquaintance or neighbour arrived, the waiting ones were always ready to volunteer information and advice they thought were indispensable for the newcomers. "You better know what is awaiting you here," someone I hardly knew told me as soon as I descended from the truck. "In a few days," he continued, "after the medical checkups and the army recruitments, they will call you to tell you where and when you are going to be sent for temporary settlement. Since you do not want to go to some godforsaken desert moshav or maʿbara, ask to

be settled somewhere near the metropolis, where you probably have
relatives already settled there." Here came a short list of the choice
ma'barot then available: Ramat Hasharon, Pardess Katz, Zakiyya,
Khayriyya, Yahud, Petah Tikva, and so on. Unless, of course, you
have some special reason to want to be sent to Jerusalem or vicinity.

"To be sure," I was told further, "the official will want to send
you somewhere else—to the Galilee or the Negev or to some other
wilderness. Under no circumstances should you agree to go—and if
the son-of-a-bitch gets tough and insists there was no more room in
the place of your choice, the best way to persuade him will be for you
to get violent. You can seize a chair, the inkpot, any instrument you
can lay your hands on, and hurl it at him. This is the only language
these bastards understand around here!"

"Individual bargaining by blows"—that is what it amounted to.
But I was too "civilized" for that, and I rather sided secretly with the
poor Jewish Agency official who, I decided, was only trying to make
ends meet in a situation I thought was extremely difficult to cope
with. It took me a few months to realize how callously and heartlessly Jewish Agency officials and others dealing with the affairs of
immigrants from Middle Eastern and North African lands were in
reality—and a few more years to see how effective and legitimate a
way for collective bargaining riots and blows could be. The instincts
of those newcomers in *Sha'ar Ha'aliyya*—and after them the organiz-
ers of the riots in Wadi Salib in the late 1950s and the Black Panthers'
demonstrations in Jerusalem in the early 1970s—were immeasurably healthier and much more effective than the understanding and
moderation I often advocated in private talks.

However, while I was fairly understanding—even sympathetic—
about the difficulties and hardships the new state faced coping with
such a flood of newcomers, I seem to have been rather severe where
"culture" and intellectual attitudes were concerned. In fact, I found
the place and the people shockingly provincial, compared even to
the society and the cultural milieu I had left behind. I mentioned
this in a letter I wrote my Baghdadi friend Jacob a few short weeks
after our arrival. "There is much truth in what you say," Jacob wrote
in a letter dated March 20, 1951, referring to my letter of the 17th,
"about the cultural position and the Sabra [native-born Israeli] type.
I am surprised that you had no definite notion about it before. I myself remember hearing that the general atmosphere is, as you put
it, 'anti-cultural.' I gathered that from the leader of the Movement

(*Ha-Tenuʿah*, the Zionist underground in Iraq, in which Jacob was involved only as one of the many Jewish youngsters who attended the movement's clandestine Hebrew classes). People here have one notion: Work.

"There is not much hope in the Sabra, but there is hope in the new immigrants. In time you will come to realize that, generally speaking, the people here are not only uncivil and uncivilized, but downright inhuman (this is being decried by newcomers from all lands); it is as if to counteract the measure of social justice and equality that is found in this country."

Now, over 50 long years after my plane landed at Lydda Airport, I cannot help marveling at the amount of sheer chutzpa needed for me—and for Jacob—to pass such harsh judgments on a country whose official language I did not know and after a stay of only 37 days.

JERUSALEM 1951

My first glimpses of Jerusalem were at least as uninspiring as they were disappointing. I arrived there one day in early May 1951, armed with the documents needed for registration at the Hebrew University. It was late in the afternoon, and the only person with whom I had been in touch and whose address I knew was Jacob, who had arrived in the city a few months before.

I had previously approached Jacob on the subject and asked for guidance, now that he had spent one semester at the institution. In those days almost the whole of the university was housed in Terra Sancta, and the only decent—and free—place for the likes of us to meet was the YMCA, opposite the King David Hotel and not far from Terra Sancta. Like many other new immigrant students, Jacob was a member of what I think was called the YMCA club, a status that enabled him to use the swimming pool and the showers—in addition to the library and its spacious reading room, where one could read, do some homework, and drowse on a classes-free afternoon. I made my way by foot from the Central Bus Station, then situated in the very center of town, had a long chat with Jacob in the halls of the building, went with him to the "mensa" where we were served some sort of supper, and then headed for the students' dormitory in Musrara, hardly a block from the border, where he put me up for the night.

A friend in Baghdad had asked me to inquire about relatives of his who lived "in Jerusalem." It did not take much effort to find the place; they lived somewhere in the complex generally known as Mahane Yehuda. I duly paid them a visit, having promised my friend to report to him via a London address he gave me—and what I saw taught me a great deal of what I eventually was to learn from my readings and in my anthropology classes at Tel Aviv University.

To put it simply, these Jews, whose parents and grandparents had trudged their way from Baghdad to the Holy City some three decades previously, led exactly the same kind of life they had in their hometown. None of the far-reaching, radical changes that their former neighbors and fellow Jews had undergone in the course of those long years appeared to have affected them in the least. What was even more striking, none of the habits, mores, and innovations that characterized their immediate surroundings were noticeable in their behavior and way of life. This was so much the case, indeed, that on that occasion and in years to come, I often found that I was hardly able to communicate with them, so great the gap between us had become, owing to the process of modernization that Iraqi Jews went through in their native land and that, for some reason that seemed to me mysterious at the time, had somehow bypassed them.

Years later, when taking courses in sociology and anthropology, I was to come back to this same theme in a paper I wrote under the title "Cultural Stagnation and the Workings of the Self-Fulfilling Prophecy" and for which my lecturer gave me a grade of AA. I quote it here because it represented my very first attempt at a "scholarly" approach to a problem that I thought I could be of help with.

I opened my paper with references to Robert Merton's book *Social Theory and Social Structure,* in which he devotes a chapter to what he calls the self-fulfilling prophecy. The thesis elaborated by Merton, as he himself states, is not a new one, and is certainly older than modern sociology. In various forms, we find it in the work of at least two older sociologists. Max Weber had already pointed out that an essential element of the interpretation of human action was the effort to seize upon the subjectively intended meaning of the participants in it. A little later, in their classic study of the Polish peasant in America and Europe, W. I. Thomas and Florian Znaniecki advanced the thesis that in our study of man it is essential to find out how men define situations in which they find themselves, because if men define situations as real, they are real in their consequences.

Since the time of Thomas and Znaniecki, I added, the idea of the self-fulfilling prophecy had become one of the axioms of sociological research. One of the latest statements of the thesis was to be found in R. Dewey and W. J. Humber, *An Introduction to Social Psychology*, in which they formulate the hypothesis as a sort of vicious circle—the prejudices and discriminatory attitudes of the dominant groups result in restricted socioeconomic life chances for members of the disadvantaged minority group, and resentment of these burdens in turn leads to the development by the minority group of traits and attitudes that provide the dominant groups with bases for rationalizing their habitual prejudices . . . The operation of the vicious circle reveals itself in the life experiences of disadvantaged individuals and groups, very few of whom are able to avoid the consequences of this circular process.

Now, my own feeling is that this concept of a circular process, which I thought was of the highest relevance to the Israeli situation, can help us understand another phenomenon to which I once gave much thought and which I shall call cultural stagnation, but which may be given other, more "sociological" descriptions. I first noticed this phenomenon shortly after I arrived in Israel early in 1951, as an immigrant from Iraq.

This occurred when I had to visit friends who had come to Israel shortly before I did and who, in the meantime, had managed to rent a room or two in an old house in the Mahane Yehuda quarter in Jerusalem. I spent the night with my friends, and in the morning had my first real look at the quarter, the marketplace, and the people of Mahane Yehuda. As is well known, Mahane Yehuda is inhabited mainly by Oriental Jews, many of them hailing from Baghdad and Aleppo. In the late 1910s and the early 1920s there was a small-scale immigration of Jews from Baghdad, mostly, it appears, from lower-middle-class and poor families. Now the point about these Jews was that they came from roughly the same socioeconomic milieu as my own family did—lower-middle-class people who used to inhabit the poorer quarters of Baghdad, which, in those days, were a bunch of damp, drab, overcrowded, dirty, and disease-infested slums that, for the most part, lacked running water.

The way these Baghdadi Jews lived in Mahane Yehuda in the early 1950s, their behavior, their level of education, even their norms—all these struck me as being vastly different from the way of life, the behavior, educational level, etc. not only of myself, my family, and my social circle, but also of the whole socioeconomic milieu from which they themselves originally hailed. In other words, assuming that parts of the same family separated sometime in the 1920s, some staying in Baghdad and others moving to Jerusalem and Mahane Yehuda, what we find in the 1950s are two or more families belonging to, not two different cultures, but certainly two different "phases" of cultural development, acculturation, or, if you like, Westernization. And the question is what had happened in those three or four decades, socioculturally speaking, to these two parts of the same family. More concretely and personally, I kept asking myself what, approximately, would have happened to *me* had my own family decided sometime in the early 1920s to pack up and immigrate to Eretz Israel, most probably landing in Mahane Yehuda or the Hatikva quarter in Tel Aviv (which strongly resembled Mahane Yehuda).

It is impossible to give here an adequate idea of the manifestations of cultural stagnation that I thought I spotted in these people, but a few instances will do. While, for example, the Jews who had continued living in Baghdad had gradually adopted the use of knives and forks, cooked European dishes, worn European clothes, listened to Western music, learned one or more foreign languages, and entered into modern marriages, the same generation of Baghdadi Jews who lived in Mahane Yehuda in 1951 cooked dishes that we had almost forgotten about; they spoke the same vernacular of Judeo-Arabic as they did forty years previously, whereas ours was replete with words from Arabic and other languages; their marriages were made in the old fashion; the young among them knew no foreign languages; and their educational level struck one as shockingly low. In short, they were in a state of obvious cultural stagnation.

These were my first glimpses of the phenomenon. With the passage of years, two more related phenomena began to intrigue me.

First, as I came to know about the Meah Sha'arim quarter and the group called Neturei Karta (Aramaic for "Guardians of the City"), I wanted to find out whether the same kind of process was operating there as the one I have just described. And in fact, the Neturei Karta did show signs of stagnation. Moreover, this whole business made, and makes, me wonder sometimes whether a similar process of stagnation has been operating to varying degrees on *all* communal, cultural, and perhaps ideological groups in this country. (To take one example: the tenacity with which the old Eastern European Zionist establishment holds on to ways and concepts that to many younger people seem simply incomprehensible.)

Second, during my visits abroad, when I had a chance to meet people from my own generation of Baghdadi Jews—and also when they came here in the 1960s direct from Baghdad—I often find myself wondering how different *I* have become from these people. Whether, in other words, the same process of stagnation and fossilization apparent in the Baghdadi emigrants of the 1920s is operating on the 140,000 Jews who immigrated into Israel from Iraq in 1951–1952?

I concluded the paper in the form of a plainly rhetorical question: "Assuming," I asked, "that this process is at work, in what way has it originated, been helped or accelerated by what Merton calls the self-fulfilling prophecy and what Dewey and Humber term the vicious circle?"

Chapter 2 | ₽ROBINGS

One historian of ideas has called it "that unquench-able and irresistible thirst of the soul that demands an explanation of the world in which it finds itself. Akin to such aspiration," he adds, "is that of the historian, who also seeks law and order in the universe. History, like science, like religion, is a constant search for such law, which yet always just eludes the grasp" (Charles Singer, *A Short History of Scientific Ideas*).

It was in my fourth year of schooling, in the course of a history class, and our teacher was relating how the Prophet Muhammad died and how his successor was chosen. The story was fascinating, and I was listening with a good deal of concentration. The account, however, was occasionally marred by what I thought were annoying remarks and phrases, such as "It is said . . ." "Certain sources have it that . . ." and "On this point reports tend to conflict with each other." To my young and apparently far too orderly mind, this was incomprehensible, and I finally raised my hand and asked for permission to speak. "You say, O Master," I began, in a tone of protest and frustration, "that the episode you related was 're-ported' by one source but denied by another. Does this mean we can never be certain that it did take place? And how come we don't know exactly what had happened? Isn't everything duly recorded and known?"

I don't quite recall what the teacher's exact answer was, but I have since learned that my protest at that early age was symptomatic of a temperament and a frame of mind that were to characterize my general approach and my attitudes to things all my life. This search for certainties and the conviction that they are available and accessible were, I believe, the sources of a general predilection for definitions. This predisposition, which has plagued me both as a private person and as a sometimes-committed intellectual, amounted to a passion, and it caused me a great deal of trouble and embarrassment at various stages of my life.

I remember, for instance, that in my fervent, if short-lived, Marxist days, I once pressed my friend and mentor Abdallah Mas'ood—a Shi'i Muslim whose loyalties seemed to me to be equally divided between internationalism and his underprivileged community—on the vexed question of how it was possible for Comrade Stalin to be regarded as the number one man in the Soviet Union and in world communism. After all, he was only general secretary of the Communist Party of the Soviet Union, whereas the prime minister and even the president of the USSR seemed to enjoy far less authority, power, and prestige. A true believer and quite devoid of a sense of humor when it came to ideological and party business, Mas'ood took me to task severely for entertaining such forbidden thoughts—although, of course, he failed to provide anything like a satisfactory explanation.

But it was in Israel that my passion for exact definitions was to land me in the most trouble. It came soon after my first encounter with what I still perceive to be a general Israeli-Zionist aversion to definitions and clear thinking. After a relatively short period of time in Israel, I discovered that definitions of any kind were almost anathema to the establishment—especially when they had to do with such crucial subjects as Jews, Arabs, Judaism, Zionism, ethnicity, and similar explosive topics. At one point early in 1965, some high-ranking government official made one typically mindless remark that so incensed me that I found I had to do something about it. Which I did in the form of a Marginal Column, printed in the *Jerusalem Post* on January 21 under the headline "Semantic Niceties." It reads in full:

> There is a tendency among official spokesmen generally, and Israeli spokesmen in particular, to seize on any argument which sounds even remotely suitable to a given purpose. This is understandable in many cases —and may even work. But like anything else it can be overdone. Speaking recently of Arab attempts to establish a "Palestine Entity" Mr. Arye Levavi, director-general of the ministry of foreign affairs, asserted that the project was no more than an artificial attempt to invest Arab enmity towards Israel with the attributes of a people's struggle for its homeland. This claim has no foundation, Mr. Levavi is reported to have added. There had never been a "Palestine People," and never under the British Mandate had Arab nationalists spoken of such an entity as "Palestine." Palestine, he recalled, was then termed "Southern Syria."
>
> One wonders where our foreign ministry gets its historical facts. The term Southern Syria was out of circulation in Arab nationalist circles almost as soon as the mandate was put into effect. Instead, "the Arab people of Palestine" became the accepted way of describing the inhabitants of

mandatory Palestine. Besides, there are signs that the growth of a separate national identity among these people has continued and even become intensified. This is one of the most interesting developments in the Middle East in recent years, and it seems to be true alike of the refugees and of those who have managed to stay where they were before 1948. This is in many ways paradoxical, for it comes at a time when the general trend in the Arab world is away from local nationalisms and towards Pan-Arabism. At a time when the Arabs of Syria, Iraq, Egypt, and Yemen profess a belief in one great Pan-Arab entity, it is certainly curious to find one group of Arabs clinging desperately to a national identity which they never really had in the political sense.

It does, however, seem that there are good reasons for the growth of this paradox. Some time ago the Beirut literary monthly *Al-Adab* published a remarkable story by Samira 'Azzam, a gifted short story writer hailing from Jaffa who now lives in Lebanon. The story, entitled "Palestinian," tells of the misfortunes of a refugee from the Galilee village of Rama who, though now a fairly well-established grocer in Beirut, is unhappy because he is never allowed to forget that he is a Palestinian. In fact, "Palestinian" is his only known name, a fate which he resents intensely, and he makes desperate but unsuccessful attempts to escape by getting naturalized as a Lebanese. When an opportunity finally presents itself of acquiring an identity card, he decides to take it though it cost him a fortune — only to find that the card was forged.

In other words, the Palestinian identity of the ex-Palestinians is partly imposed on them by the outside world and partly by a combination of outside pressures and frustrations. The situation is reminiscent of Jean-Paul Sartre's statement of the dilemma of the modern Jew: what makes the Jew a Jew is not so much his own decision as the opinion of outsiders. The Palestinian, whether he is in Beirut, Baghdad, Haifa, Nazareth, Gaza, or Ramallah, cannot escape his Palestinian identity, even if he chooses to do so. Thus "the Palestinian People" now exist, if for no better reason than that the outside world — in this case other Arabs — has decided that they do.

There are other reasons for hoping that Mr. Levavi's argument is not going to be the basis of Israel's case against Arab attempts to create a "Palestinian Entity." As a historical argument it does not hold water. Nor is it going to convince many people. It cannot possibly convince the emerging nations of Africa and Asia, many of whom have had no definable national identity until a mere decade or so ago. It is not going to convince the Arabs of Palestine, to whom semantic niceties may sound rather irrelevant.

Finally, one has the feeling that it cannot convince even the Israelis. At least, it fails to convince this one, who, after 14 years in Israel, is still daily plagued by such unanswered questions as to what is a Jew, what is an Israeli, and who, precisely, is a Zionist.

EXODUS TALE INCOMPLETE

Where what I would call my incurable passion for certainties was to prove something of an impediment was in the case of the article I promised to the editors of the American Jewish monthly *Commentary* but never wrote. Sometime in the summer of 1951, shortly after settling in the Talpiot ma'bara and after securing a post office box, I wrote to the editor of *Commentary*, which was published by the American Jewish Committee and which I had become familiar with in Baghdad back in the mid-1940s, asking if he would be interested in an article setting out the story of the exodus of the Jews of Iraq. The answer came promptly, signed by Nathan Glazer, then associate editor. It was dated September 26, 1951, and reads in part:

> We read your letter of September 16 with interest, and we agree with you that we should get an article on Iraqi Jewry. I would like to suggest, however, that you concentrate as much as possible on an account of the life of Iraqi Jewry before its dissolution under pressure, and perhaps it would be possible for you to do this by introducing a certain amount of personal experience. For example, to what extent were Iraqi Jews educated? Prosperous? Westernized? Integrated into the life of Iraq? Perhaps the most important theme you could take up is an explanation of why the Jews of Iraq were eventually forced to leave the country while, for example, the Jews of Egypt managed to weather the storm. Was there enmity between the Iraqi Jews and the general population and if so, which class?
>
> In short, we would like to propose that you try a portrait of a large Middle Eastern community whose experiences might throw light on the future of the Jews of Egypt and North Africa. The other side of the story — how the Iraqi Jews were brought to Israel, and their future there — could be handled, I think, much more briefly, since that subject will be treated in the near future in articles on Israel we plan to run. We look forward to seeing what you write on the subject.
>
> SINCERELY YOURS . . .

I duly sat down to write the piece—alternating between the British Council Library at Terra Sancta and the YMCA reading room, the only two places where it was possible to get a chair and a desk. Not yet having purchased a typewriter, I wrote in longhand, some sixteen packed pages in which I tried to sketch the events that had led to the exodus, starting with the *farhud* of June 1941, which marked the end of Rashid 'Ali's revolt and the short "war" with the British, and ending with the promulgation nine years later of the law allowing Jews to emigrate, provided they surrendered their Iraqi nationality.

All went well until I set out to record the background—the events following the signing of the Portsmouth Agreement with Britain, made public in December 1947, the involvement of the predominantly Jewish "Anti-Zionist League" (*'Usbat Mukafahat al-Suhioniyya*), rumors about the participation of members of the Zionist underground in violent demonstrations as an act of provocation.

The account gradually became too involved and too long—and the implications (the active involvement of the Zionist underground, first in provoking the authorities, which resulted in harsh measures against the movement, and later in trying to accelerate the exodus, reportedly by throwing bombs in the synagogue where Jews were registering for emigration and in a Jewish cafe on the Tigris, acts of terror that resulted in tens of thousands of Jews rushing to surrender their Iraqi citizenship) were too sweeping and too damning for the kind of article I wanted to write. It was certainly not the sort of article Glazer had in mind. I wrote Glazer to that effect, apologizing for not being able to furnish the account he wanted.

Scanning the now battered manuscript, I think the most interesting facts I stressed there were the numbers of Jews registering for emigration in the early days of the law. These were as follows:

TABLE 1

	Baghdad	Basra
May 6, 1950	614	0
May 7, 1950	1,752	0
May 8, 1950	2,980	331
May 9, 1950	2,920	532
May 10, 1950	2,400	362
May 11, 1950	1,114	0
Total	11,780	1,225

After these 13,000 registered, reports started to come from the new arrivals to their relatives, warning them against following in their footsteps—and a general lull prevailed. Then came the bombings. The bomb in the synagogue exploded on January 14, 1951, and was soon followed by another in the coffee shop. By March 9 of the same year, the day the law ended, 103,866 Jews were registered for emigration.

The real reason for my failure to finish and send that report to *Commentary* was, of course, that I did not want to be rash with my conclusions. I wanted first to learn more—not only about what actually happened in Iraq that led to the mass exodus of its ancient and prosperous Jewish community, but also about the outside forces that were obviously at work there. These included, first and foremost, the local Zionist underground—generally known as the *Tenu'ah*, the Movement—and the emissaries of Aliya Beth (clandestine immigration) and other sectors of the Zionist movement in Palestine and later in Israel.

To do this in a way that would satisfy me and convince others, rather than merely add to the heat and bitterness of the argument, I had of course to consult the views of "the other side," the Jewish quarters and groups not officially associated with the Zionist establishment. During the first years of the new state, such groups and institutions were still influential in their own way. *Commentary* and its sponsor, the American Jewish Committee, were deemed non-Zionist, and often openly criticized Israel. Ultra-Orthodox Jewish groups were even more critical, some ideologically opposed to the establishment of a state for the Jews in our time—or at any time for that matter, since for such an event we are supposed to await the coming of the Messiah. Few of these latter positions, however, were expounded persuasively in a reasoned, authoritative, and nonpolemical manner, especially in English, the language on which I still had to depend for my information.

OPENING SHOTS

When I arrived in Israel, one of the first things I did was to arrange for a post office box and send notifications of change of address, or subscription renewals, to my then favorite periodicals—*Partisan Review, Horizon*, the *New Yorker, Commentary*, and the *New Statesman*, while Elie in London sent me his copy of the *Times Literary Supplement*, the *Cambridge Journal*, and a few other sources of intellectual nourishment. With so much time on my hands, I also used to spend days on end at the well-stocked and efficiently run British Council library, which was housed in Terra Sancta in a room adjoining the reading room of the Hebrew University library. The YMCA library too was also fairly well stocked, and the librarian used to give me special and courteous service, partly because, on my arrival in Jerusalem, I had brought him regards and good wishes from Jabra Ibrahim Jabra, his friend and fellow Orthodox Christian from Bethlehem. Jabra had fled to Baghdad in 1947 and gotten a post as teacher of English literature at the Baghdad College of Arts; I had become friendly with him through my work for Al-Rabita Bookshop, my contributions to the *Iraq Times*, and my circle of local literati and dilettantes.

It was with this kind of intellectual and literary bent that I came to Israel. While I was studying Islamic civilization and Arabic literature at Hebrew University, I needed a job or some other source of income—and here, too, Elie proved instrumental, though at second remove.

While studying at the London School of Economics, Elie had met Yohanan Ramati, a young London Jew who was taking the same courses and who was then going out with (or was engaged to) a fellow student from Israel. This was Datya, daughter of Israel's first finance minister, Eliezer Kaplan. In 1951, the two were married and living in a nice apartment in Katamon. Yohanan was then a civil servant, Datya had a job at the Bank of Israel, and they had connections in influential places.

Ramati had worked for a brief spell for the *Jerusalem Post*, and when I approached him, he gave me a recommendation to the manager of that paper. Since it was then virtually unheard of in Israel for a person whose mother tongue was not English to know the language well enough to work for that paper in an editorial capacity, the only work I was deemed capable of doing was proofreading—if that. And so I was given a chance, tested, and admitted—and actually started working there in July 1951, when still attending the morning Hebrew ulpan in Rehov Hillel.

What with the sordid physical conditions in which I was living, the ulpan, and the start in November of a new semester at the university, I had quite a hard time of it. The plight of Iraqi Jewry, the overwhelming majority of whom had by then arrived in Israel; the public debate raging about the mass immigration from the countries of the Middle East and North Africa; the incredibly stupid and utterly illiterate and prejudiced things that were being said; and the absence of serious challengers and spokesmen—all these had the effect of slowly making me perceive what I had stubbornly refused to see; namely, that there indeed existed a basic prejudice against these Jews and that this prejudice was inevitably being translated into discrimination, active and passive, against them. The impact of this discovery was quite shattering, especially since I had started with an extremely optimistic, open-minded, and rather understanding attitude to the great difficulties facing a young state trying to grapple with mass immigration, the treatment of immigrants, and the hardships they faced.

During this time, all the writing I did was in the form of personal letters, school papers, and copious notes made in the course of the long days I spent in libraries. For one reason or other, I made no attempt to contribute to the pages of the *Jerusalem Post*. However, when the literary editor, Dr. Eugene Meyer, asked me to write a review of Majid Khadduri's *Independent Iraq,* which he had borrowed from a colleague, I complied, and my review was printed in the issue dated August 8, 1952.

Sometime toward the end of 1952, the YMCA librarian suggested that I speak to his club, adding that I could choose a book as a subject. He then suggested one of his new acquisitions, a slim volume by various hands — Arthur Koestler, Stephen Spender, Raymond Aron, and other leading lights of the day — with the title *America and the Mind of Europe.* I duly wrote a substantial review and read it before the readers' club. It was well received, and a few weeks later I submitted it to Meyer for consideration. He printed it as it was, although as a matter of fact it had been written for a different audience and was more a survey of the book than a proper book review (whatever that is). The review "adorned" the book page of Friday, January 30, 1953 — but already on the previous day, having read the piece in page proof, Agron had sent me the following note:

> I have read with much pleasure and interest your review-cum-summary of *America and the Mind of Europe* in this week's book page.
> This is not a criticism of an excellent summary but a suggestion which the Literary Editor will have made long before this. The suggestion is that a "proper" review tells more about the book in fewer words; in other words, such notices should be shorter. In my own opinion, the shorter the writing, the more disciplined it is, which means that there is more meaty reaction and fewer quotations.
> But I do congratulate you on the readability of the whole thing.

I replied to this obviously loaded note with a remark about how there were "hundreds of ways to write a book review" and why I thought the one in which I had chosen to write mine legitimately belonged to these. Be that as it may, the review came out under a title chosen by the literary editor—"An Atlantic Dialogue"—and I insert here an excerpt:

> There is a sense in which it would be true to say that there were two European discoveries of America. The merchant and the politician have credit for the historic first discovery, whereas the second is a process rather than a single operation. This process has, in the last 50 years or so, undergone many fluctuations and setbacks. Not only did the European intellectual show total indifference to the American phenomenon, but also some of the best creative minds in America itself felt so estranged there that they spent most of their lives and wrote much of their work in Europe. Henry James, T. S. Eliot, Ezra Pound, and Gertrude Stein are the first names to come to mind.
>
> Melvin J. Lasky, an American who has been watching the European scene closely for a number of years, contributes an essay on literature and the arts. He holds that the creation of a common European-American spiritual community is the primary life-preserving task of Western culture. He appeals for the discarding of "the old, tortured formula," on both sides: "The Jeffersonian version: America is young, vigorous, progressive; Europe is old, tired, decadent. The Jamesian version: America is raw, innocent, susceptible; Europe is dark, engaging, profound. The Rooseveltian version: America is practical, experimental, promising; Europe is helpless, reactionary, tragic."
>
> Lasky's essay concludes with a highly pertinent admonition: "If a truce should ever be called, possibly then we can remind ourselves, as Eliot once said, that it may still be the destiny of the American to become a European in a way that no European ever could become."

INVOKING ORWELL, TOLSTOY

What with my ulpan classes and the few distractions available, I was not able to do any "real work." Nevertheless, I managed to obtain two interesting new books—one of them sent to me by Elie, who was always worrying about the dearth of reading material available to me at that time—and decided to try my hand at what by then I thought I was fairly good at doing—book reviews. The result was these two pieces, which for one reason or other never made it to print. Not surprisingly, the first dealt with George Orwell, who at the time was one of my few culture heroes; I had first made his acquaintance in the mid-1940s in his weekly column, "I Write as I Please," in the London weekly *Tribune*. It was a slim pamphlet of forty pages, written by Tom Hopkinson and published by Longman for the British Council. I wrote:

Mixing literary criticism with personal impressions is a dangerous thing. Tom Hopkinson's second sentence reads: "Orwell had little imagination, little understanding of human relationships, little sympathy with individual human beings — though much with humanity in general."

Which Orwell, the man or the writer? If the writer, we find no evidence in his books to bear out the claim; if the man, why not specify? A few lines further we are told that writing was so deeply a part of Orwell's nature that "qualities are manifest in his work which did not reveal themselves in his life." The more the pity that Mr. Hopkinson chose unfairly to take advantage of this ambiguity.

After giving a partial list of Orwell's weaknesses, Hopkinson proceeds to inform us that his subject's strength and weakness relate to a single cause: he was "without historical perspective." The author of *1984*, it is maintained, saw the world of his day with peculiar intensity because "he saw very little of its past and regarded the future as simply a continuation and extension of the particular present which he knew." This preoccupation with the present is said to have prevented Orwell's seeing not only the past and future, but also the present as it really is.

At a first glance this sounds very pertinent. A man lacking historical perspective tends to exaggerate his immediate situation and become obsessed with the evil surrounding him. Yet, it may well be asked, what is this historical perspective supposed to be? Is it an innate quality of mind or is it something that can be acquired? Can you have it at all times and without reference to the particular historical phase you are passing through?

Orwell was born in 1903. For those who reached their maturity in the years between the two world wars, historical perspective could have provided little solace. For how could it have helped make their world less unintelligible and perplexing? How could it have explained the subtle perversity of the Moscow trials, the general failure of nerve that made possible Franco and Munich, the Soviet-German pact, and the partition of Poland — culminating in the supreme tragedy of Europe's attempt at a "final solution" of its Jewish Question?

If "historical perspective" can be of use in explaining away such phenomena, then it can indeed be very dangerous and objectionable. It can deprive men of their sense of right and wrong, and can be made to justify any crime however gross, only provided that it involves whole groups of human beings and thereby takes on "historical" proportions.

Another book that came my way was Isaiah Berlin's *The Hedgehog and the Fox: An Essay on Tolstoy's View of History*. I don't think the review was ever published, and I give it here:

The question most likely to spring to mind on reading this slim volume is: Can history be of any appreciable use as a guide for understanding the present — or, for that matter, the past itself? Has history any meaning, any significance or message?

The answer, of course, depends on our idea of the forces at play in history, the power — if such it is — which moves the destinies of peoples and civilizations.

The nature of history has always puzzled thinkers. The problem was thus formulated by Henri Frédéric Amiel when he wrote:

At first sight history seems to us accident and confusion; looked at for the second time, it seems to us logical and necessary; looked at for the third time, it appears to us a mixture of necessity and liberty; on the fourth examination we scarcely know what to think of it, for if force is the source of right, and chance the origin of force, we come back to our first explanation, only with a heavier heart than when we began.

(Translated by Mary A. Ward)

This is a far-reaching conclusion. Once you subscribe to the theory that history is nothing but accident and confusion — especially if you do so with a heavy heart — you are only one step from the mystical, deterministic, tragic, or otherwise fatalistic view of history.

It was at some such explanation that Count Lev Mikolaevich Tolstoy arrived. An absorbed and life-long interest in history led him to a "violently unhistorical and indeed anti-historical rejection of all efforts to explain or justify human action or character in terms of social or individual growth, or 'roots' in the past."

Finding in this a paradox which "surely deserves attention" Isaiah Berlin comes to the conclusion that, both in his preoccupation with history and in his interpretation of it, Tolstoy was trying to be something which he in fact was not, something which in fact contradicts Tolstoy's own nature. For the author of *War and Peace*, Berlin tells us, was a "fox," indeed an arch-fox, and what he was pretending to be was a "hedgehog."

The fox-hedgehog opposition comes from the Greek poet Archilo-
chus, a line of whose poetry reads: "The fox knows many things, but
the hedgehog knows one big thing." Applying the epigram to writers
and thinkers, Berlin makes this seemingly innocuous statement yield a
sense in which it describes one of the deepest differences which divide
them.

The fox, curious, sceptical, pursuing many ends, reveling in life's in-
exhaustible diversity and plurality; the hedgehog, dedicated, obstinate,
relating everything to a central vision, and reducing life's great variety to a
single system or principle. Thus, according to Berlin, Plato, Dante, Hegel,
Dostoevsky, and Nietzsche are obviously hedgehogs; Aristotle, Shakespeare, Goethe, Pushkin, and Balzac are foxes.

The problem which Tolstoy poses — at least to Berlin — is that he cannot be fitted into either of these categories. We do not know whether he
was "a monist or a pluralist, whether his vision was of one or of many . . ."
Through a careful examination of Tolstoy's philosophy of history embodied in *War and Peace* and from a consideration of the influence on him
of the ideas of the French thinker Count Joseph de Maistre, the author of
The Hedgehog and the Fox decides that Tolstoy was by nature a fox, but
that he believed in being a hedgehog. Berlin detects a discrepancy between
Tolstoy the man and Tolstoy the artist-thinker, and claims that Tolstoy's
view of history — and the impact of that view on his beliefs and attitudes
and presumably also on his art — was in conflict with his own nature as a
man "compounded of heterogenous elements."

It is not quite clear whether Berlin is implying that the contradiction
renders Tolstoy a lesser artist, a lesser thinker, a lesser "philosopher of
history" — or perhaps all these combined. Yet it is quite obvious that an
artist trying to be something other than what he actually is cannot possibly produce the best work he is capable of. Berlin quotes Flaubert on
War and Peace: "*Il se repete! et il philosophise!*" He also quotes a contemporary Russian source as reporting that literary specialists "find that the
intellectual element of the novel is very weak, the philosophy of history
trivial and superficial . . . but apart from this the artistic gift of the author
is beyond dispute."

Tolstoy is further convicted on a charge of willful falsification of historical detail, "falsification perpetrated, it seems, in the interests not so much
of an artistic as of an 'ideological' purpose." The "ideological" content
of *War and Peace,* embodied mainly in the long Epilogue, is said to have
been either ignored by later critics or put down to a combination of "the
well-known Russian tendency to preach" and the "half-baked infatuation

with general ideas characteristic of young intellectuals in countries remote from the centres of civilization."

Tolstoy's view of history seems to amount to a rejection of its validity and effectiveness as a guide to the actual happenings of the past, the present, or the future. At first he was passionately interested in it, thinking that "only history, only the sum of the concrete events in time and space . . . of the actual experience of actual men and women in their relations to one another and to an actual . . . environment — this alone contained the truth, the material from which genuine answers . . . might be constructed." He set out to discover the forces that move history and the laws governing that movement, and arrived, with his hero Pierre, at seeing only a succession of accidents "whose origins and consequences are . . . untraceable and unpredictable; only loosely strung groups of events forming an ever varying pattern, following no discernable order." From which it followed that it is a great illusion to think that individuals can, by their own resources, understand and control the course of events.

The Hedgehog and the Fox is so well-documented and contains so great a wealth of supporting evidence for its argument that no reasonable doubts can be entertained as to the validity of its scholarship . . . The arbitrary division of writers into the two categories of hedgehogs and foxes, however, would seem even looser than Berlin is prepared to admit. There are so many borderline cases that the whole theory tends to crumble. To cite one example, Proust is claimed by the author to be a hedgehog; but there is an equally valid case for considering him a fox, indeed an arch-fox.

But perhaps the book should be read as an oblique comment on a modern phenomenon — that of conversion. Conversion has been widespread among present-day writers in the West. There is little doubt that for Isaiah Berlin a whole procession of contemporary writers, ranging from T. S. Eliot to Christopher Isherwood and including such names as Aldous Huxley, Auden, Greene, Waugh, Malraux, and Camus, provides good examples of the apparently damaging attempt to attain the metamorphosis from fox to hedgehog.

OPERATION EZRA AND NEHEMIAH

It was shortly after the publication of my review of *America and the Mind of Europe* that David Grossman (Vital), who was then on the paper's editorial staff and was asked to prepare a special Pessah supplement devoted to the subject of immigration and the absorption of immigrants, was looking for someone, preferably an immigrant, to contribute an article on the Iraqi *aliya* (*ascent,* the word chosen to define the immigration of the Jews of Iraq to Israel), which had also been dubbed Operation Ezra and Nehemiah, invoking the biblical story of the exodus of Jews to Babylon in the early sixth century BCE. His choice fell on me, and despite the mixed feelings I recall having, I accepted the assignment readily. I consider the piece to be of special value, representing my first attempt to plead the case of my fellow Iraqi Jews before the general Israeli public. The article—for which the editor chose the heading "Operation Ezra and Nehemiah: Attempt to Maintain Living Standard, Attain Genuine Absorption"—was outspoken. The gist of it was that not enough was being done to really absorb new immigrants from the Middle East and North Africa.

I also had some words of praise for Iraqi immigrants. "The average Iraqi immigrant," I wrote,

> has both the will and the ability to make himself a useful and organic part of this land, and can provide much of the sense of stability and solidity which is so lacking here. The Iraqi immigrants have many characteristics which should have provided invaluable assets: their having come in whole families, the fact that they cannot return to their country of origin, their exceptional proficiency in learning the language, the comparatively large number of professional people among them, the fact that they are quite familiar with modern standards of work and organization, and their experience in commerce, finance, and administration.

I suspect that the article, printed in the issue dated March 30, 1953, now reads like a piece of special pleading—and perhaps it was!

> It seems to me that at the root of the problem lies a fundamental misunderstanding. The immigration and settlement authorities, knowing nothing of the history, the way of life, the culture, and the aspirations of Iraqi Jewry, expected a mass of primitive Orientals who, they thought, would inevitably and naturally settle at the bottom of the social scale. In this the immigration authorities are not to blame; they acted according to their own lights and what flimsy information they were supplied by *shlihim* (Jewish Agency emissaries) more intent on getting Jews here than on a comparative study of cultures.
>
> On the other hand the prospective Iraqi emigrants, having no direct contact with Israel, deprived of all normal sources of information and

bamboozled by irresponsible fanatics, made *their* calculations according to a set of different assumptions. Once here, they had to sustain the shock the discovery of such a state of affairs was bound to create.

This seems to have gone on even after the facts became evident for anyone willing to see. To cite one glaring example: after the Iraqi immigration was concluded, no less an authority on the subject than the head of the Jewish Agency's Immigration Department informed the 23rd World Zionist Congress in Jerusalem that the country was being overburdened by mass immigration from Oriental countries like Yemen and Iraq, which brought the country no doctors, teachers, or nurses. It was also pointed out that, this being so, Israel was bound to turn into a country of "hewers of wood and carriers of water." Speakers proceeded to implore the Congress to intensify its efforts to encourage professional immigration from the West.

There is a kind of bitter truth in this view. The country is indeed in danger of becoming one of carriers of water and gatherers of wood, but this is *not* partly due to the fact that the Iraqi aliya did not include enough professionals. The danger lies in these immigrants being confronted with a situation in which they find themselves having to adopt primitive ways, where they have to stop sending their children to school or taking adequate care of their health. It would, of course, be foolish and redundant to assert here that the Iraqi aliya is self-sufficient in doctors, teachers, etc., because it is measurably more than self-sufficient.

One hopes that, sooner or later, it will be realized that the future of this country depends on the use it makes of the material it now possesses, not in mere clamoring for professionals from the West. The contribution of the Iraqi aliya to the cultural and physical building-up of the country, though in no way small so far, depends in large measure on the opportunities it is given and on the attitudes taken toward it.

The article — my first ever to touch on the ethnic problem — received a mixed reception from the editorial staff. One member, an American newcomer, described it as the best piece in the whole supplement — or even "the only good piece," I don't remember exactly — although another, a sabra by the name of Dan Bavli, considered it the limit of chutzpa for a newcomer from Iraq to venture the thought that the Israelis could possibly *learn* something from Orientals of any provenance. Be that as it may, for me personally the article was one of those one-time pronouncements, never to be pursued further or, an even remoter possibility, made into the subject of a crusade. To be sure, my next few contributions to the *Post* were confined to the book pages.

By that time it was becoming evident — though I continued doggedly to resist the thought — that the people at the *Post* had something of a blind spot where non-"Anglo-Saxons" and non-Westerners were concerned. And abroad in the Israeli world was a kind of consensus that virtually all educated young men from Iraq were communists. There was a good deal of other nonsense — such as the fear of "Levantinization," concern about "lowering standards," and other claims calculated to safeguard the interests and position of the in-group against the danger of encroachment by an out-group. In the case of the *Jerusalem Post,* I figure, it was a combination of all these factors plus a certain amount of disbelief.

A year after my article on Iraqi immigration appeared, another occasion presented itself for me to delve into the subject. Shlomo Hillel, who originally hailed from Iraq and who played what is thought to be a decisive role in accelerating the exodus of Jews from there, protested in the course of a Knesset debate on foreign affairs against "the American suggestion that compensation should be paid by Israel to Arab refugees," and against that part of the prime minister's statement in which reference was made to this country's readiness to pay such compensation. His protests were being made, said Hillel, "in the name of the Iraqi Jews, whose entire property was confiscated after they had already received their Israel immigration permits and were on the way of becoming Israeli citizens." This was followed by a claim that the value of confiscated Iraqi Jewish property "by far exceeded" that of abandoned Arab property in Israel.

This prompted me to write an article in which I said, among other things, that while it was quite possible that Mr. Hillel's speech was incorrectly reported — especially his estimate of the value of the Jewish property seized by the government of Iraq — it must be said that here was an example of a valid case spoiled by overpleading. For it seemed to me that, with the exception of a few fanatics, no one would contest the idea of compensating Arab refugees as a move both morally right and politically expedient. Moreover, to suggest that Iraqi immigrants should be compensated at the expense of Palestine Arabs was equally indefensible.

I then proceeded to give the facts as I knew them: On March 10, 1951, a secret session of parliament in Baghdad passed a bill decreeing that the possessions of the emigrating Jews were to be frozen and put under the administration of a "Secretariat-General of Frozen Jewish Property." The law was put into effect the same day. At that time well over half of the Iraqi

Jews were still awaiting transportation to Israel—generally the better-off part of the community. People who were about to liquidate their businesses, sell their houses and household effects, or close out their bank accounts found themselves denuded and dispossessed overnight.

A week later the Israeli government issued a formal statement of protest in which it said, among other things, that in retaliation it would use funds due to be paid as compensation for Arab refugees' property in Israel to compensate the emigrating Iraqi Jews affected by the new law. On the other hand, one of the reasons advanced by the Iraqi government in justification of its move was, of course, that it was seeking to retaliate against Israel's "confiscation" of Palestine Arab property in this country.

Three years after these declarations were made, the Palestine Arab refugees still live under truly subhuman conditions . . . Israel's complete and inexplicable silence on the subject of confiscated Jewish property in Iraq, moreover, has perceptibly helped the Arabs in giving a wholly one-sided picture of the situation . . .

The article was not published, though Agron for some reason ordered the accounts department to pay me a fee.

| $\mathcal{A}$RAB AFFAIRS ANALYST
OF SORTS

THE WEST, RUSSIA, AND ISLAM

*T*he few words of appreciation said in praise of the
article I wrote for the *Jerusalem Post* on the Iraqi
immigration gave me some encouragement, though they did not come
from people who mattered. In those days I used to buy the *Listener* regularly, and was thus familiar with the latest Reith Lectures, which the BBC
weekly printed in six consecutive issues as they were delivered. That year
the lectures were given by Arnold Toynbee, and the subject was "The
World and the West." As soon as they were brought out in book form, by
Oxford University Press, I seized the opportunity and promptly wrote a
review, considerably before the book itself could have reached Jerusalem.
I think now that the review would have been accepted and published by
Meyer if I had not made the silly mistake of showing it first to Agron, who
told me he would pass it on to the book page editor. But the rejection slip
was not late in coming, and, typically, it came from poor Meyer rather than
from Agron himself. Unfortunately, the note said, the book had already
been dealt with by George Lichtheim in one of his London Letters. I had
read the letter in question, and I wrote to Meyer and pointed out, quoting
dates and facts, that Lichtheim's piece had been written and sent in not
only before the book was published, but even before Toynbee's last two
lectures had been broadcast.

I ought to have realized—but again I failed to do so—that the reason
for the rejection lay somewhere deeper. It was plainly just a little too much
for a paper like the *Jerusalem Post* to publish a rather sympathetic review of anything written by Toynbee, an anti-Zionist and allegedly "anti-
Jewish"—and written by a newcomer from an Arab land, to boot. But
Meyer tried to smooth out the matter the best he could. "Thank you for
your note and the review," he wrote. "You are no doubt right in what
you say about Lichtheim's review which was apparently written before
he could have known the last two lectures with Toynbee's conclusions.

At all events, as I told you, we cannot now revert to the subject . . ." The note was dated April 29, 1953. What actually caused the editor's rejection was the somewhat sympathetic view I took of Toynbee's main theme, which was that for the four or five centuries ending in 1945, the West, in its encounters with "the world," had been the archaggressor.

*A*lthough by now my standing as a book reviewer was quietly gaining recognition, the higher-ups at the *Post* had their reservations. Among the books I still managed to review was one on a purely American theme, a *Partisan Review* symposium entitled *America and the Intellectuals.* I had read the text when it was first published in the periodical, and in my review I expounded the thesis that intellectuals have no business meddling in public affairs, nor ought they to conform or in other ways identify with the powers that be. On the contrary, I asserted, dissent and alienation were the normal attitude expected of the intellectual vis-à-vis the government of the day and society in general. The book page editor's response to this review came in the form of a memorandum:

> I regret that I must return your *Partisan Review* piece.
> On reconsideration you will, I hope, agree that this is a mixture of editorial and Marginal Column writing rather than a brief notice which alone could come into question for the book page.

One review I wrote on my own initiative must have been prompted by things that certain ethnic groups of Jews, including my fellow Iraqi immigrants, were witnessing and experiencing in their new home in the mid-1950s. None of this, of course, could have been openly referred to in the review itself—which, in the course of the writing, became something of a brief survey of the book's contents—hence the studied neutrality of the treatment. One problem related to the title of the book, *The Colour Problem: A Study in Racial Relations,* the very mention of "colour" being usually avoided when speaking of the "one people" the Jews were. I don't now recall who chose the heading for the piece, but "Anatomy of Prejudice" was a fairly apt one, and the review was printed in the *Post* on July 29, 1955. I quote one paragraph here:

> Ethnocentrism and colour prejudice have, moreover, a respectable psychological function. They represent "a defence mechanism enabling the individual to handle inner conflicts engendered by a failure

to make a completely successful adjustment to society," thus providing "a means . . . of handling anxieties the origins of which are largely unconscious." The prejudiced are therefore to be pitied no less than those at whom their prejudicial practices are directed, for the people most inclined to be intolerant are "those who feel insecure and are afraid of losing their present social status." The aggressiveness this insecurity breeds finds socially accepted outlets in the many targets provided in a heterogeneous society by the existence of other cultural or social groups.

Another rather loaded review, containing a distinctly unflattering appraisal of the West's attitudes and of its dealings with the rest of the world, appeared on March 25, 1955. It purported to be a review of two books: *Moslems on the March* by F. W. Fernau and *Islam* by Alfred Guillaume. Excerpts:

The trouble lies in the schism in the soul of the modern man of the East, torn between two cultures and in full possession of neither. His future well-being depends on his reaching a workable compromise that can restore his self-confidence. The Moslems' most pressing problem today is the same as that with which they have been grappling for the last century or so: how best to adjust themselves to the new conditions in which they have been plunged by the intrusion of the West. It is a vast and many-sided problem, further complicated by the West's own by no means light ailments.

In the dealings of the West with the rest of the world, a fundamental ambiguity has always arisen from the fact that the West did not practise and, perhaps, did not even believe what it professed. It preached reason and used force; it taught equality and despised "natives"; and it failed to adopt either a coherent attitude or a comprehensible policy. This has added to the pains of adjustment, for non-Westerners were led to believe in the superiority of their own ideals and way of life at one and the same time as they had to recognize the West's superiority in technology and the arts of warfare.

This seemingly harmless compromise has resulted in the very conflict from which the Moslem's mind suffers. A culture is an organic whole and cannot be separated into so-called "good" and "bad" components without each losing its original characteristics. And so the Moslems, along with other non-Westerners, find themselves in the grip of a dilemma which manifests itself from time to time in a show of varying degrees of violence.

WITH SEPHARDI CHIEF RABBI NISSIM

By now, unwillingly but almost inevitably, I was being fast drawn into the business of writing on Arab and Middle Eastern affairs. Gradually, against my natural inclinations toward more "intellectual" topics and concerns, I found myself giving in.

At first it was strictly book reviews — which Agron never failed to praise in note after note as long as they remained confined to the subject that he had decided a newcomer from Iraq could write about best. Incidentally, Agron seems to have taken a special interest in the book page: It so happened that whenever I wanted to review a book of general history or world affairs, it was always he, rather than Meyer, who found some objection or other to my doing so.

It was thus that I finally found myself becoming an acknowledged "expert" on Arab affairs. Apart from the *Post*, I was also sought after by the editors of the short-lived weekly *Here and Now*, and was already contributing to their pages — mainly book reviews but occasionally full-length articles on Arab topics — as well as one profile, whose subject was Iraqi-born rabbi Yitzhak Nissim, who had just been elected Sephardi Chief Rabbi of Israel. The profile, which I wrote under one of my pen names, N. B. Argaman, is of some interest in the context of this personal account, since it persuaded me that I should have to take up Arab affairs as my fate and destiny as a newspaperman in Israel. The piece on Rabbi Nissim was printed in the weekly's issue dated April 14, 1955. It came out under the title "First in Zion."

Yitzhak Nissim Rahamim, joint Chief Rabbi of Israel, Rishon le-Zion (First in Zion), is an erect, energetic, prominent-featured, and alert-eyed man of fifty-nine. He is the author and annotator of several treatises on Jewish Law and a close personal friend of President Ben Zvi. Rabbi Nissim was a young scholar of thirty when, together with his much younger wife, he decided to leave his hometown, Baghdad, and set out for the Holy City, where he had already established contacts with prominent rabbis and learned dignitaries.

This was not the first time he had seen the Promised Land; in 1906, as a boy of ten, he was brought along by his late brother Yehezkel on a visit. Over a cup of tea he will recall this first long journey and relate, with his unfailing sense of humour, how it took their caravan a full thirty days to cover the distance between Baghdad and Aleppo. His stay was very short, and his impressions are naturally somewhat dimmed by the lapse of time.

Shortly after their arrival in 1926, the young couple took up residence in David Yellin Street in Jerusalem. They still occupy, with their four sons and three daughters, the same small flat—now sadly outgrown. Rabbi Nissim took up his studies and researches exactly where he had left them in Baghdad, while his wife assumed the strenuous duties of keeping house and bringing up the children.

In his imposing study, its walls entirely covered with thousands of old fading volumes, the Chief Rabbi explained to me why he never assumed official rabbinical duties: he wanted to devote all his time to study, and—with modest private means and God's help—he never felt the lack of remuneration. With a look of satisfaction he pointed to the rows of books written by his illustrious predecessors, who were the fount of authority on the Law not only in the Land of Israel but in the whole Sephardic Diaspora.

When asked how so much came to be written in this country on disputed points in the Law (*Halakha*), he obligingly offered to explain the reason. In their dealings with their Jewish and other minorities, the Osmanli Turks, who ruled Palestine till the British conquest in 1917, seem to have practised their own brand of liberalism. The Jewish communities under Ottoman rule were granted a large measure of autonomous communal life. They raised their children in the manner they themselves chose and settled their personal status cases in their own rabbinical courts. The Rishon le-Zion, as well as the chief rabbis in other Ottoman provinces, was not only invested with absolute authority where the Jews were concerned, but he could arbitrate in cases involving the Sultan's Moslem subjects whenever these chose to go to him. Hence the massive treatises and controversies.

Rabbi Nissim was twenty-one years old when the British entered Baghdad in 1917, and his community is considered to have been, numerically and economically, the most important single element in the town. Despite their inadequate experience in the crooked ways of power politics, Baghdad's Jews seem already to have had an inkling of what lay in store for them. They petitioned the British High Commissioner, asking that they be granted British nationality. The reasons they gave make interesting reading these days. The Arabs, they pleaded, were politically irresponsible; they had no administrative experience; and they could be fanatical and intolerant.

The dispute now raging over the new Rishon le-Zion's election must be an issue of profound obscurity to the ordinary citizen. Apart from the claim that he has not been a practising and officiating rabbi, the bone of contention seems to lie in the common belief that the Rishon le-Zion must be a Sephardi, while Rabbi Nissim belongs to the Iraqi community. It is doubtful, however, whether this claim has any foundation. In the first place, the title was never the monopoly of one community in Jewry (the first Ashkenazi Chief Rabbi was installed only in 1922). Moreover, the title was always granted on grounds of merit alone. Rishon le-Zion Yitzhak Hacohen Rappaport (1749) was an Ashkenazi rabbi; another, Rabbi Nissim Hayim Moshe Mizrahi (1730), author of *Admat Kodesh,* was of Baghdadi origin. With a modesty that is truly disarming, Rabbi Nissim points out that the tradition of his seat required abilities which he is aware he does not possess, adding that his election was a measure of the decline of Sephardic Jewry.

Chief Rabbi Nissim holds very definite opinions on the role which Judaism is destined to play in this "constructive epoch of toil and labour." In the face of numerous differences of culture, origin, and approach, the most effective way of uniting and moulding the tribes of Israel into one nation, he believes, is the diffusion of the spirit of the Torah — the decisive factor in preserving Jewry's national character through the centuries of exile. It is essential to go ahead with the task of building and strengthening the state, but, he adds, "it seems to me that the eagerness to achieve material results unwittingly makes for checking the aspirations for reinforcing the spiritual power of the people." Spiritual values must therefore be maintained and fostered, and close cooperation must be established between the state and the spiritual leaders.

Moreover, the Diaspora faces an increasing danger of assimilation, and it looks to Israel "not for help in attaining European culture and civilization, but for Judaism, Torah, religious precepts, and tradition," he declares. "If in Israel itself these will not form part and parcel of our life, how can we bring them to bear on the Diaspora? Even those righteous Gentiles who have lent their support to the cause of Israel wish to see in Israel the people of the Bible. We must not disappoint them . . .

What I did not mention in my profile was how much I enjoyed conducting our interview in the colloquial Arabic spoken by the Jews of Iraq, on the false pretense — I believe — of not being sufficiently well-versed in Hebrew.

TAKING THE AIR

Apart from a brief sojourn in Persia in the mid-1930s and my immigration to Israel, the first twenty-seven years of my life were spent without my ever setting foot abroad. My first real journey in foreign parts came late in the summer of 1955, when I joined Elie and his wife Sylvia in their trip back to London after they had spent a short first visit in Israel.

Elie's arrival in Jerusalem one day early in September 1955 was an event I considered so singular and so exciting that, when his brother Maurice told me of Elie's arrival (accompanied by Sylvia and their firstborn of a few months), I decided to leave my proofs practically unfinished, telling my immediate superior that I had to leave because of the arrival of a friend.

It was the first time I had seen Elie in almost nine years — and my first opportunity really to get to know Sylvia. I must say that, with my expectations being so great and disproportionate and my basically romantic bent, I was a little disappointed, though by no means discouraged. What with the baby, Sylvia's increasingly clear tendency to be domineering, and Elie himself doing research of one kind or other the whole day in the Hebrew University library, there was no way of renewing our old intimacies and sharing common interests and passions. And besides the factors already mentioned, Elie seemed to have lost interest in literature and literary works and to have become immersed in things and subjects that did not really interest me in the least. My apparent refusal to grow up, or at any rate to outgrow what he later rather disparagingly termed my "literary approach" to things, seemed completely inexplicable to him — and I suspect that he and Sylvia shared the feeling that here was a man of thirty-one or thereabouts, talented in many ways, good looking, and in other ways quite charming and certainly "eligible," virtually wasting his time and probably his life on things so intangible and ungainly as to be absurd.

I am not suggesting that they were wrong or unfair. They knew that I had made a mess of my university courses — and twice over! They saw how I was wasting my time and energy reading galley proofs for a daily newspaper. They sensed that I was not even looking seriously for a wife and suspected I was largely philandering. They, on the other hand, were bent on building Elie's career as a teacher at the London School of Economics, where he had just received an appointment as junior lecturer.

All this, however, did not affect our friendship in any serious way, and during their stay I saw much of Elie and his wife when they were free. Elie then was totally unknown in Israel, nor did he have much sympathy for the Zionist enterprise or for the brand of ethnic nationalism that informed Israel and its rulers. In fact, during the early 1950s Elie had come under the powerful influence of the late Emile Marmorstein, an English Jew of Hungarian descent; for some years in the early 1940s he had taught English at the Shamash School in Baghdad and had left an indelible impression

on a number of his students. He was deeply religious and a lifelong anti-
Zionist—and his affiliation with and active work for the ultra-Orthodox
group known as Neturei Karta were no secret.

In 1951, soon after my arrival in Israel, I wrote Elie a long account of
what I thought had led to the destruction of the Iraqi Jewish community.
In that letter I had a good deal to say about the role I thought the Zionists had played in the disturbances that followed the signing, late in 1947,
of the Portsmouth Agreement between Iraq and Britain, and how those
disturbances and the role the Jews played in them actually marked the beginning of the end of Iraqi Jewry. Elie informed me in reply that he had
passed my report on to someone who would make use of the information
contained in it—and although he did not mention Marmorstein's name,
I gathered subsequently that he had been the recipient.

My first meeting with Marmorstein took place in London in his room
at the BBC, where he was either the head or one of the senior executives
of the Oriental Languages Department. I found I had a lot in common
with him, and I agreed with much of what he said about Israel and Zionism. In his home, where I had dinner with him and his wife one evening,
I noticed that he was engaged in reading the proofs of the book that he
had been working on for some years and that was to take about eight more
years to come out. I had seen a reference to the book in an essay written by
Elie—in a footnote that described the book as forthcoming. The book,
which finally came out in 1969 under the title *Heaven at Bay,* published
by Oxford University Press with the imprint of Chatham House, must
have been an agonizing affair to write, judging at least by the time it took
Marmorstein to write and revise it time and again. It was a little disappointing in that it dwelt at disproportionate length on detailed accounts
of cases in which Neturei Karta activists sought to preserve Judaism from
the secular assaults of the Zionists. I myself had come under the spell of
Marmorstein's ideas after reading his 1952 article "Anti-Semitism and the
State of Israel."

Marmorstein's ideas were not in themselves new, nor did they origi-
nate in the Neturei Karta ideology. That Zionism contains some of the
notions advanced by European anti-Semites was a thesis expounded by
no less a Zionist historian than Yehezkiel Kaufmann in a memorable essay;
also familiar were his objections to the Zionists' lock, stock, and, barrel
embrace of an ethnic-racial concept of nationality that had its roots in
central and eastern Europe. What really caught my attention in Marmorstein's work was the thesis, introduced in his concluding paragraphs, that
what the Eastern European Zionist establishment in Israel really found

objectionable and obnoxious about the masses of Middle Eastern and North African immigrants pouring into the country was that these reminded them of the conditions prevailing in their own *shtetls* and ghettos of Eastern Europe only a few decades earlier. I quoted this passage — without mentioning its author's name — in the concluding part of my article "Israel's Communal Controversy," which appeared in the American Jewish monthly *Midstream* in 1964.

Although he held distinctly anti-Zionist and antinationalist opinions, Elie was far more careful and circumspect. In his letters to me he was quite specific and outspoken, pointing out once that the real conflict in Palestine was one not between Arabs and Jews but rather between Arabs and Europeans. To the best of my knowledge, he first went public on the subject in the *Manchester Guardian* late in 1951 with an anonymous article titled "Iraqi Jewry: An Obituary."

In that article he did not mince words concerning the part the Zionists played in the affair. He sent me a cutting of the article, and I showed it to, among others, Professor Goitein one afternoon when I walked with him to his home nearby after class. To my surprise, Goitein, after reading the piece carefully, said he agreed with its central thesis. A few months later, Elie sent me a *Cambridge Journal* in which he had published a lengthy article on the subject, signed, "Antiochus," of all improbable names.

It was a brilliant piece of angry historical discourse, linking the fate of the Jews of Iraq to that of the Armenians in Turkey and the Assyrians in north Iraq and showing how the ideas of European nationalism had disrupted Middle Eastern society since 1900. Above all, he was scathing about the Zionists and their approach to Iraqi Jewry, and bitterly critical of their antics. The article, in its entirety, was reprinted almost ten years later in *The Chatham House Version,* updated with copious footnotes. I could not help noticing, however, that Elie had deleted a footnote from the original article — one referring to the work of Arnold Toynbee and his ideas concerning the basic difference in approach and temperament between Sephardi and Ashkenazi Jews.

The apparent affinity between my views and those of Marmorstein and Elie did not last long. The fact that I was living the Israeli reality while they were contemplating it from afar landed me somewhere in the middle — between Marmorstein's religious extremism and Elie's growing "realism" and increasingly petulant assaults not only on Arab nationalism and Pan-Arabism but also on Arabs and "Sunni Islam" in general. In later years, what with the influence wielded by the scholarly *Middle Eastern Studies,* which he launched in 1964, his growing status, and his allegedly "anti-Arab" stance, Elie became an extremely sought-after guest for the many seminars and symposia organized by various Israeli universities. In a sense, I felt that I was left alone in the field of battle, deserted by the person from whom I had learned much of what now I was being penalized for saying.

LONDON AT FIRSTHAND

Although—or rather because—it was uneventful, my stay in London in the autumn of 1955 served to cure me of some of my romantic ideas about England and the English. We arrived in London one afternoon after spending a few days in Istanbul and a couple of days in Athens. Before our arrival I had already begun to feel that I was not going to have an easy time of it being a houseguest of the Kedouries' for as long as a few weeks, but I accepted it with some stoicism, since I had no other plan of my own and also because I did not want to give any appearance of being disappointed.

What really disappointed me was that throughout my stay in London I never actually had an opportunity to have a real chat with Elie, something for which I had waited all those years. At first I attributed this to Sylvia's continuous presence, but later I discovered, to my dismay, that Elie himself had little to say about the kinds of subjects and ideas that I thought we still shared. I seemed to exhaust his patience one day when he finally spelled it out—telling me in so many words that the time had come for me to outgrow those "literary ideas"!

I spent much of my time in England either traveling alone or studying in the Reading Room of the British Museum Library (where I gained entry only thanks to a pass obtained for me by Elie). One person with whom I spent much time was Abboudi Dangoor, who had left Israel and joined his brother, who ran some export-import business of his own in London. The two brothers, both unmarried, lived in what seemed to me a mansion, in a very good neighborhood in London. Abboudi cooked some Iraqi dishes, and I often had a meal there. One day, out of the blue, he told me that should I, for any reason, decide to move out of the Kedouries' place, I would be more than welcome to spend the rest of my stay in London with them. I had no idea what prompted the offer; I had not breathed a word about my relations with Elie and his wife or of my mixed feelings about my stay with them. But I declined the offer, saying it was completely unnecessary, since I was quite happy right where I was. Abboudi's reaction to this was that the offer stood anyway, just in case.

I left London for Paris roughly on the day I had planned to leave originally. Paris was a different world, largely because I was finally on my own
and did not have to account for anything. Edmond Samuel, a good friend
from Baghdad, had arranged a room for me in the hotel in which he was
staying, the Hotel de Lisbonne, in the heart of the Latin Quarter—and
we breakfasted together regularly in his room. He was then already in his
second year of chemistry studies at the Sorbonne, and he used to go out
every morning for rolls or croissants, which we had with coffee and often
with butter and cheese supplied to the Jewish students who ate at a certain Jewish restaurant run by the Jewish community or some other Jewish
organization. Somehow Edmond managed to obtain tickets entitling me
to have cheap and fairly good meals there for my lunch—and in the evening we used to go to a nearby Turkish restaurant, where we had kebab and
rice, and usually yogurt and sugar for dessert. The rest of the day, when
Edmond was at his studies, I spent with some acquaintances, mostly in
cafes, where I used to play pinball machines endlessly.

As usual, I couldn't do without bookshops, and since my knowledge
of French was scanty, I managed to find an Arabic bookshop run by an
elderly Armenian and situated in some obscure corner not far from where
I was staying. By that time I had spent more than four years without so
much as *seeing* an Arabic newspaper or magazine, let alone books. Apart
from the few books there that I felt I could afford, the most interesting
items I encountered were back issues of a new Arabic monthly called
Al Adaab. I think *Al Adaab* then was in its second or third year, and it
was undeniably something new in the world of Arabic letters and culture—a periodical combining literary interests with rather advanced and
often outspoken political articles leaning toward a new kind of radical
nationalism.

In a very real sense those back issues of *Al Adaab* launched me on my
career as a specialist in Arab politics, culture, and ideology. Shortly after
returning to Jerusalem, I was able to make good use of the material contained in those magazines, and through Marmorstein I was able to receive
it regularly from a Lebanese who was a colleague of his at the BBC and
who used to run something called the Arabic Publications Distribution
Bureau.

At that time there was a running controversy in *Al Adaab* about the
nature of Arab nationalist ideology—and when Zeev Laqueur wrote to
me from London, asking me to contribute a paper to an anthology he
was editing of articles and studies on the Middle East, I suggested one on
this subject. He gladly accepted the offer, and the result was a substantial

paper, "Arab Nationalism in Search of an Ideology," which appeared in *The Middle East in Transition,* published by Routledge and Kegan Paul early in 1957. In that paper I quoted copiously from two long dissertations written by Sa'dun Hammadi, a young Iraqi student in Wisconsin — and the same Hammadi who was to become the foreign minister of Iraq for many years. The article was well received, and I continue to see it mentioned or quoted in new books on that subject.

By the time I left Paris, I was fairly penniless. An added difficulty was that I could not use my air ticket to Rome — included in my original flight ticket — because of a strike at Paris airport. And since I had no money to stay in Paris and wait for the strike to end, and because things were not so well organized in air travel as they are now, I took the train to Rome at my own expense and was thus rendered even more nearly penniless. But Rome was apparently some sort of last stop for many Israelis, and the Israeli embassy or consulate there was quite ready to help. Through middlemen and some Israeli stalwarts, small amounts of money were lent to Israelis stuck in Rome without money — against checks or just promises or whatever. I wrote out a check — a good one — and received a certain amount of money that helped me pay for my pension and meals. I wrote a postcard to Elie and Sylvia, some sort of farewell letter while I was still on European soil. I don't think the postcard was suitably polite or even free of bitterness — and a long period was to follow in which our relationship left much to be desired.

Chapter 4 | ‎RACHEL

RENEWING CONTACTS

*B*ack in Jerusalem after an absence of over two months, I felt an urge to renew contacts with members of my family near and far. Apart from Mother, who lived with me and used the kitchen as a bedroom, none of my near relatives lived in Jerusalem. My aunt Regina's family, the Jijis, were in Ramat Gan; my brother, Eliahu, and his family had by then managed to rent a flat in Ramat Yitzhak nearby; my younger sister, Simha, was married and living in a village, Ein Sarid, which I had never visited. Eliahu's two elder daughters, Daurice and Evelyn, now married to two brothers with whom they had some family relation on their mother's side, were in Ramat Gan and almost always not exactly on speaking terms with either Hella (their mother) or Eliahu or both.

In my spare time and on short weekends I started going occasionally to Ramat Gan, where I spent the nights generally at the Jijis'. Their flat was large enough, and there was the added attraction of their younger daughter, Rachel, by then in her twenties and eminently eligible. I started inviting her on outings I could afford, and I had the impression that Moshe Jiji, ever the patriarch, looked approvingly on what seemed to be a growing relationship.

In the end nothing came of it. On the one hand I thought the girl, good-hearted and good-looking though she was, just a little bit too "simple" for my taste; on the other, she perhaps found me unsuitable for the selfsame reasons, and also as a result of feeling that I did not care for her enough. In any event, Rachel soon married one of her many cousins from her father's side. She seems to have made a good judgment, and the two have since lived happily and raised their children in something like affluence. I had to look elsewhere — and I did.

In a sense, it was one of those attempts — said never to have succeeded — to "go home again." My estrangement from the family, and from anything that had to do with the old ways, was complete. For years I had had no proper Sabbath eve blessings and meal (*kabbalat shabbat*), at least not a traditional one in the manner of Iraqi Jews—not to speak of going to synagogue or actually observing the Sabbath. Nor did I attend the various weddings, *brit millah* (circumcisions), and bar mitzvah to which I was invited by members of the family—at least not if I could find an excuse not to go. What is more, my family somehow accepted this state of affairs, peculiar as it might have seemed to them, as something that couldn't be helped or done much about, knowing as they did the kind of life I was leading, living in Jerusalem instead of somewhere on the coastal plain and adopting a modern outlook about things in general.

It was therefore with some surprise and delight that I was received back by members of my family. For instance, sometime after returning from Europe I decided to spend Sabbath eve with Eliahu and his family—and I was astonished, and not a little touched, by the fact that almost nothing seemed to have changed after something like a generation of separation—neither the blessings nor the food nor the festive atmosphere. It was the first time I had attended this particular celebration conducted by someone other than my late father, and what I found striking was that no change was discernible. With equal diligence and care, too, my sister-in-law, Hella, laid the table in the same old way and with the same variety of *b'rakhoth* (benedictions) and dishes, including things that are not usually to be found in Israeli shops and greengrocers. Even the *kiddush* drink was the traditional homemade juice extracted from raisins.

It was roundabout this time that one afternoon, while working on my proofs at the *Post*, I received a call from Professor Samuel Klausner, who introduced himself as an American psychologist conducting research in Israel on the Iraqi community and its integration in Israel. He asked whether he could interview me at his home in the Greek Colony, and I agreed. At that time I was already getting increasingly involved—theoretically rather than in any practical capacity—in the subject of immigrant absorption in Israel, the ethnic problem, and related matters, and I was delighted that someone—and an American academic at that—was taking the trouble to study the subject.

After the difficult first "business" session—in which I submitted to the indignity of a Rorschach test and of actually being recorded on tape—Klausner and I developed the kind of relationship that was close to real friendship. I found him open, understanding, and—unlike the usual run of American Jews—not unduly affected, or almost not affected at all, by the kind of systematic brainwashing to which Zionist fund-raisers in

North America were subjecting prospective Jewish donors at the time. As a matter of fact, Klausner confessed to me that he had feelings of guilt and an uneasy conscience when he reflected that he himself at one point had helped promote nonsense about Iraqi Jews among his Jewish compatriots in the United States. He also showed me some of the photographs he used to be given to peddle — mostly snapshots of Kurdish and Persian families from far-off villages and townlets, to be presented as "Iraqi Jewish families" needing rescue from certain death by being transported to the land of dreams and promise. We were both very glad to have discovered each other and to have such common ground and a common language and inclinations.

I no longer remember what Klausner's "verdict" was concerning my emotional and psychological state or what the Rorschach test revealed, although he himself was quite frank and open about it. But I do know that I felt a lot better after I had related to him my feelings about redis-covering my family and the emotional response I had had when reliving part of my childhood memories at my brother's Sabbath eve table. I have no doubt that the long session with him and the numerous chats that fol-lowed influenced me greatly, though perhaps not quite consciously, in my subsequent decision to seek a wife who shared my background, rather than to continue my flirtations and minor affairs with young women from Europe and North America.

It was Klausner who introduced me to Aharon Amir, who then lived in a fairly spacious house in the Greek Colony with his wife, Hanna. Aha-ron at that time had just finished the translation of the six bulky volumes of Winston Churchill's war memoirs, and felt that he and Hanna could afford a stay abroad for some length of time — a trip made easier because they were childless. During the initial stages of our acquaintance, Amir and I thought there was or should be a natural affinity of views and ap-proach between us, or rather between the movement of which he was one of the leading ideologists — variously called the Young Hebrews or the Canaanites — and the community or group of communities to which I belonged, namely the Sephardi-Oriental camp in Israel.

This affinity would have been based on the solid foundation of what I will call shared alienation from the dominant ideology: The Canaan-ites were fiercely opposed to the idea of Pan-Jewish nationalism, and the Sephardi-Orientals were in a very valid sense excluded from it. The Young Hebrews did not consider the Arabs — inside Israel or outside of it — alien in culture or nationality or ethnicity, and Jews coming from the Arab world were for all intents and purposes Arab. Finally, unlike the Zionists, neither the Canaanites nor the "Arab Jews" subscribed to the ideology of an exclusive, ethnicity-oriented Pan-Arab nationalism, the kind that the Israeli establishment was actively, even openly, fostering, although largely in the negative sense of viewing Israeli Arabs as belonging to an "Arab" nationality and speaking of the "Arab world" as the true homeland of the Palestinians.

The trouble, however, was that Amir and his Canaanites sought to go much further than that: the Arabs of Israel—and by implication the Arabs of the Middle East as a whole—were not ethnically and nationally "Arabs," but were in fact "Hebrews," or at any rate had to be made into Hebrews. Were they not Canaanites and the descendants of Canaanites— exactly as the Jews were?

And so on. I myself never could accept this atavistic, pre-Judaic brand of ethnicity, and in the course of our long friendship and association I came to accuse Amir and his friends of actually being the logical perpetuators and true heirs of the Zionist ideology, with its emphasis on the secular, ethnic-racial aspect of Jewishness. In due course, Amir and at least one of his leading fellow Canaanites, Ezra Sohar, joined the Greater Israel Movement, which after the Six-Day War advocated the annexation of the West Bank, the Gaza Strip, and the Sinai to Israel. Ironically, when his true intentions and his basically anti-Zionist approach were "discovered," Amir was expelled from the leadership of the movement. But he went on advocating annexation, and later extended his interests to south Lebanon: the establishment of an Israeli foothold there through the efforts of mercenary Major Saʿad Haddad would be another step toward the lofty goal of a Hebrew commonwealth.

Meanwhile my association with the *Post* and as a contributor to *Here and Now* continued, and in some ways I became more in demand there as a result of the natural competition between the two publications. Moreover, the appearance in the *Post* of my book reviews in the course of the years 1953 and 1954 tended to give rise to some kind of controversy between the paper's main editors. Meyer found them handy and sought to encourage me, although he did this with extraordinary wariness; Lurie was chiefly somewhat perplexed at the prospect of an outsider—and one suspected of being "an Egyptian Communist" at that—making regular appearances in the paper; and Agron likewise did not know how to digest me. The main problem, in fact, was whether I was to be encouraged to grow into a full-fledged member of the *Post*'s family.

In a way I was caught in a kind of cross fire. It was known in the *Post* that Lurie, who was the actual boss as far as daily management of the editorial department was concerned, was the sort of boss who did not like anyone else, even the editor in chief, to interfere in what he considered his exclusive sphere of authority. However, being a novice in these matters, and encouraged by his tireless attentions, I turned to Agron when I thought it was time to move from the drudgery of proofreading to the authority of the editorial department.

It took Agron a long time to respond—and only after I had reminded him of the subject. It transpired that after he had urgently consulted Lurie, the latter had objected for some reason or other—but reputedly merely because I had not applied to him for the move. Agron wrote me a note: "I have been thinking about your suggestion to move to the Editorial Department, but after looking over the ground very carefully, I regret to say I see no vacancy or prospect of one in the near future. Have you followed up my suggestion with regard to *Here and Now?*"

The implication was clear: rather than try to get into the editorial department, better look elsewhere for advancement! I did, but there was no offer attractive enough to make me move.

GOING OUT WITH IRAQI NEWCOMERS

In Tel Aviv in the early 1950s, in banks and similar institutions in which newly arrived Iraqi young men found employment, it became the custom among veteran fellow employees to dub any girl who went out with an Iraqi "a harlot." The reason: These Iraqi young men were interested in sex rather than in meaningful relationships, and once they had had sex with a girl, they would then rule her out completely as a potential wife. Some put it another way: even if they initially had considered a girl worthy of marriage, the minute she surrendered to them she became unfit to be a wife.

There is, I suppose, nothing surprising or extraordinary about this, considering the kind of society Iraqi Jews had been bred in. In that society, a girl's loss of virginity was considered a calamity so great that no family would dare seek a husband for her. Even in the most "modern" and educated of milieus, in which a girl could conceivably go out with a young man, he first had to be approved of by her family. It was totally unthinkable for a girl to go out with an unmarried man and sleep with him, or even live with him, before marrying him.

Initially at least, Israeli girls who disapproved of dating young Iraqi immigrants were thus basically right in assuming that having sex with such young men was tantamount to prostitution — only without even the benefit of the money! It has to be added here, however, that this state of affairs changed fairly quickly. Some girls still refused to give up so easily and found a way of enticing their suitors, but the outlook of these young men underwent a basic change, and they soon adapted themselves and their attitudes to the new situation.

I was twenty-six when I arrived in Israel, and judging by the considerable measure of popularity I enjoyed among women I encountered, I was probably also "eligible." The difficulty, however, was that I did not think the time had come for me to enter any kind of permanent relationship. In the confusion I felt in those days, too, what with the destitute conditions in which I lived, the uncertainty about my career, the studies I took up immediately after I arrived in Jerusalem, and a dozen other worries and anxieties, I did not think I could establish the kind of household and family that would fit into my own vision of such things.

Not that there was at all a dearth of suitable candidates. The morning Hebrew ulpan was full of eligible young women, at least five of whom competed for my attentions. There was first Vera, a Jewish American young woman in her late twenties; she subsequently married a world-famous musician. Vera came to the ulpan very elegantly dressed and fairly heavily made-up. She was a rather sophisticated person and, what was more important to me at the time, not totally unacquainted with things of the mind. One day she came to class holding a small parcel wrapped in paper bearing the name of a good Jerusalem bookshop. I asked her to show me the book — and lo and behold, it was none other than Burckhardt's volume on the Renaissance in Italy. I could not hide my surprise, and she said that she had purchased the book to give as a birthday present to a friend — which impressed me even more.

Vera took a real interest in me, and one day she invited me to the place where she had a room — in the most fashionable quarter in town — saying it was her night of babysitting and the flat was empty. It was a clear enough gesture, but for some reason I lied, saying that I had another date or appointment. But Vera was looking for a husband in a hurry and could not cope with my pace of doing things. In the middle of the ulpan course she left for Tel Aviv — and after a few months I heard she had married Isaac Stern, the famed violinist.

Then there was Naomie. Naomie too was looking for a spouse — and rather more earnestly, since compared to most girls, she was less good-looking, far more modest, and more observant, though in a modern kind of way. She hailed from Switzerland, but her English was quite adequate, and our friendship outlasted the ulpan for some time — until she gave me up as a hopeless case and married some young engineer in Haifa. During the first weeks of our acquaintance she ventured to accompany me at night on strolls in the city's then main park, and these strolls inevitably developed into embraces and kisses and some modest necking. But she would never go beyond that, even when later on she invited me to an occasional light dinner in her furnished room. I became quite fond of her, and at a certain juncture she even wrote to her mother, asking her to come to Jerusalem, presumably to meet and inspect the eligible suitor. I had the impression that the mother was pleased with what she saw — but then I was making it quite clear that my plans did not go that far. It was shortly after that visit of her mother's that Naomie sent me an invitation to her wedding.

Esther was from Romania. Not quite twenty, she was intelligent, quick-witted, and surprisingly well read — and she knew several languages, including German and Russian and some French and English. She was richly endowed physically, well built and well proportioned. With no makeup and no hairdo, she looked like my idea of a simple country girl. And she had the added attraction of being poor and living in an immigrant girls' hostel run by the Jewish Agency. We had a lot in common, in short, and her love of languages and her knowledge of literature tended to strengthen our friendship. She was especially impressed by the fact that, having learned something about the derivation of certain words in Romanian, I was able often to use "Romanian" words by the simple device of substituting the ending -tzia for -tion — modernizatzia for "modernization," implicatzia, rotatzia, and so on; I once even used the word constipatzia, just in case it would work, and it did. But Esther was also quick to pick up Hebrew, and we often had to make do with our knowledge of that language.

After finishing our ulpan course, Esther joined the army — and one day while I was sweating over proofs at work, Esther suddenly made an appearance, her first at the newspaper, duly clad in uniform, her tendency to obesity seemingly more pronounced. She was not quite happy in the army, she told me, what with all those young Israeli and new immigrant girls with whom she could not find a common language. She waited for me until I finished my afternoon shift — and it being already dinnertime, we had something to eat, and then I took her to the room that by then I had acquired in Princess Mary Avenue. After what seemed to be hours of necking, she finally agreed to spend the night with me.

I was becoming quite fond of Esther, and had our relationship lasted for a sufficient period of time, I think it would have ended in marriage. However, one day when we were supposed to meet somewhere, Esther failed to turn up—and since that day I have not been able to discover what happened then or her whereabouts now. Our one common acquaintance, a Romanian woman who lived with her husband not far from where I lived, didn't know any more than I did; at least, that was what she said.

Although those were the days of mass emigration from Iraq, there were very few Iraqi newcomers in the ulpan I attended. The reasons for that are too complicated to go into here. Suffice it to say that, though armed with a secondary school certificate and a letter of admittance from the Hebrew University, I had to bring a letter of recommendation from Goitein before I could register for the ulpan!

MATCHMAKING MADE EASY

One of the two Iraqi newcomers whom I remember meeting in the ulpan was a girl in her early twenties by name of Mary, the other a young man of no special interest or appeal to me. Nor was Mary for that matter, although she did her very best to show me that she was no less bright or intelligent than the girls I seemed to be courting. And the truth was that she wasn't. Eager and a good learner, she also had quite a sense of humor—and was full of life and its expectations. But I failed to be impressed or attracted— at least for the duration of our Hebrew lessons. Subsequently, however, after she and her parents moved to Ramat Gan and following Esther's disappearance, I wrote to her. We met one Saturday evening somewhere near where she lived (I was staying with the Jijis).

To my surprise and disappointment, Mary's response to what she must have known was a serious attempt at knowing her better, made with the most "honorable" of intentions, was not quite up to my expectations— and after a short correspondence (which I made a point of conducting in English), we again lost sight of each other. Later I learned of her marriage to some bank clerk. Many years later we met somewhere, and when I learned that she was on the point of getting a divorce, I managed to broach the subject of our nonrelationship and what I thought was her large share in not allowing a meaningful and perhaps lasting relationship to develop. She admitted the charge, saying only that she had thought me too "self-centered."

In a way, there was a fundamental inconsistency in my decision to marry into my own community and social milieu. Not only did I think I was more at home in the society of Westerners, but I also had the feeling that Iraqi girls and Iraqis in general tended to consider me some kind of queer fish—bookish, overly preoccupied with ideas, not sufficiently modern, and somewhat antisocial—and in any case not worldly enough. One of the things that tended to disqualify me in a certain section of the society was the fact that I had never bothered to learn to dance and took no part in any sport. This put me in a very peculiar position. On the one hand, no Iraqi Jewish girl who was of the right age group and educated enough to be considered eligible could be expected to be intellectual enough to contemplate marriage to a man who had not taken the trouble to learn to dance; on the other hand, girls who did not take notice of such things were usually not educated and came from a social class that was not normally one with whose members I and my friends associated.

There was another difficulty. In 1956, when I finally felt I had better settle down, I was coming up on thirty-two, an age that was not the most convenient if you were looking for a wife of suitable age. A girl of what age is suitable for a man of thirty-two? The question is not easy to answer, and perhaps should not be asked at all, since the answer seems to differ for each case. As far as I was concerned, although I made no hard and fast rules about it, I felt that at such an age a difference of about ten years would not be too great, but a girl over twenty-six would probably be a bit too old unless an attachment should develop that was strong enough to make all other considerations irrelevant.

It was quite a tricky situation. In Iraqi Jewish society, even after five years of "modernization" in Israel, going out with a girl for any length of time without a formal engagement was not a common practice. And I felt that I had no time to spend on such complex affairs, especially in Jerusalem, where the Iraqi community was small, counting out the old-timers with whom I could find no common social or cultural language. Besides, as the saying goes, all the nice girls had already got themselves husbands, and girls under twenty-five were both too young and probably too acculturated to the new society and the new social norms to be quite acceptable or responsive enough.

I kept vaguely trying to find a way out, to try to decide on the person with whom I would want to share a lifetime. One day in the summer of 1956, however, a sort of solution to this tricky problem presented itself. It came in the form of an indirect suggestion made by my friend Aharon Nathan. I had known Aharon in Baghdad only superficially, when he used to frequent the Al-Rabita Bookshop, usually looking for a classic or for something recommended by the English teacher at the Shamash School, where he was preparing for the London matriculation. In Israel, I came across him in the days when I attended the Hebrew University, where he was taking a degree in Middle Eastern studies — and at one stage I was instrumental in finding partial employment for him as a proofreader at the *Post.*

In those early days of immigrant absorption, both Aharon and I lived in the Talpiot maʿbara — he with his father and three sisters, I with Mother and Simha. This, however, was before my journey to Europe and before I made my decision about marriage and about the community into which I wanted to marry. By the time I had decided, two of Aharon's sisters were already married and the third was somewhat too young, besides being unresponsive.

By that time Aharon knew me well enough to know about my personal plans, and one day he told me he would like to introduce me to the family of his eldest sister, Hanna; by that time they had moved from the maʿbara to a house in Arnona, a few dozen meters from Kibbutz Ramat Rahel. It was the first time I had learned of the existence of that family, since there had been no occasion for Aharon to tell me about it previously. To be sure, he told me what the real aim of the visit would be, although he made it clear that that was not the sole aim — namely, to make the acquaintance of the family's eldest daughter, Rachel-Dahlia, who was in her twenty-fifth year and was working in some government office, doing something with computers, which were then in their infancy, at least where Israel was concerned.

The story of Rachel's family was like that of any of thousands of Iraqi Jewish families still groping their way in new and rather bewildering circumstances. Apart from Rachel — at home they insisted on calling her Dahlia, her other name — there were two sons and two daughters, all but one already out of school and working. My future father-in-law, Moshe, who was my senior by probably no more than thirteen years, used to work in the export-import business in Baghdad and earned a respectable enough living there to raise his children in fairly comfortable circumstances and send them to the best schools.

Rachel, being the firstborn, had just managed to finish her secondary schooling before she came to Israel illegally in 1950, where she joined a kibbutz while awaiting the arrival of her family. When the family arrived the next year, however, she was forced to leave the kibbutz and take a job to help pay for the family's grocery bill. All seven members of the family lived in a tin hut in the Talpiot maʿbara, then situated close to the border with Jordan. Eventually, Moshe found a job in the accounts department of the Ministry of Trade and Industry, the children started to go to school, and the elder of Rachel's brothers and sisters found jobs and were earning some money. In the meantime, using savings and money from the sale of some jewelry, the family rented a ground-floor flat, moved out of the ma'bara, and started some sort of normal life again.

I did not know — and never bothered to ask — about Rachel's previous experiences, or whether she had had any suitors. But in the course of long talks we had during our excursions and in my room, I was given to understand that at least two of her brother Jacob's friends had sought her hand, and that for some reason or other she had declined. For the engagement, officiated by her mother's father, I gave her a ring, and we spent the few months until the wedding mostly looking for a suitable place to live, since my room was far too small.

However, when the appointed date approached, it became all too clear that the wedding couldn't take place: November 5, 1956, was only a few days after the start of Operation Kadesh — the name given by Israel to the war with Egypt in the Sinai — and I was doing reserve duty in the army. There was some trepidation on both sides about the postponement — interpreted as a bad omen — and in the end November 12 was set as the final date. It was a very modest wedding celebration — at the Ohel Mo'ed Synagogue in Tel Aviv, where most of the relatives and friends invited could come without too much trouble. The honeymoon lasted exactly seven days — the seven days that the army agreed to grant me for the occasion. We spent most of it in a hotel near Ramat Gan, and the evenings we spent visiting relatives and friends in the vicinity — an opportunity for the two of us to meet and get to know each other's family.

After spending some weeks in the crowdedness of my little room, we finally moved to the two rooms we had taken in the German Colony for key money (a payment for taking possession of the key to an apartment). They were large enough rooms in themselves, and my mother was able to stay on with us. Rachel had her job at the government Bureau of Statistics, and I continued with my proofreading — and all of us waited for my wife to become pregnant! By that time I had acquired a large ancient typewriter and was able to type my occasional articles and columns by day while working afternoon or night shifts at the paper.

ISRAEL ARABIC BROADCASTS

Before I was released from my reserve duties, however, I was ordered by the army to do work for the Arabic section of Israel Radio as part of my service. As far as I was concerned, the arrangement could not have been more convenient, since I did the work in Jerusalem, in shifts, and was thus given an opportunity to spend more time at home and in normal social activities.

When Lurie got wind of this, however, he at first became furious, and then immediately saw his opportunity and seized it. He contacted the paper's lawyer and made sure that he was right to insist that the army had no business employing reserve soldiers in civilian jobs as part of their service; he then wrote to the army to that effect; and he finally started sounding out the director of Arabic broadcasts, Shaul Bar-Haim, on the possibility of his taking me on as a full-time news editor. He was to succeed on all counts.

Dealing with me was a real problem for Lurie. Although my English was good enough, as a proofreader I was reportedly not sufficiently careful, and some errors were left in the stuff I read. On the other hand, from what I had written for publication until then, he judged that I would be rather more than merely adequate as an analyst and commentator on Arab affairs, someone whom the paper needed desperately, since their salaried Arab affairs man was deemed unqualified for the task. Lurie's idea was that I should either replace him or become the paper's Arab affairs analyst as a freelancer. What tended to complicate matters was that shortly before the Suez War, Lurie had finally decided to move me to the editorial department as subeditor, both to encourage me to write more articles and to appease his chief proofreader, who had been complaining about my performance.

In the editorial department, however, although no one complained about the quality of my work as copy editor, my superiors said I was rather slow — and for all I knew they were probably right. Lurie thus found himself in a pretty tricky situation. He could not very well antagonize me by simply giving me the sack; he could not force the editorial department to keep me; he was determined that his Arab affairs man either leave the paper or else continue to be content with merely monitoring Arab news; and he was not about to employ an additional man to do the job of analyst-commentator on these affairs. For all these reasons, Lurie decided that the best way was for me to work for the Arabic radio.

He won his case with the army easily enough. But another development having to do with Arabic broadcasts intervened in his favor. Following the Sinai campaign and the apparently resounding victory for Egypt under Abdel Nasser, the powers that be suddenly became aware of the importance of these Israeli broadcasts, and decided to expand them very considerably. For this there was a need for people who knew Arabic well enough to edit news, write talks, and produce programs. As a matter of fact, it was this that had led the army to post me at the radio station.

When the army found that it couldn't continue with this, the radio people offered to employ me temporarily on a shift basis, and I agreed — without, however, terminating my relations with the *Post* as an employee. This arrangement continued for a short time only, and in the spring of 1957 I was formally appointed a news editor in Kol Yisrael's (the Voice of Israel's) Arabic section. Lurie had good reason to be pleased with himself, and I, having actually lost nothing by the arrangement, started contributing more regularly to the paper, and also filling in for its Arab affairs reporter, Gideon Weigert, when he was on leave.

As a kind of summing up, I wrote Lurie a letter dated January 1, 1957:

Following your suggestion the other day re: the possibility of using material broadcast over our Arabic radio, I have just had a meeting with Shaul Bar-Haim on the subject. It appears that there are three groups of material which can be of use to us:

1. Political talks written by people who have access to special information.
2. Army intelligence handouts which can be cooked and served as substantial background stories.
3. Extracts from newspapers and broadcasts in Arabic.

Needless to say, any or all of the above material can just be reported as coming from Kol Yisrael Arabic broadcasts or "an official spokesman" or such. However, the deciding must be made by you, and I await further instructions.

Lurie was quite happy with the arrangement — as indeed he should've been! Lurie was in fact killing two birds with one stone — finding what he thought was a decent way of easing Weigert out of his job and having me as a part-time Arab affairs analyst and commentator.

The arrangement worked fairly smoothly: I contributed my weekly column, "The Middle East Scene," under the pen name Amnon Bartur, and at the same time discharged my duties as news editor at the Arabic section of Kol Yisrael.

This went on for nearly a year and a half, during which the only hitches I recall were Weigert's complaints to the Journalists Association and some mysterious protestations from the Mossad — no less! — that in my Bartur reports I was using material and information that were strictly secret and that nevertheless somehow reached me. These claims I found vastly amusing, not only because they had absolutely no foundation in fact, but also — and chiefly — because I thought they reflected upon the sources the Mossad had for its "secret" information regarding the Arab scene. After all, all my sources were limited to Arab radio broadcasts and the few Jordanian newspapers published practically next door, in Arab Jerusalem.

EDITOR IN CHIEF

Some time in 1958 another development came up. By then Rachel was expecting, Mother continued to keep house, and things seemed to have settled more or less nicely for us. In the meantime, too, our uncle Aharon Nathan (he is quite a few years my junior and only five years older than Rachel) had been working in the office of the prime minister's advisor on Arab affairs, at that time Shmuel (Ziama) Divon. In 1958, he became one of Divon's two assistants — the other being Uri Lubrani.

It was during the last few months of Divon's service that the outcry came for a drastic change at the semiofficial Arabic daily *Al Yawm,* and acting on a cue from the then director-general of the prime minister's office, Teddy Kollek, Aharon started sounding me out about taking up the job of the paper's editor in chief. It was of course understood that the paper's budget would be increased and that I was first to plan the necessary changes, which included, besides expansion and improvement of services, the drastic step of making the paper a morning newspaper. The offer also entailed our moving to Tel Aviv, since there was no question of moving the paper to Jerusalem or, alternatively, of my doing the job while continuing to reside in Jerusalem.

It was a very difficult decision to have to make. The pros were as weighty as the cons — or so it seemed to me at the time. On the one hand, the shift implied a considerable increase in my salary and a certain improvement in status; it also meant the end of the drudgery of news editing at the radio, where I was not exactly happy with the way things were conducted generally. There were, in addition, no political strings attached. Although I never was a member of the ruling party, Mapai (the Israel Workers' Party), no questions were asked on that score. Tel Aviv, too, had its attractions, and by that time I felt I had had enough of Jerusalem.

On the other hand, I felt that by then I was somehow on the right road — fast becoming an acknowledged authority on Arab affairs, writing as a freelancer not only for the *Jerusalem Post* but also for some periodicals abroad, including *Commentary,* one of whose editors—George Lichtheim (former writer of the London Letters for the *Post*)—had invited me to contribute an article and had duly published it. My friend Aharon Amir had also just launched his quarterly, *Keshet* (*Rainbow*), and I began writing for him some stuff that went considerably beyond what normally went by the name of journalism—real heavyweight papers on such subjects as Arab nationalism, the Muslim Brethren, and the modernist movement in Islam.

I also had an offer through my friend Alfred (Alef) Sherman—whom I had met at the *Post* and who knew Elie from the London School of Economics—to do a book jointly with him on some Arab ideological subject. However, although I felt that taking the job at *Al Yawm* was tantamount to asking for trouble, I must admit that these were vague feelings. In the end a combination of factors led me to give my consent, factors having to do mainly with the challenge that I saw in the assignment and the material improvements that the new job was bound to bring with it.

I had my first taste of the shape of things to come quite early in the proceedings—and had I been a little more careful, a little smarter, or a little more far-sighted, it would have been enough to keep me away from the job. As I mentioned, despite the fact that the funds for *Al Yawm* came from the prime minister's office, the Histadrut (the national labor federation) had a strong foothold in it: *Al Yawm*'s editor, Michael Assaf, and his assistant, Tawfiq Shamosh. When the idea was discussed of making far-reaching changes, therefore, the Histadrut was considered a legitimate party to the deliberations, especially since it had hinted that it intended to contribute to the increased subsidy.

It was thus deemed suitable for me to have an interview with Mr. Reuben Barkat, the chairman of the Histadrut's political department. An appointment was arranged, and one afternoon I went to see him at the labor federation's headquarters in Tel Aviv. I was totally unprepared, and was taken quite by surprise when he opened by saying something about the paper's becoming a Histadrut organ, implying ever so subtly that that was not exactly the same as being a semiofficial paper. I mobilized what presence of mind I had and mumbled something to the effect that I saw no basic contradiction there, and that at least as far as local Arab affairs were concerned, I really could detect no difference in approach between the government and the Histadrut.

Barkat was shrewd enough not to press the point any further, and we parted fairly amicably. A week or so later I was chatting with Lurie one afternoon about an idea for a leader, and he suddenly mentioned something about *Al Yawm,* saying he understood that I had rejected the offer — he did not even try to hide his pleasure at the development. When I asked him how he knew I had rejected the offer, he said he had been told about it by no less a man than Uri Lubrani, who by then was in the active stages of replacing Divon as the prime minister's advisor on Arab affairs. Lubrani, it soon transpired, was told by Barkat that I was not interested in the job — and the matter would have rested there had Lurie not been shocked when I told him that I had said nothing to give Barkat that impression, and that in fact I was still interested in the job.

Lurie then telephoned Lubrani and related to him my version of that interview with Barkat, thereupon restarting the ball rolling. Apparently the prime minister's office, then run almost single-handedly by Teddy Kollek, went on with the negotiations despite the Histadrut's objections to my appointment, deciding to go it alone as far as budgetary considerations were concerned. For my part, although I had nothing against the Histadrut as such, I was really annoyed at how Barkat had apparently tried to prevent my appointment. I thought it was repulsive, and was thus glad that the Histadrut was out of it.

I was to be proved wrong on both counts. For repulsive as Barkat's stratagem seemed to me to be at the time, it was nothing compared to what was to come. Moreover, the Histadrut never really remained out of it, even for a moment; what it wanted was just to gain time. There were two possibilities, according to its calculations. The job of renovating and enlarging *Al Yawm* — and turning it into a morning paper — was so difficult that my failure was inevitable, after which it would be able easily to take over publication. Or the operation would succeed, and it would find another way to call the shots. In any event, the operation did succeed — and the Histadrut did find a way of taking almost total control.

It is remarkable how party functionaries in Israel tend to survive — and prevail — against all odds. Sometime in 1960 Reuben Barkat was ousted by Histadrut Secretary-General Pinchas Lavon during the peak days of the so-called Lavon Affair, a naked struggle between the Histadrut and the government. The conflict originated in a "security mishap," the blame for which had been placed on Lavon while he served as minister of defense in the early 1950s.

The so-called mishap had to do with certain acts of sabotage that Israeli agents had directed against a number of American institutions in Cairo, with a view to creating tension and discord between Washington and Cairo. The operation was executed in such an amateurish way, and subsequently failed so dismally, that no one in Tel Aviv was willing to take responsibility. As minister of defense, Lavon, however, was held responsible, and was accordingly demoted to the job of Histadrut secretary-general. While waiting for the dust to settle, Lavon entrenched himself in the monstrous Histadrut citadel, and a few years later he reopened the case in public, now blaming David Ben-Gurion for what he said was a total fabrication against himself.

The house of labor became fiercely divided upon itself, and Barkat, a longtime faithful follower of the party's machine, apparently sided with Ben-Gurion's camp. Lavon promptly sacked him, together with certain of his stooges. Equally promptly, Barkat was rehabilitated by the party, and became secretary of Mapai.

As far as I am able to discover, it was Barkat who first actively tried to get me out of the way. It all started with a Marginal Column I had written for the *Post;* it was given a title not of my doing—"Non-Ashkenazi Justice" (August 13, 1963).

But first a few words about *Al Yawm,* its checkered history, and the circumstances leading to my becoming so deeply—and disastrously—involved in it.

Al Yawm was launched sometime in late 1948 by a group of establishment Arabists, and its editorship was entrusted to Michael Assaf. A lifelong Mapai member and Histadrut ideologist, Assaf was officially the Arab affairs commentator for the Histadrut's daily, *Davar,* but was also responsible for an Arabic weekly the Histadrut had been putting out, *Haqiqat el Amr* (*The Truth of the Matter*). Since Assaf could not, because of his limited knowledge of Arabic and because of the time required to do both jobs, do all the work himself, he used the services of a younger man, an associate of his and Histadrut employee by the name of Toubia (Tawfiq) Shamosh. Both Assaf and Shamosh were answerable, at least formally, to whoever happened to head the Histadrut's political and Arab departments, which always had the same boss, although the latter department was "managed" by some trusted Arabic-literate employee of the federation. When *Al Yawm* was launched, Assaf naturally became editor in chief and Shamosh, his "editorial secretary"—the Israeli equivalent of a managing editor or executive editor.

There was, in reality, not much for real live reporters or even editors to do at the paper. Conveniently appearing at noontime, *Al Yawm* consisted of four tabloid pages: three carried summarized and often caricatured versions of the main news stories from that same morning's *Davar,* minus various items judged too sensitive to bring to the notice of the Arab readers, plus a few usually dated short reports from stringers in the larger villages, reporting mainly on visits from some government official, the building of a road or a school, and similar stories of a "positive" nature. Some space was also given to summaries of articles on the Arab world written by Assaf for *Davar*, rare letters from readers, even rarer original contributions, as well as a weekly literary page in which some of the poets and writers who were subsequently to be the leading ones in the field — Rashid Hussein and Mahmud Darwish among them — made their first appearance.

As the Arab population gradually achieved greater education and political awareness, however, *Al Yawm* became increasingly unpopular, and in fact was treated as a laughingstock by the same intelligentsia that it was supposed to serve and give expression to. Moreover, the two political parties of the left, the Communists and Mapam (the United Workers' Party), were already producing Arabic-language newspapers that, though neither was a daily, looked far more like proper journalistic enterprises than *Al Yawm* ever managed to do — and that also employed and printed contributions by Arab writers and publicists. Faced with this state of affairs and overwhelmed by criticism of the scope and policies of the paper and its professional standards, the office of the prime minister's advisor on Arab affairs was finally moved to do something about it.

The reason why that office had to take action was simple: although the paper was actually run by Histadrut hacks, and its general orientation was decided by the federation's Arabic Department, the money was paid from government funds, specifically from the budget of the prime minister's advisor on Arab affairs. And so, some eight years after its launch, *Al Yawm* was finally judged ripe for drastic changes, and the search for a new editor and a new format started.

However, once I stopped drawing a regular salary from the *Post*, my relations with Lurie improved, and apparently my pieces became something of an attraction. As far as real knowledge of what was then going on in the Arab world was concerned, mine must have been a classic case of learning while doing, my main initial contribution to the field being no more than a certain felicity of expression and a refusal to say things that were either insufficiently backed by facts or a mere repetition of what had already been said hundreds of times by others. The method worked, and it worked so well that I myself was surprised.

My contributions to the *Jerusalem Post* in those days fell into four categories: one Marginal Column a week under my own name; a Friday article, "The Middle East Scene," featuring the week's main event and signed "Amnon Bartur"; one or two unsigned leading articles on Arab and Middle Eastern affairs; and book reviews. It was only in my book reviews that I allowed myself the privilege of writing about things that really interested me — general cultural subjects, intellectual trends, novels, Jewish topics and books on Arab and Middle East subjects. This helped me keep in touch with literary, cultural, and intellectual trends in the world as a whole. I also accepted an assignment to do a column of short reviews, which the paper used to run under the heading "Round the Bookshops."

My work for the radio as a news editor, since it was done in shifts and thus tied me to the place for no specified hours of the day, helped me in these rather hectic activities. Apart from my work for the radio and my regular contributions to the *Post,* I was able to accept other small assignments — articles for the American Jewish Congress's *Congress Biweekly,* a serious contribution to an anthology of Middle East studies then being prepared by Walter Laqueur for Routledge, some translations, and contributions to local publications in English.

Chapter 5 | ＴHE LEVANTINISM SCARE

JACQUELINE KAHANOFF

ＴHe only fan letter I remember writing went to Jacqueline Kahanoff. This was in the spring of 1958, when the newly published Israel supplement of *The Jewish Frontier* (the journal of the Labor Zionist Alliance) carried an article with the intriguing title "Reflections of a Levantine."

The piece was written by Mrs. Kahanoff in defense of the much-maligned "Levantine," and the thrust of her argument was that European Zionists, who had been set apart in Europe as a foreign, Oriental people — "Levantines" — and had retained their Jewish identity by remaining un-assimilated, would have been expected to return to the Holy Land as if returning to the Semitic, Levantine, Oriental world in which the Jewish people had its roots. That the very opposite had occurred — that these men had actually rejected the Levant and its peoples — was a paradox that Jacqueline Kahanoff could not easily comprehend.

In her opinion, those European Israelis who were constantly voicing fears of "Levantinization" and "Orientalization" and extolling the virtues of Western civilization and Western culture had forgotten "that the exploitation of colonial peoples, race prejudice, death camps and nuclear warfare are also part of Western civilization." Their attitude, she thought, reflected "a lack of cultural re-evaluation of themselves in the light of their tragic experience in Europe which ended in mass extermination and their presence in a State of Israel planted on the outer fringe of a vociferously anti-European and anti-Western world."

Needless to say, at a time when the so-called Levantines were being shamed into disowning their cultural distinctiveness, such ideas as those put forward by Kahanoff I found refreshing and welcome in the extreme. Eventually I was to discover that, whatever else it was being made to mean, the appellation "Levantine" suited Jacqueline Kahanoff superbly — both in the geographical and cultural sense.

How else can one describe a Jewish woman who was born in Cairo of an Iraqi father and a Tunisian mother, got her schooling in a French school in the Egyptian capital yet managed to speak not a word of Arabic, studied in Paris, lived and worked in the United States, wrote a novel in English, married a Cairo-born Jew of Russian extraction, and came to Israel in the mid-1950s to find herself defending the cause of the Levantine underdog?

By far the best and weightiest of Jacqueline's writings were first published in the Hebrew quarterly *Keshet*. It was also in 1958 that I drew Aharon Amir's attention to her work and arranged a meeting between them. It was just after the first issue of *Keshet* had come out, and the meeting took place in our tiny residence in the German Colony in Jerusalem. In the second issue of the magazine, the first of her autobiographical sketches— "A Generation of Levantines"—was published in Amir's own Hebrew translation. Apart from the rest of this series, virtually all the essays she wrote were to appear in *Keshet,* including her detailed and moving long piece, "To Die a Modern Death," in which she described the death of her father in a home for the aged in Tel Aviv. A few of her other essays and articles were published in a variety of Hebrew papers and periodicals, especially *Ma'ariv* and the woman's magazine *At.*

In a preface that he contributed to a collection of her essays published after her untimely death in 1980, Amir rightly points out that Jacqueline Kahanoff's essays and recollections became hallmarks of his quarterly, an avenue to the hearts of sensitive and discriminating readers of the magazine. And indeed the collection was welcomed in literary and cultural circles in Israel with warmth and enthusiasm—deservedly, if only as a possible means of introducing a new Israeli generation to a world and a culture that it was taught to underestimate and denigrate.

The correspondence that followed my original fan letter to Jacqueline was rather short, since we were soon to move to Ramat Gan, where meetings and dinners were to take place fairly regularly, almost always with the participation of Aharon and his charming first wife, Hanna. The following are extracts from two of the few letters Jacqueline wrote to me while we were still in Jerusalem.

May 28, 1958
Dear Mr. Rejwan:

First let me tell you how very much I appreciated your letter and your response to the article in the *Jewish Frontier*. Oddly enough . . .

as a faithful reader of your editorials in the *Jerusalem Post,* while I wrote the article I often thought of them and of the difference in our point of view, and wondered if we would ever meet to discuss these ideas which have consequence in which we are all involved. I am very happy that the opportunity has now come . . .

To return to your letter. You have touched on the weak spot of my article. I frankly admit it and feel this more now than a year ago when I wrote the article. Yet I don't think that the M.E. [Middle East] is only a matter of Arab States vs. Israel, but of other minorities too. Very much depends on politics, I know, and these are real worries. My point of view is speculative and can be mistaken. It is that after the present fury, there might be a reaction towards a great many of the good things in the Levantine tradition because politics will not completely change people. Just to take the example of Nasser, he had not become so that he killed the Jews in Egypt, he let them come to Israel, knowing that after all they would serve in the Army here. He and his consorts are still Levantine enough not to apply the extreme logical consequences of these beliefs, and I know, at least from my parents who have recently come, that in Egypt itself opinion is not all of a piece — nor for that matter is it in the FLN [Front for National Liberation, an Algerian political party set up in Egypt]. My point is that we and our neighbors may rediscover that not everything in the Levantine was bad, they have to discover that, and we can't force them to. But I don't think it helps that we should ignore either the real problems which led them to their actual revolt which is anti-Levantine and anti-European, nor that this might be a way through which another generation might find a way to speak of the possibility of a common way of feeling and not be dismissed at the outset as inferior and undesirable and impossible. I do not know, nor do I think there is a clear Yes or No. But I do know that had I been born Moslem I would have been pro-Nasser now as a necessary reaction to the last 50 years, and having then another set of values. I would have reacted against these extremes. I suppose this is confused dashed off from a cafe table — but maybe we can discuss this further. I am much looking forward to meeting you.

BEST REGARDS,
JACQUELINE S. KAHANOFF

June 12, 1958
Dear Nissim,

I really feel embarrassed for not having written to you sooner as I
had the intention of doing to tell you how glad I was to meet you and
your wife and to thank you both for the very pleasant and interesting
evening . . .

I also enjoyed meeting your friends and hearing what they feel
here in Israel. I think there ought to be some form of action or pressure because that's how things get done in the modern world. But it
should have a neutral and appealing name. After all a lobby or pressure group is never called that way. The American oil lobby is called
I think the American-Arab Friendship League. This might be called
the Association for Cultural Advancement — with a membership
open to all. The first thing is not to be put on the defensive about
"separatism." What do you think? . . .

AHARON AMIR AND *KESHET*

Despite our basic differences of opinion, Aharon Amir and I became good
friends, and throughout the eleven years that I and the family spent in
Ramat Gan, our social life very often intermingled with that of the Amirs.
They were invited practically to every social function we gave; we went out
to eat together, often to the little Iraqi place in Ramat Gan called Shemesh;
and on a few occasions we went together to a nightclub in Jaffa's entertain-
ment center. There was real friendship between Rachel and Amir's first
wife, Hanna, and my continued association with *Keshet*, which Aharon
edited, gave us an added reason to be together fairly frequently.

Amir had started *Keshet* as a cultural quarterly some time in 1957 —
and already in the first issue I had a contribution, a Hebrew translation of
my article "Arab Nationalism in Search of Ideology," which had just appeared in *The Middle East in Transition*, a book of essays edited by W. Z.
Laqueur and published in England by Routledge. At first Aharon did not
like the article, but on showing it to his then editorial secretary, Hedda
Boshes, he changed his mind — and apologized at length for his earlier
judgment! In the second issue, however, I offered him an original contribution, to my mind an even weightier one, on the Muslim Brethren. And
after that, what with my growing interest in the study of modern Islam
and the roots of the nationalist movement in Egypt and in the Arab world

generally, my contributions continued, covering such a wide variety of subjects as surveys of the religious thought of Jamaleddin al-Afghani and Muhammad 'Abdu, the rise of Egyptian nationalism, the cultural upsurge that followed the modernist movement of Afghani and his followers, Ibn Khaldun and his philosophy of history, and even an article on the communal problem in Israel—an incomplete rendering of my *Midstream* article "Israel's Communal Controversy."

Amir "did" *Keshet* virtually single-handedly—taking care of the editing, translating, proofreading, assembling of pages, advertising, and promoting. And this in addition to the huge volume of translations he had to do to earn a living. Amir was in fact one of the two best translators I was fortunate to have for the occasional article or review that I chose to publish in Hebrew. The other was Boaz Evron, who, for a brief period of time, worked as literary editor of the evening daily *Yediot Aharonot*. With the exception of two appearances that I made in the bimonthly *Amot*—published by the American Jewish Committee and edited throughout its short and stormy existence by Shlomo Grodzenski—practically all the occasional journalism and book reviews I published in Hebrew appeared in *Keshet* and *Yediot Aharonot*.

During Evron's literary editorship of the latter, he somehow managed to have a long review-article of mine in his pages practically every week. I once asked him how he managed to translate them while also doing the work usually involved in editing the book pages. His reply was so flattering that I record it here only with some embarrassment. He said: "Nissim, believe me when I tell you that translating an article of yours takes me considerably less time and trouble than editing an average Hebrew piece of the same length and putting it in good shape for the typesetters." Not particularly disliking praise, I made sure he meant what I thought he did!

I had only a few quarrels with Amir over editorial policy or contents. He printed my article on the ethnic problem after a certain amount of hesitation—and then only after he made me agree to take out the first few paragraphs dealing with Kalman Katznelson's notorious *The Ashkenazi Revolution*. Otherwise, faithful to his Canaanite creed though he continued to be, he refrained from narrow sectarianism and dogmatism and produced a fairly open cultural and literary platform. However, from my long association with him and from the innumerable occasions on which we discussed the matter, I came to the conclusion that Amir's recipe for *Keshet* was a very shrewd and intelligent one. Although he probably would not have published any direct attack on the Young Hebrews' ideology (or perhaps he would have, on the assumption that even such a piece would serve the cause in some way), his outlook was so broad that he managed to detect some "positive" aspect in practically everything he published.

I have never stopped marveling at this aspect of Amir's conduct as *Keshet*'s editor. For one thing, it showed a welcome broadness of vision; for another, more significant consideration, his policy seemed to me to signify a measure of self-confidence and a strength of belief in his own way and outlook that were rarely encountered in doctrinaires and true believers. Another aspect of his approach and his way of trying to make virtually everything serve his ideological purposes was the care he took when translating for the quarterly: he was diligent about using words and expressions drawn from pre-Judaic Hebrew (and not from Rabbinic Hebrew), thus reflecting the Hebrew of the old Hebrews, of whom the Young ones were supposed to be the inheritors.

Not that he gave up the more practical aspects of the good fight. In the early 1960s, coming to an understanding with at least some of his old comrades in the movement—notably Dr. Ezra Sohar and 'Adia Gurevitch—he founded the so-called "Hebrew Thought Club," a discussion group meeting once every fortnight (at the premises of 'Am Ha-Sefer, the publishing house owned by Amir's father and run by himself) to deal with some politico-cultural topic thought to be of relevance either to the affairs of the day or to "Hebrew thought" or both. I used to attend the meetings, and on one occasion I took it upon myself to give the opening presentation. The subject was Arab nationalism and Pan-Arabism, and in it I expounded my views on what I considered the basically Pan-Arab orientation of the Zionist establishment in Israel and how it had come to pass that the last of the Pan-Arabs were then sitting in the Israeli Foreign Ministry in Jerusalem!

The paper was received with enthusiasm by Sohar and by Amir, who were particularly anxious to enroll me in their group. But it was evident, as it had been almost a decade before, that my views and those of the Canaanites coincided only up to a point; after that point, our paths parted in most meaningful senses. Shortly after my leaving the editorship of *Al Yawm*, in fact, a delegation comprising the three big shots of the movement—or of that part of it that was working under the guise of the club— came to see me at our home in Ramat Gan, hoping to persuade me to get organizationally more involved in their activity, for what it was. But all I could do was to repeat my old and familiar argument with Amir.

In any event, even that tiny band of three ageing Young Hebrews was to be dismantled because of equally tiny differences of opinion. It is, after all, in the nature of all such small and highly ideologically oriented groups to be torn by such differences. Death, too, eventually played a certain part: Gurevitch died, Ezra Sohar turned his attention to more practical goals and submitted his candidacy to the Knesset as the leader of a small group concerned mainly with taxes and the quality of life, and Amir continued in his chosen path as a solitary fighter for the good old cause, turning more and more to original writing, although he had to go on with his work as a professional translator. During 1980 and 1981, in fact, you could hardly leaf through the literary pages of any local newspaper without coming across Amir's name, as either author or translator of at least one of the titles mentioned or reviewed.

FASHIONING A "NATIONAL MINORITY"

Shortly after taking up the editorship of *Al Yawm,* in April 1959, I found myself increasingly exposed to the variety of dilemmas and issues comprised in what is known as the problem of the Arabs of Israel. The exposure sprang largely from my day-to-day contact with what was virtually a new generation of Israeli Arabs—journalists, poets, teachers, and intellectuals who had hardly reached the age of ten when the state was established in 1948. Partly, too, it was due to the way that I found myself looking at the problem: simply as one part of the more general issue of Israel's bewildering posture as a self-styled "European," or "Western," country—despite the fact that, on the one hand, over half of its people were Middle Easterners, and, on the other, it is situated in the heart of the Arab area and surrounded by Arabs.

My quarrel with Mapam (the United Workers' Party), for instance, was not that it was wooing Arab voters by bandying about Arab nationalist concepts and doctrines; the real reason was that, while pretending to offer Israel's Arabs more than the ruling Mapai party did, they would not or could not compromise on one cardinal issue—namely, defining Israel as a Jewish state and its nationality as Jewish. What I considered even more objectionable was that, in reality, the kind of ethnic nationalism that they advocated among the Arabs followed the same ideological lines as did the nationalism advocated by all Zionist parties, not excluding Mapam— Pan-Jews wooing and commiserating with Pan-Arabs, so to speak. I took up this subject in a few columns I wrote for the *Post* in 1961–1964:

My central thesis was that in their attempt to discredit the Communists, Mapam spokesmen used two sets of charges—one meant for the Jewish and the other for the Arab voter. On the one hand, they accused the Communist Party of the cardinal sin of "hypocrisy"; to the Jews of Israel it says that the Communists are willing to cooperate with Mapam despite the two parties' different attitudes towards Zionism, and that its Arabic organ, *Al Ittihad,* condemns Zionism and "Zionist parties from Mapam to Herut."

Again, whereas for Mapam's Hebrew organ the Communists' chief drawback was their anti-Zionist agitation, for its Arabic daily their real offence was their anti-Nasserist stand. To put it briefly, to the Jew, Mapam says that the Communists are anti-Zionist and should therefore not get his vote; to the Arab it says that they are anti-Nasserist, and therefore anti-Arab nationalist and unworthy of his vote. The Communists, in turn, take pains to explain to their Arab reader that Mapam is merely a Zionist party like all other Zionist parties and that it would therefore be criminal to give it his vote! . . .

("What Price a Vote?", JUNE 6, 1961)

At some point in the early 1960s I finally came to the conclusion that something was basically wrong with Israeli society's attitudes toward the out-groups living in its midst and actually surrounding it on all sides. I refer, of course, to the so-called "Sephardi Jews," the Arabs of Israel, and the Middle Eastern world as a whole. Not being the fighting type, I felt no inclination to confront the phenomenon face-to-face, expose it, or proceed to wage a private holy war. Instead, I often tried to express my dissatisfaction and my general outlook in oblique, indirect ways. In book reviews, in columns, and in general articles I tended to choose topics with some relevance, hidden or open, to the situation that I was facing and that I thought the society as a whole ought to confront and tackle squarely and unambiguously.

I cannot now recall the precise state of mind in which I found myself when I first read Czeslaw Milosz's *The Captive Mind*—whether I perceived an analogy between the situation he described in the book and in my own situation as I saw it. The fact remains, however, that I found the book sufficiently interesting for me to devote a column to it—with special reference to a chapter in which Milosz made references to "ketman," a concept that in the circumstances I found both fascinating and relevant. Excerpts:

The word "ketman" occurs for the first time in Western writing in a book by the notorious Comte de Gobineau, who spent many years in Persia in the 1850s, first as secretary in the French Legation and then as Minister.

In his book, *Religions and Philosophies of Central Asia,* Gobineau gives a brief account of *ketman*—which seems to be a Persian corruption of the Arabic *kitman,* meaning reserve or secretiveness.

The people of the Mussulman East, Gobineau writes, believe that "he who is in possession of truth must not expose his person, his relatives or his reputation to the blindness, the folly, and the perversity of those whom it has pleased God to place and maintain in error." One must, therefore, keep silent about one's true convictions as long as possible. Nevertheless, says Gobineau, "there are occasions when silence no longer suffices, when it may pass as an avowal." In which case one must not hesitate to take the plunge and pass to what may be termed active ketman.

Not only must one deny one's true opinion, Gobineau continues, describing this variety of ketman, "but one is commanded to resort to all ruses in order to deceive one's adversary. One makes all the protestations of faith that can please him, one performs all the rites one recognizes to be the most vain, one falsifies one's own books, one exhausts all possible means of deceit."

The satisfactions and merits of such a course of action are multiple: By practising ketman one places oneself and one's relatives under cover, saves a venerable faith (one's own) from the horrible contact of the infidel, and cheats the latter and confirms him in his error, imposing on him the shame and spiritual misery that he deserves.

Moreover, we are told, "ketman fills the man who practises it with pride. Thanks to it, a believer raises himself to a permanent state of superiority over the man he deceives, be he a minister of state or a powerful king... It is an unintelligent being that you make sport of; it is a dangerous beast that you disarm. What a wealth of pleasure!"

(QUOTED IN CZESLAW MILOSZ, *The Captive Mind,* pp. 54–55)

Following this short introduction, I wrote:

Analogies between Islamic ketman and the ketman of 20th Century Europe are drawn by Milosz in connection with the state of the intellectuals in the People's Democracies today, especially in his own country, Poland. But ketman, or some variety of it, seems to be common to all totalitarian regimes, and its practice in the modern Arab East is extremely, and understandably, widespread.

Nowhere is this more evident than it is in Egypt which, having for decades been the acknowledged centre of Arabic and Islamic culture, produced during the twenties, thirties and forties a great number of scholars and writers who held pronouncedly liberal views and openly looked on Europe as a model and an example to emulate. When the army officers made their advent in 1952 and chose the path of chauvinism and xeno-phobia, the old-time intellectual leaders had to go into a kind of mental hiding.

This proved to be good enough for the time being, and men like Ahmad Lutfi al-Sayyid, Taha Hussein, Tawfiq al-Hakim and ʿAbbas Mahmoud al-ʿAqqad managed to keep out of harm's reach by mostly maintaining silence about their true opinions and by occasionally throwing in a good word about the regime. But what with the bitterness of the Syrian debacle and the feverish drive towards "Arab Socialism" this does not seem to be adequate any longer, and there are clear signs that a sort of literary purge is already on.

That simple, amateurish ketman can no longer save a man's skin is shown, among many other examples, in a fierce polemic published in Cairo's leading political weekly, *Rose el Yussuf,* on November 27, 1961. The article, entitled "Armchair Socialism," is a vicious attack on a book called *Cooperative Democratic Socialism,* which appears to be a truly in-genious piece of ketman. The author, whose name is not given, is said to have written a devastating critique of the socialist doctrine while seem-ingly defending Nasser's socialist measures — and was awarded a national book prize into the bargain . . .

("Varieties of Ketman," DECEMBER 26, 1960)

COMMUNAL ISSUE TO THE FORE

This was not the first column in which I tried to introduce a more serious, almost philosophical note to the subjects that really interested me and that were then, in Israel, usually treated as caprices or just a family quarrel — or, far worse, as side issues raised by people who had one or another kind of axe to grind. The column for which I chose the title "Self-Propagating Malady" was one of these. For one reason or other, the *Post* did not publish it. I give excerpts from it here, following one published exactly a month earlier, as the two also reflect the kind of intellectual pursuits that were and continue to be my chosen sphere.

Since that day in the autumn of 1951 when, deciding that the Hebrew I had picked up in the Ulpan was enough to enable me to plough through a Hebrew daily, we bought our first copy of *Ha'aretz,* I have always been wondering who reads all those solid stacks of unrelieved columns of print which continue to make up the Friday "supplements" of the Hebrew Press. The idea that the week-end issue of a daily can be offered as an adequate substitute for a weekly journal was still quite foreign to me, but with the passage of time — and with the continued absence of weekly journals of opinion to fill the need—I became used to the anomaly. And so, grumbling as always, I applied myself one Friday early in 1962 to the job of scanning *all* the Hebrew papers, and, as always, there was the usual crop of "ideological" dissertations — this time, too, dealing largely with the perennial theme: What Has Gone Wrong with Israeli Society?

The Labour press seemed especially worried: "The State and the Disillusionment of Our Generation" ran the title of one article in *Davar* (Histadrut); "The Lighted Side—and the Shadowed" was the title of another article in *'Al Hamishmar* (Mapam); while the subject of *Lamerhav*'s (Ahdut Ha'avoda) first page two feature was the kibbutz movement's attempts to cleanse itself of the terrible stain of hired labour. The three articles have one leading conviction in common: something basic has gone wrong. There was a time, *Lamerhav* recalled, when the term "hired labour" denoted something entirely different from its current usage, namely when members of the kibbutz themselves went out to work as hired labourers in neighbouring towns and cities; today the words evoke the picture of groups of labourers from adjoining immigrant settlements coming to the kibbutz every morning, each with a bundle containing his lunch, or a phone call to the labour exchange in the same immigrant town . . . To the *'Al Hamishmar* writer, the root of all evil lay in the fact that the life-giving concept of the class war was abandoned by "the intelligentsia," while the *Davar* contributor blamed it all on the State, which he said was "displaying an astounding apathy toward what takes place inside the soul of the citizen."

Examined a little more closely, this phenomenon can perhaps be traced back to a deeper, far more decisive factor, which for want of a better term I will call uprootedness or the lack of roots. As Simone Weil, writing at a time of great distress, noted, to be rooted is perhaps the most important, though may be the least recognized, need of man. "A human being (she wrote in connection with the Nazi occupation of her country) has roots by virtue of his active, real and natural participation in the life of a community, which preserves in living shape certain particular treasures of the past and certain particular expectations for the future." This participation is a natural one in the sense that it is automatically brought about by the place, condition of birth, profession and social surroundings. Such multiple roots are necessary for every human being, for man draws "well nigh the whole of his normal, intellectual and spiritual life by way of the environment of which he forms a natural part."

Of how many Israelis can this much be said?

("The Need for Roots," FEBRUARY 4, 1962)

In one column — again not published — I quote Simone Weil as saying that uprootedness is dangerous because it is a malady that tends to be self-propagating. "For people who are really uprooted there remain only two possible sorts of behaviour; either to fall into a spiritual lethargy resembling death, like the majority of the slaves in the days of the Roman Empire, or to hurl themselves into some form of activity necessarily designed to uproot, often by the most violent methods, those who are not yet uprooted, or only partly so."

"The Romans, for instance," I quoted further, "were a handful of fugitives who banded themselves together artificially to form a city, and deprived the Mediterranean peoples of their individual manner of life, their country, traditions, and past history to such an extent that posterity has taken them, at their own evaluation, for the founders of civilization in these conquered territories." The Hebrews "were escaped slaves, and they either exterminated or reduced to servitude all the peoples of Palestine." The Germans, the Spaniards, the English and the French all behaved in the same way.

Under the impact of war, the disease of uprootedness encompassed all Europe. Weil again: "As for the Oriental countries, to which during the last few centuries, but especially in the last 50 years, the white man has carried the disease of uprootedness from which he is suffering, Japan gives ample proof of the intensity reached there by the active form of this disease. Indochina offers an example of its passive form. India, where a living tradition still persists, has been sufficiently contaminated for even those who speak publicly in the name of this tradition to dream, nevertheless, of building in their land a nation according to a modern Western type. China remains very mysterious; Russia, which is, as always, half European, half Oriental, just as much so . . ."

As for the American continent, "since its population has for several centuries been founded above all on immigration, the dominating influence which it will probably exercise greatly increases the danger!"

In this "almost desperate situation," all that Weil saw that one could look to for encouragement here below was "those historical atolls of the living past left upon the surface of the earth." For several centuries now, she observed, "men of the white race have everywhere destroyed the past, stupidly, blindly, both at home and abroad." If in certain respects there has, nevertheless, been real progress during this period, she concluded, "it is not because of this frenzy, but in spite of it, under the impulse of what little of the past remained alive."

LEVANTINISM DEFINED

At one stage in my ongoing attempts aimed at debunking some of the establishment's basic assumptions, reacting to the then rampant talk about Levantinism and about the alleged dangers it posed to the "Western" society of Israel, its culture, and its values, I wrote a column, which appeared in the *Post* on May 16, 1961, under the title "What is Levantinism?"

Levantinism is a notoriously elusive concept. It is scarcely possible to find two serious persons who can agree on a single definition of the term; each one of us usually makes it mean what he wants it to mean.

On another, and higher, level of confusion, it seems that any political opponent in Israel may with impunity be branded a Levantine — or at the very least, a Levantinizer. When the good old *Manchester Guardian* recently found itself at variance with the Israeli prime minister, it accused him of plunging the country into Levantinism. When a distinguished Israeli Socialist at odds with his party's leadership the other day wanted to prove the "uniqueness" of the Israeli labour movement, he said this uniqueness lay in the fact that the movement was capable of preventing us from deteriorating into the Levantine society towards which we were heading.

What, then, is a Levantine? Before attempting to answer this question we must dispose of one minor difficulty. Geographically speaking, a Levantine is he who is born and bred in the Levant — and on that score there are many of us who are Levantines — and Israel is and has always been a Levantine country.

But besides being a geographical concept Levantinism is also (and it is here that the term is used pejoratively) a cultural one — and here the confusion is monumental. For, culturally, you can come from the Levant and be the opposite of a Levantine; you can hail from Europe — even from Western Europe — and be the epitome of Levantinism. Again, you may think that you are checking Levantinism and then shout your way into a perfect Levantine mood. Finally, and perhaps most distressing of all, you can be a Levantine and blissfully oblivious of it—and at the same time never stop being vocal about the danger of Levantinization.

At this point I suggested what I described as the best definition of Levantinism (cultural). This is that to be a Levantine is to live in two worlds or more at once without belonging to either—to be able to go through the external forms that indicate the possession of a certain culture without actually possessing it. According to this definition, Levantinism is a condition in which one no longer has a standard of values of one's own— a state of mind that reveals itself in lostness, pretentiousness, cynicism, and despair.

If we accept this definition, it becomes obvious that in Israel Levantinism is and can be the monopoly of no particular community or group of communities. Israel, in fact, must be teeming with Levantines. For, come to think of it, it is by no means self-evident that an Israeli hailing from Egypt, the Levant countries, or Iraq should find it more difficult to meet the challenge of Westernization than one who hails from the countries of eastern Europe and tries to disown his cultural background.

I concluded the piece by quoting a passage from the section on "Phanariots, Qazanlis and Levantines" in Arnold Toynbee's *Study of History*. "In the earlier centuries of their dominance," Toynbee relates, "the Osmanlis, knowing the people of Western Christendom—the Franks, as they called them—only through their Levantine representatives, assumed that Western Europe was wholly inhabited by such 'lesser breeds without the law.' A wider experience led them to revise their opinion, and the Osmanlis came to draw a sharp distinction between the 'fresh-water Franks' and their 'salt-water' namesakes. The 'fresh-water Franks' were those who had been born and bred in Turkey in the Levantine atmosphere and had responded by developing the Levantine character. The 'salt-water Franks' were those who had been born and bred at home in Frankland and had come out in Turkey as adults with their characters already formed. The Turks were puzzled to find that the great psychological gulf which divided them from the 'fresh-water Franks' who had always lived in their midst did not intervene when they had to deal with the Franks from beyond the seas . . ."

The reason why the Turks could easily understand "salt-water Franks," yet find the native-born Franks, who were geographically their neighbors and compatriots, psychologically alien, was that there existed "a broad similarity between their respective social backgrounds." Both, Toynbee explains, had grown up in environments in which they were the masters of their own houses. On the other hand, both the Turk and the European-born Frank had difficulty understanding or respecting the "fresh-water Frank" because this latter had a social background that was equally foreign to both of them: "He was not a son of the house but a child of the ghetto; and this penalized existence had developed in him an ethos from which the Franks brought up in Frankland and the Turk brought up in Turkey had both remained free."

ANTHROPOLOGY? SEZ WHO?

All, except one, thought I was joking. They were a pleasingly mixed group of men sharing roughly the same intellectual and public interests, and the subject of the evening's discussion was the direction that Israeli research should take in the sphere of Oriental and African studies.

"What about anthropology?" I asked. "Is anthropology taught in our universities?" The query came abruptly and somewhat provocatively. But it was certainly no joke. Indeed it was one of the oddest things about our institutions of higher learning that until comparatively recently they showed so little interest in this important discipline. In a country that is a human laboratory, where over seventy cultures rub shoulders with one another and where cultural contacts and the diffusion of cultures take place daily under one's very nose, this neglect seemed to me to verge on the ridiculous. And it is not only our universities that were to blame: it was chiefly those bodies that were in any way connected with the work of immigrant absorption and integration — the Jewish Agency, the Ministry of Education, the army. The columns that follow were partly a result of that discussion.

> Time was when anthropologists were content with the study of problems which were remote from the concerns of daily life — theoretical preoccupation with cultural evolution or diffusion and the systematic description of cultural "curiosities." The emergence of modern anthropological studies, mainly in America, a few decades ago made the discipline and its findings very relevant to the contemporary scene. The emphasis was shifted from the purely theoretical plane to that of current problems of conflict and adjustment coming to the surface within expanding cultures . . .
> It was in the U.S. that anthropologists were first given a share in laying

down practical policies, and it was therefore there that the great names in modern anthropology emerged — Boas, Sapir, Benedict, Kroeber, Linton, Mead and Herskovits.

But if anthropology is the science of culture and culture is the sum total of a people's customs and ways of behaviour and thought, what is the upshot of this study for our contemporary thinking? Writing 34 years ago, Ruth Benedict asked this same question — and her answer was: anthropology makes us "culture-conscious." In her words: "The culture we are born into is also, as the earth is in the solar scheme, one of a series of similar phenomena all driven by the same compulsions."

In accepting such a view of culture, Benedict continued, "what we give up is a dogged attachment to absolutes; what we gain is a sense of the intriguing variety of possible forms of behaviour, and of the social function that is served by these communal patternings. We become culture-conscious. We perceive with new force the ties that bind us to those who share our culture. Ways of thinking, ways of acting, goals of effort, that we tend so easily to accept as the order of the universe, become rather the precious and special symbols we share together . . . For the social function of custom is that it makes our acts intelligible to our neighbours. It binds us together with a common symbolism, a common religion, a common set of values."

We do not stand to lose by such a tolerant and objective view of man's institutions and morals and ways of thought. Benedict again: "On the one hand, we shall value the bold imagination that is written in all great systems of behaviour; on the other, we shall not fear for the future of the world because some item in that system is undergoing contemporary change."

Few things can be as apt and as relevant to the contemporary Israeli scene as these reflections.

("The Science of Ourselves," AUGUST 27, 1963)

Dr. Fernando Henriques, a social anthropologist on a short visit to Israel to study immigrant absorption, is on record that the continuing process of the mixing of "races" in this country will produce, within 100 years, "a pure Israeli [type] compounded of all the ethnic elements," and that by then the current distinction between "European" and "Oriental" will have disappeared . . . However, while it is everybody's wish that the process should be quick and successful, the hazards involved are so great that the subject should be tackled with the utmost care. Above all, it is essential that no confusion of concepts be allowed.

Nor should one allow oneself to be swayed by any undue optimism or wishful thinking. Some three months ago, addressing a gathering of working youth instructors, Premier Levi Eshkol confessed that "in the past I believed that we would, within 10 to 15 years, succeed in changing the face of Israel society after we have processed the young generation through the educational melting pot—the kindergarten, the elementary school and the post-elementary classes." Now, Mr. Eshkol added, "I have come to see this as a long process and a matter of generations." Clearly, the Prime Minister's past optimism was shared by many Israelis. In fact, the Israeli attitude, official and non-official, towards what for lack of a better term we will call "cultural integration" seems to have been greatly influenced by the simple belief that nothing is impossible. However, since human beings are made somewhat differently from mere metals, this optimism was misplaced, and the melting-pot theory has not proved itself.

The optimism has, indeed, almost backfired. Instead of slowly, sympathetically, consciously and purposefully setting about the job—instead of making the change tolerable and as "natural" as possible in the circumstances—the means employed to arrive at the desired end have in many cases produced some most undesirable results which can serve only to slow down the process of change, if not actually stop or reverse it. It would be no exaggeration to say that the rise of communal political groupings is attributable at least as much to cultural pressures as it is to considerations of "political representation."

The sad and dismaying thing is, of course, that all this would have appeared quite elementary had modern socio-psychological and anthropological findings been heeded. Other societies undergoing the same kind of technical and cultural changes have not thought it unnecessary to consult experts. UNESCO, for example, saw fit to use the expertise of prominent social workers and anthropologists to find out, among other things, the mental health implications of technical change and how best to avoid undue suffering and maladjustment when setting about introducing such change. In a manual published by UNESCO eight years ago, a list is given of psychological principles seen as guiding the process of technical change. One of these is addressed to the "agents of change"—the teacher, the agricultural extension worker, the nurse—and it lays it down that the beliefs and attitudes of the people among whom these agents work must be seen as having "functional utility."

For each individual, we are told, these beliefs and attitudes "give continuity to his personality, permit him to feel that he is a named, identified person, the same person—only older, or more important, although fatter,

or just elected to office — than he was yesterday . . . If the teacher or extension agent recognizes such clinging to old beliefs and practices as having
real usefulness for an individual, rather than interpreting it as evidence
of stubbornness, uncooperativeness, ignorance, inability to learn, etc., he
will be better able to introduce changes."

Failure to grasp these principles can result only in rousing "violent re-
sistances and attempts at compensation and retaliation from those whose
feelings of self-esteem have been violated . . . [They] may come to repudiate the possibility of learning anything at all or of sharing anything at all
except 'bread' with those who have so denigrated their cherished ways
of life."

Clearly, this is not the kind of "cultural integration" to which Israel
aspires. She simply can't afford it!

("Ends and Means," SEPTEMBER 10, 1963)

When we first make his acquaintance in Leonard Q. Ross's unforgettable
Education, Mr. Hyman Kaplan's entire store of knowledge about American Literature consists of the somewhat controversial proposition that the
"most famous tree American wriders" were Jeck Laundon, Valt Viterman
and the author of Hawk L. Barry-Feen, one Mocktvain. At the time this
happens, Kaplan is in his forties, one of the 30-odd adults in the beginners'
grade of the American Night Preparatory School for Adults ("English —
Americanization Civics — Preparation for Naturalization"). Now Kaplan
and his 30 schoolmates may have been a lost deal as far as the reading and
enjoying of American literature were concerned, but one would not be
surprised if one learned that one of them was to be the father of a Henry
Roth, a Lionel Trilling or an Alfred Kazin.

We were struck by this thought while reading a symposium on newcomers and literature conducted by a *Ma'ariv* reporter and printed in that
paper's New Year issue. The reporter sought the opinion of several Israeli
writers, young and old, as to the prospects of bringing the new immigration nearer to original Hebrew literature. He also asked what could be
done so that this literature might become "a sort of bridge between the
various communities."

The trouble, of course, was that the main assumption behind the questions were either vague, or mistaken, or both. The very use of the term
"new immigration" in this context, with the implicit assumption that it
is *only* this massive body of Israelis that needs "bringing nearer" to local
literature, tends to raise doubts and difficulties. Are the veterans, then, all

avid readers of Hebrew literature? Are there not among new immigrants a considerable number of men and women who do take an interest in local literary output?

Above all, what is this all-purpose term "new immigration" supposed to denote, precisely? There are dozens of ways of classifying populations—such as rich and poor, educated and illiterate, Left and Right, well-mannered and ill-mannered, white and coloured, and the customary classification of Israelis into "new immigrants" and "veterans," which seems to be one of the more hazardous among them. The error becomes rather drastic when, in making this classification, "new immigration" is consciously or subconsciously identified with immigrants from Asian and African countries or, which also happens often, with the entire Oriental population of Israel . . .

It is therefore rather refreshing to see that a number of those questioned by *Ma'ariv* were themselves becoming aware of the absurdity of such generalizations. Poet Haim Guri rightly pointed out that "before we ask the question as to when the newcomers would *start* reading us, the question emerges as to when did the veterans cease reading us?" Before reproaching Dimona, he added, we have to settle accounts with North Tel Aviv.

"What new immigrants are we talking about, precisely?" Hanoch Bartov asked in almost visible rage. "This veteran *Yishuv*, from whose grapes warm wine cellars now produce 100 barrels of Fine Old every day, was once all new immigrants, green and completely raw . . . If my father was here three years earlier than your father, does this make of me your spiritual provider?" Turning to the problem of literature, Bartov asked how many contemporary Hebrew books the veterans have read in recent years? "How many of our Ministers so much as touched a Hebrew work of fiction? How many of our Ambassadors? What Hebrew book has created a sensation, brought tears to people's eyes, gladdened their hearts?" . . .

Well, one should have thought it was time our publicists and other veterans of good will stopped their unsolicited patronizing of the poor immigrant!

("Immigrants and Literature," OCTOBER 1, 1963)

"This family is not yet Americanized; they are still eating Italian food." The starched young gentleman from the settlement department took stock from the middle of the immigrant family's kitchen: Were there framed pictures on the wall? Was there a piano? Books? His mind apparently at rest on these scores, he jotted down the above note and left to prepare his report." As Professor Oscar Handlin—from whose book *The Uprooted* this episode is taken—explains: Confident of their personal and social superiority and armed with the ideology of the sociologists who had trained them, the emissaries of the public and private agencies were bent on improving the immigrant to a point at which he would no longer recognize himself. Handlin further quotes a warning sounded at the time by a prominent American educator: "Our task is to break up their settlements, to assimilate and amalgamate these people and to implant in them the Anglo-Saxon conception of righteousness, law and order."

It is hard to reflect now that such things were taking place only a few decades ago in the New World, especially when one views them against the state of mind prevalent in America today on these subjects. This new American attitude has now found expression in an outstanding book published last month by the Massachusetts Institute of Technology under the title *Beyond the Melting Pot* and written by two keen-eyed social scientists, Nathan Glazer and Daniel Patrick Moynihan. The main point to be made here is that the great American melting pot, in which all ethnic groups were supposed to lose their distinguishing characteristics and to blend into a homogeneous whole, appears from the pages of Glazer and Moynihan's book to have done very little melting indeed.

It would seem from the authors' conclusions that however much these ethnic groups may have changed over the years, they have retained their identity: They differ now as much as they ever did—and what is more, Glazer and Moynihan seem to be quite pleased about it. To be sure, all of these groups feel and are wholly American; but culturally they remain hyphenated Americans. Instead of being upset about this state of affairs, however, the authors argue that these separate ethnic identities rather add to the richness of the national fabric. Armed with the necessary theoretical equipment, convinced of the fundamental unity of all human culture, and stressing similarities and harmony where their predecessors spotted differences and conflict, Glazer and Moynihan accept the U.S. as a pluralistic society in which different ethnic groups would always jockey for position and prestige.

If this seems a far cry from the climate of opinion prevailing in America a few decades ago concerning ways to integrate, assimilate or amalgamate various immigrant groups, it could hardly have been otherwise. As Handlin writes, "there was a fundamental ambiguity to the thinking of those who talked about 'assimilation' in those years. They had arrived at their own view that American culture was fixed, formed from its origins, by shutting out the great mass of immigrants who were not English or at least not Teutonic. Now it was expected that these excluded people would alter themselves to earn their portion in Americanism. That process could, however, only come about by increasing the contacts between the older and the new inhabitants, by sharing jobs, churches, residences. Yet in practice, the man who called himself an Anglo-Saxon found proximity to the other folk just come to the United States uncomfortable and distasteful and, in his own life, sought to increase rather than to lessen the gap between his position and theirs."

As usual in such cases, the blame continued to be laid at the door of the immigrants. To start with, they were accused of their very poverty: "Many benevolent citizens, distressed by the miserable conditions in the districts inhabited by the labouring people, were reluctant to believe that such social flaws were indigenous to the New World. It was tempting, rather, to ascribe them to the defects of the newcomers, to improvidence, slovenliness, and ignorance rather than to inability to earn a living." The newcomers were also accused of congregating together in their own groups and of unwillingness to mix with outsiders . . .

Finally, when the ambiguity and the contradictions in the attitude of the dominant "natives" became unbearable, an escape was still found: "It was tempting to resolve the difficulty by arguing that the differences between Americans on the one hand and Italians or Jews or Poles on the other were so deep as to admit of no conciliation. If these other stocks were cut off by their own innate nature, by the qualities of their heredity, then the original breed was justified both in asserting the fixity of its own character and in holding off from contact with the aliens . . ."

("Pluralism in Action," NOVEMBER 19, 1963)

There was a pervasive air of festivity on the empty site of the Kiryat Uno Ma'bara the other day. After 13 years of chequered existence the *ma'bara* was being finally and officially liquidated. The speakers, though mercifully brief, were full of enthusiasm. The Chairman of the Local Council expressed pride that this was the first *ma'bara* to be liquidated; another speaker claimed it was the last; and finally Mr. Yosef Almogi, the Minister of Housing, settled the historical dispute: this was neither the first nor the last of the *ma'barot* to be liquidated. Both the Chairman and Mr. Almogi expressed their regret, however, that six or seven families still lingered on in the old shanties, but both made it clear that that was the fault neither of the Local Council nor of the Ministry of Housing. These families, they said pointedly though gently, can move into their allotted flats "immediately" if they wish.

These families, then, were doggedly staying on in their shabby surroundings of their own choice. Why? The question seemed to us highly if somewhat horribly fascinating—especially as we happened at the time to be reading a new Hebrew novel on life in the *ma'bara* during the first tempestuous years. The novel, called simply *Ha-Ma'bara*, by Shimon Ballas, was written by a young man who, as a newcomer from Iraq, himself lived in a *ma'bara* and watched its fortunes closely. Writing in a direct, realistic and pleasingly unapologetic manner, Ballas does what no Israeli writer has so far managed to do. He catches the atmosphere and the very spirit of a dramatic and fateful moment in the life of a group of human beings suddenly plunged into an existence and surroundings completely foreign, and mostly hostile, to them. The main virtue of the novel is that its author does not try to sugar the pill. As early on as page two we are introduced to Shlomo Hamra who, explaining to his wife why he decided to call his planned coffee house *Maqha al-Nasr*, says: "Do you remember the coffee house of Hajji Hussein al-Ne'emi in Bab Lagha? It was called Al-Nasr. Hajji Hussein is a man the like of whom are not many. May Allah bless his memory! He told me: 'O Abu Fuad, don't go! You will regret it!' "

Yet Abu Fuad, together with some 130,000 other Iraqi Jews, did come, Hajji Hussein or no Hajji Hussein. What was the source of their disappointment on arrival? As far as can be gathered from Ballas's book, the cause of the disillusionment was not the material conditions in which they suddenly found themselves, indescribably squalid though these certainly were. Rather, it was the rude discovery that they suddenly became nameless, faceless, indistinguishable human beings with no past, no culture, no dignity and little future to speak of. The hostility and prejudice with which they felt they were received cut very deep indeed: one character in *Ha-Ma'bara* who no doubt had never before thought of such nice communal distinctions tells another who was complaining that God ceased to listen to her prayers: "The God of [the State of] Israel is also Yiddish!"

It was not the physical *ma'bara* that was the bane of these people's lives. It was, one suspects, the "other" *ma'bara*, the one of the soul, of human relationships and sentiments which constituted the real bar. Powerfully, though without labouring the point, the author of *Ha-Ma'bara* brings out the fact that what worried his characters most was not their sub-human material condition but the desire to prove, first of all to themselves but also to those "Yiddish," that they were people with dignity, with a past and with a culture—named, identifiable persons coming from clean, well-ordered homes and having their own ancient customs and way of life which they would allow no one to denigrate or laugh at. Ultimately, what Ballas's characters seem to be struggling for was not physical rehabilitation but to be allowed out of the "other" *ma'bara* of prejudice, of indignity and of enforced inferiority. This *ma'bara* is far from liquidated as yet, and one has the feeling that the six or seven families still lingering on in the Kiryat Uno Ma'bara have, with some elusive natural intelligence, come to the conclusion that it is no use abandoning the physical *ma'bara* while remaining in the other, spiritual one.

The really sad aspect of this *ma'bara* of the mind is that we all now seem to be in it — old-timer and newcomer, Occidental and Oriental, responsible leader and simple citizen alike. It is painful enough that the ex-inhabitant of the *ma'bara*, guided by his limited experience of the "First Israel," should go on referring to the old-timers as "the Yiddish" or sometimes worse; but it is alarming to find that many of the old-timers, including high-minded, responsible and dedicated leaders of the State and the Zionist movement, should often choose to be so condescending and even insulting when speaking of the "Second Israel." To judge, for instance, from some of the pronouncements made by these leaders when on fund-raising missions abroad, one would imagine that they speak only for that half of the population to which they themselves belong. It is this other, mental transit camp, which so many of us seem to inhabit, and whose spiritual squalor is no less shocking than the material squalor of the *ma'bara*, that must be liquidated before we can arrive anywhere. Then we can come to the few remaining inmates of the Kiryat Uno Ma'bara and meaningfully, and with a clear conscience, ask them to move into their allotted flats nearby.

("*Ma'bara* of the Mind," MAY 5, 1964)

Chapter 6 | THE THREE DIVIDES

The basic problems besetting Israeli society, culture, and politics are closely interwoven. In the course of the years 1960–1964 I came to identify these as three great divides — the communal-cultural, the religious, and the national. The first two divisions can be said to be largely inter-Jewish while the third pertains to Jewish-Muslim and Israeli-Arab relations. To give some idea of just how my general approach to these problems developed, I reprint here a number of representative pieces written during the first half of the 1960s.

The ethnic-cultural divide (using culture in its broader sense) was given expression in articles I wrote or planned to write for the *Post*, or intended to be published there. For the issue dated September 23, 1963, I sent the paper a column dealing with the ethnic problem. The heading I gave it was "Unity in Diversity." It was rejected and — partly to prove to the editors that there was no easy way of avoiding the issues and that the *Post* was not the sole outlet available to me — I wrote a longer article on the same theme and bearing the same title and mailed it to the editor of the *Jewish Chronicle* of London, in which it appeared under the heading "Israeli Culture: Unity in Diversity," on November 15, 1963. It reads in full:

The use of the word "culture" has undergone several mutations during the past 150 years. Before the nineteenth century it used to mean the tending of natural growth, and, by analogy, a process of human training. Later on it came to mean "a general state or habit of mind," and then "the general state of intellectual development in a society as a whole" or "the general body of the arts." It is in these particular senses, current as far back as the middle of the last century, that Israeli intellectuals continue to use the term — or its Hebrew equivalent *tarbut* — and it was obviously in that sense that the Israeli writer and playwright Binyamin Tammuz wrote his article "Israel in Search of a Culture" which appeared in the New Year number of the *Jewish Chronicle*.

I propose to deal with Israeli culture in the post-nineteenth-century sense denoting "a whole way of life, material, intellectual and spiritual," and also in its more recent connotation as being the sum total of a people's way of life, patterns of behaviour and thought and the whole social legacy which the individual acquires from his group. Clearly, used in this sense, a specific Israeli culture can be said to be non-existent—or at best to be in a process of formation. In a country of immigration, where dozens of ways of life rub shoulders with each other, it would be unrealistic to speak of a well-defined, coherent "culture."

Yet this seemingly elementary proposition is generally, sometimes stubbornly, ignored by veteran Israelis of European origin. The majority of them seem to imply that, the variety of cultures brought by new immigrants notwithstanding, there is, so to speak, a "hard core" Israeli culture whose general lines were already well drawn before the establishment of the State. According to this estimate, new immigrants, including those coming from the Orient, can and will be "absorbed" into the culture of the old *Yishuv*. As the Prime Minister, Mr. Eshkol, recently told a group of youth instructors, he had estimated that "we would, within ten to fifteen years, succeed in changing the face of Israeli society after we have processed the young generation through the educational melting pot— the kindergarten, the elementary school and the post-elementary classes." "Now," Mr. Eshkol added, "I have come to realise that this is a long process and a matter of generations."

It is significant to note that the disillusionment has come just where it was not expected—the education of immigrant children. The so-called "educational melting pot" has failed to mould even the children—many of them *sabras*—into anything like a uniform type of Israeli youth. On the contrary, it has served only to create an educational gap whose dimensions tend to become broader rather than narrower. Speaking apropos of the average Israeli university student's spiritual and literary standards, the head of the English Faculty at the Hebrew University, Professor Adam Mendilov, told the Hebrew daily *Ha'aretz* recently that he thought there was too much complacency in Israel about matters concerning education.

One of the shortcomings of Israel's educational system which he cited was the failure to solve the problems of intercommunal integration. Even graver, he added, was "the fact that we failed to take into consideration the cultural, social and language background of the masses of children who came here. We have fitted our education apparatus to the needs of certain European types, [basing it] on their social standards, their thought patterns and their economic status." In anthropological terms, Professor Mendilov concluded, "the culture of those who came to us from other places may be a high one, but it is different from the culture on whose patterns we have built our system of education."

Against this fair and level-headed view one may set the more general opinion—which also sounds quite convincing—that Israel is not meant to be the kind of society which, supposing that Chinese Jews gained numerical predominance in it tomorrow, would or should suddenly acquire the patterns of Chinese culture. But then, what kind of society is Israeli society meant to be? No specific or clear answer is generally given to this question, but the evidence makes the conclusion quite inevitable, and one cannot but agree with Mendilov's contention that our education—and not only our education—is cut to fit the social, cultural and economic patterns of "certain European types."

Indeed, what is usually meant by such a lavishly used phrase as "the integration of the new immigrant into Israeli society and culture" is often, if not always, the rather doubtful ideal of "remoulding" the newcomer from Asian and African countries into something very much like the self-image of the veteran, non-Oriental, Jewish settler. In this connection, it is worth noting that newcomers from "certain European" countries simply cease to be "new immigrants" as soon as they have acquired a smattering of Hebrew—so that in a sense the appellation "new" applies exclusively to immigrants from Oriental lands, though they may have been as long as 15 years in the country. (A friend of mine, a German Jew who has been in the State 30 years, once told me that one really never does cease to be a new immigrant, unless one happens to come from the Eastern European Pale!)

This rather extremist attitude of the veteran *Yishuv*'s spokesmen is not often articulated—it is simply too absurd to maintain openly. But it is, or has been until very recently, the basic assumption informing official integration policy, and one Israeli intellectual has written, with commendable candour, that the integration of Oriental Jews into Israeli society can be attained "only through 'Ashkenazisation'!" Another, writing twelve years earlier, declared that the order of the day in Israel was "to cleanse and purify these [Oriental] brethren from the dross of Orientalism."

Surely some way out must be found? "Ashkenazisation" in one form or other has proved impractical and may prove disastrous, while "Orientalisation" can be contemplated neither by the veteran *Yishuv* nor by the Orientals themselves. Complete "mixing," on the other hand—in which the "good" aspects of both cultures are supposed to be preserved and out of which a totally new Israeli "type," neither Ashkenazi nor Oriental, is hoped to emerge ultimately—is a mere dream which, though devoutly desired by everybody, remains a dream nonetheless.

True, confronted by the concentrated assault of a materially superior dominant culture, people coming from supposedly less "advanced" cultures may have no choice but to submit. This, however, would be disintegration rather than integration, with consequences as harmful to the assailant as they are to the assailed.

In speaking of, and working for, "cultural integration," therefore, it may be worth the Israelis' while to learn from the rich experience and the broadmindedness of the cultural anthropologist, whose main contribution would be the assumption that customs foreign to one society may be treasured by another, and that cultural differences are no indication of cultural inferiority.

Many Israelis, especially those who are used to viewing these matters in mere black and white, will no doubt object to this. What we need, one can hear them murmuring, is cultural integration, not segregation—unity, not diversity. But unity can be sought, and attained, also in diversity, and an enlightened relativist cultural approach will take care of that, too. For while insisting on the validity of every culture for those born and brought up in it, such an approach will serve to throw in bold relief the hard core of *similarities* between cultures, similarities which have so far been consistently overlooked in favour of the emphasis laid on *differences*.

In its issue dated December 6, the *Chronicle* printed this letter to its editor, in which the writer manages to accuse me—of all unlikely "failings"—of having been "Ashkenazised." Or worse:

Sir:

All honour to you for printing the timely article of Mr. Nissim Rejwan. However, I ask whether Mr. Rejwan is not himself guilty of "Ashkenazisation." His article, wide-ranging as it is, nevertheless displays what I can only call "Anglo-Saxon" under-statement. For countless scores of Oriental citizens the problem he discusses has a bitter immediacy which the average English-Jewish reader would not suspect from his article. The nearest analogy could probably be expressed by saying that the Sephardi Jew in Israel who wishes to retain his own identity is being cajoled and tormented by the same pressures as face many Jews in the Diaspora.

If he remains true to his identity he is made to feel inferior and primitive; his chances of fulfilling himself in public life are frustrated; countless pressures are exerted to make him adopt a culture which is as alien to him as that of the East is to the average Westerner.

We cannot hold our heads high here in Israel: many North African, French-speaking Jews often tell others that they come from Marseilles or Lyons. This is one example. Another is the extraordinary phenomenon of Oriental Jews adopting Ashkenazi surnames.

It is in a way understandable that Jews in the Diaspora succumb from time to time to the pressures of assimilation. What cruel injustice it is that the same pressures should be exerted on Jews in Israel itself.

ABRAHAM MISRACHI, JERUSALEM

AN EXCHANGE WITH SHLOMO KATZ

The publication of my article "Israel's Communal Controversy" in *Midstream*—followed by one on James Parkes's vision of a future Israel—provoked no readers' reactions. But the editor, Shlomo Katz—a man of intelligence and fairly deeply involved in Zionist and Israeli topics—conducted a long correspondence with me on the views I expressed there. The two letters excerpted here ended the second round of a long and unwieldy exchange.

New York, August 2, 1964
Dear Mr. Rejwan:

It seems we are talking at cross purposes . . . You say, "There is no such thing as a secular Jewish culture . . . it is plainly European culture." Could be. What of it? There is no secular Arab, Chinese, Indian, or Congolese culture today either—even less than Jewish. Today, when Arab, Chinese etc. modernize and industrialize they willy-nilly become European. The trouble is they become superficially, trivially so. The Jew need not because through Marx and Freud and Einstein (and perhaps also Spinoza) he has in considerable part helped shape this European culture. The modern Baghdadi or Cairene is European to the extent that he is modern. If it is destined that the world be "European" the next couple of centuries then it cannot be helped. It will do no good to try to escape it by putting on either a *shtreimel* or a *kefiya*. Even the Arabs are discarding the *kefiyas* and *fezzes*.

Should we regard the Arab as we did the Christian goy, you ask. I say, let us regard the Arab as he deserves to be regarded. If he behaves like a Christian goy we should regard him as such. The world, also our world, is expanding. We now encounter peoples we never before encountered in our history—black Africa, eastern Asia. Our attitudes to them will be governed by events. There exists a sentimentality about Arabs—cousin Ishmael. Fine and good, if it can be used to purpose. But let us not endow it with more importance than it possesses. They have not been behaving very "cousinly." . . .

In any case, trying to curry favor with those who reject us by denying our essence (Jesus was a Jew, his name was Yeshua; or, We are really Middle Easterners, native boys . . .) is neither dignified, nor useful and totally contrary to our entire history.

As for Israel, I believe we, Jews, all Jews, have a prior right to it over everybody else (in terms of national center). Jerusalem has great meaning for the entire world west of China because we made it so, not just today, but always. As El Quds it has no significance. Shechem has meaning as Shechem (Jacob and Mt. Gerizim and Mt. Ebal) but as Nablus it is just an irrelevant and not too lovable little town.

Once again, if European culture in the broad sense is the fate of the next century, then English is as likely to be used in Israel as Hebrew. Let's not forget: the Maccabees fought for an independent Jewish state but their own children were already named Hyrcanus and Aristobulus etc. But they did *not* become Samaritans or Arabs or Moabites. And I am not terribly upset that Tanaim and Amoraim bore such non-Jewish and non–Middle Eastern names as Rabbi Tarfon (Tryphon?).

I read that Jews from Iraq in Israel sing soulfully and nostalgically about the Hidekel [Tigris]. Fine. Thirty years from now they won't. People of the second and third *aliyot* used to sing longingly about Mother Volga (which most of them never saw). They forgot the Volga songs. But I would say, let us not make a fetish of remembered customs from the *shtetl*, whether in the Ukraine or Morocco. At most this can only lead to a kind of "artsy-folksy" activities—a song festival from Morocco, a dance festival from Iraq etc. We have a lot of this in America, but there is no real cultural pluralism here (with the possible exception of the Negroes, but they differ not because of jazz but because their history and memories of slavery and their state of rightlessness set them aside).

Ramat Gan, September 1, 1964
Dear Mr. Katz:

. . . You say, I don't know on the strength of what, that Jews from Iraq in Israel sing soulfully about the Tigris, but that this signifies nothing since, in 30 years' time, "they won't." Granted. But the calamity is that in 30 years' time their children, now growing up under indescribable cultural pressures, will be *cultural orphans.* The analogy with the Russian Jews and the Volga strikes me as not quite relevant since, though even then they leave much to be desired culturally, the children of these Jews here still grow up in their own culture, more or less. The Oriental's children, on the other hand, now grow up in homes where the grown-ups are *invariably* alienated, feeling either superior or inferior to the prevalent culture. It needs no pedagogue to tell us that a child whose parents have such feelings towards the culture in which it is brought up at school etc. cannot be a normal child or grow up into a normal, integrated adult. So any consolation which we may draw from the fact that the Iraqis will in 30 years' time cease to sit down on the banks of the Jordan and weep for the Tigris is, at best, cold comfort.

I agree with you in deploring the "artsy-folksy" activities of the Oriental communities, because it is simply not enough to accept Oriental culture just on such an artsy-folksy level (I need not point out that these antics are not really the Orientals' own). Oriental culture must be accepted as the way of life and the whole existence of over 60 per cent of the country's population — not on the folklore level only. And please don't tell me about the future: I am no believer in sacrificing one generation — not one man even — for the sake of the next. We know from experience that the process can never really end.

Now for the final point. You say: Let's regard the Arab as he deserves to be regarded . . . They have not been behaving very "cousinly." Now, again invoking the intellectual level of this discussion, and also remembering that we are not speaking from the rostrum of the U.N. or some similar forum: How in the name of God could we *dare* expect the Arabs to behave like cousins at this hour of day — or any hour of Zionism's day for that matter? Do you really go so far as to suggest, the rights and wrongs of the situation notwithstanding, that any decent, self-respecting Arab could or should be expected to forget the events of 1948 and their tragic aftermath? It is always the victor, I thought, who had to make the first gesture; and what we have been doing, let's face it, is nothing but repeating worn-out and meaningless cliches. The fact is, as I implied in one of my letters, that the natural thing should be to expect that it is the Arabs who have *heshbonot* [accounts] with us, not the other way around — and to prepare our case accordingly. You say we should treat the Arab as we did the Christian goy if he behaves like one. My whole point is that you cannot, should not and need not treat an Arab as you did a Christian goy *even if he behaves like one.* It would be totally contrary to the essence of both Jewish and Arab history — all Jewish history and all Arab history. Here — and I am about to finish — the experience of the Orientals (not the ephemeral, utilitarian experience but the historical one) ought to be made use of. I think this experience is useful in the religious realm, too, but this is another story perhaps . . .

This seems somehow to have ended our long and rather heated debate. There was however a curious little addendum. Hearing from friends that my Parkes article, to which Katz took exception, was being circulated by the Foreign Ministry itself in special reprints obviously ordered from *Midstream,* I wrote Katz to inquire — and also of course to boast that the essay to which he so objected was acceptable to no less a genuine Zionist body than the government of Israel. His reply — dated December 14, 1964 — betrays a certain measure of impatience. "I have no idea of what motivated the Consulate in New York to order reprints and, since the making of reprints is not the duty of the editor, I prefer not to enquire . . ."

JUDAISM: EXTINCTION OR REBIRTH?

It was not until the early 1960s that I found the time and the occasion to reflect on one aspect of Israeli society and Israeli culture that had not usually struck me as odd — the place of religion in the socio-cultural setup, or, if you like, the relationship between the state and religion.

Relations between religion and the state in Israel being unique — the state was virtually the sole employer and the ministers of religion were its paid employees — the subject was bound to draw my attention. One episode from my first days in Israel, my very first encounter with the problem, is worth relating here. During the campaign for the elections of the

Second Knesset, in the autumn of 1951, one of the subjects contested was compulsory military service for young women. Leading those opposed to the measure was the ultraorthodox Agudat Yisrael Party, and one of the points at issue was the recruitment of girls recently arrived from countries of the Middle East and North Africa. The argument against the recruitment was, mainly, that such a course would be a violation of or at variance with the religious, cultural, and social backgrounds of these young women. The debate was fierce and rather noisy, and what with a natural inclination I have against cultural coercion and the manipulation of human beings, I gave my vote to Agudat Yisrael. This however was a private sort of protest. Publicly, in my writing, I took every opportunity of presenting my somewhat dissenting approach to the subject of the rather peculiar state of relations between religion and the state in Israel. Here are some of the things I wrote on the subject, the first three as Marginal Columns for the *Post:*

In a book which has just been published, *Modern Trends in Jewish Education* by Zvi E. Kurzweil (Thomas Yoseloff, New York & London, $5), there is a chapter on Jewish education in Israel, with the interesting heading: "How Jewish are Israel's General Schools?" It will be recalled that the government educational programme adopted by the Knesset in 1956 included a section on "Jewish consciousness," which the government undertook to endeavour to deepen among Israeli youth in the elementary and secondary schools. The programme further stipulated that the authorities would try to root Israeli youth "in the past of the Jewish people and its historic heritage, and to imbue them with the feeling of belonging to World Jewry, springing from an awareness of their common destiny and historic continuity, which unites the Jews throughout the world in all countries and throughout all generations . . ."

Three years after this programme was adopted, in September 1959, the Ministry of Education decided to take steps towards its implementation. Two committees were appointed, which between them found that, roughly speaking, there was a need to introduce "Jewish consciousness" into general State schools and "Israeli consciousness" in State religious schools. This was called "Jewish-Israeli consciousness," and it stipulated that in the general schools emphasis would be laid on the religious aspect of the subject, while in the religious schools it was to be placed on fostering national Israeli consciousness.

How *Jewish* is Jewish consciousness, then? To appreciate the full significance of the problem it may be advisable to quote further from the

Knesset debate on the subject five years ago. In his concluding speech, in fact, Minister of Education Zalman Aranne hit the nail squarely on the head when he told the House: "We respect religion, because religious faith in its pure form elevates man. We adopt the Jewish tradition which embodies both national and religious elements, because it epitomizes the glory of former times and ancient glory never wanes . . . Therefore love and respect for tradition must permeate our national schools — not in order to educate for religion but in order to maintain the national character of our educational system." Dr. Kurzweil argues that "Jewish consciousness" is thus not meant to provide an education toward religion and the observance of religious rules. "What [Aranne] meant was that *information* about Jewish tradition is to be imparted, i.e., pupils are merely to be instructed about the various facets of Jewish life and customs." In other words, what is to be imparted to the children is a historical concept of Judaism.

The indifference of much of our youth to religious tradition has often been commented upon. "Jewish consciousness" as it is now imparted does not seem capable of changing this situation. To quote Kurzweil again: "In the Diaspora the difference between Jew and Gentile is mainly religious. The *sabra,* having no religion, has nothing in common with the Jews of the Diaspora; and the Jewish people, once united, are thus in danger of becoming divided."

The truth, of course, is that — as in so many other spheres — we have been trying to have it both ways. Two of the baffling questions facing the Hebrew school in Israel — as summed up in Mr. Aranne's speech quoted above — are cases in point. The first is "How to reconcile the Zionist teaching of 'rejection of the Diaspora' with the official wish to 'inculcate in Israeli youth an awareness of the unity of the Jewish people?'" The second is "how to bring closer to children educated in secular schools a culture permeated with religion?"

("Having it Both Ways," JULY 28, 1964)

Whatever else may be said about the present state of religious affairs in this country, it is obvious that no one is quite happy about it. The out-and-out secularists complain — often plausibly enough — of religious coercion; the strictly Orthodox, having won a considerable number of victories for their own point of view, are beginning to wonder whether they are not in fact pushing things too hard — and whether "spiritual" victories won through political manipulation and pressure may not ultimately prove pyrrhic; and those in the middle, simple Jews who do not want to make a public political issue of their faith or lack of it, cannot help looking with sorrow and even disbelief on the way in which both the Orthodox and the secularist extremists are degrading religion—the former by peddling it in the political marketplaces, the latter by their noisy rejection of it.

Clearly, some way must be found out of this tangle. It cannot be an easy one, and it may well entail a major operation. Some two months ago the Klausenberger Rebbe, in a strident three-hour address to his congregation, came out for an independent, autonomous Chief Rabbinate not linked in any way to the State. His plea, though persuasive, was rejected by the main religious group in the country—the National Religious Party. "Independent, yes. Separate, no!" they replied. Needless to say, in the final analysis their reservations had little if anything to do with purely religious considerations: Separation of Synagogue and State—which is what an independent and autonomous Chief Rabbinate would amount to—would deprive the religious parties of their positions of power and influence, positions from which it seems easier to promote *formalistic* religious ends—a poor substitute indeed for the tremendous educational and spiritual effort needed to promote *genuine* religious ends.

That there is a strong Orthodox case for separation is becoming obvious to many. The Klausenberger Rebbe may have been dismissed as an extremist or a fanatic. Not so Rabbi Joseph Soloveitchik, the *Gaon* of America's Orthodox Jewry and widely considered a spokesman of the Mizrahi Movement. Rabbi Soloveitchik has recently given an interview to the New York correspondent of the *Jewish Chronicle* in which he made known his views on the relations between religion and state in Israel. In this interview he made it clear that he was now all for separation. A rabbinate linked up with a state cannot be completely free, he asserted, and "the mere fact that *halachic* problems are discussed as political issues at cabinet meetings is an infringement of the sovereignty of the Rabbinate." Above and beyond this, the rabbi expressed grave doubts as to whether the whole struggle to maintain religious observance through political action was worthwhile. "More might have been accomplished had there been complete separation," he asserted, adding that had such a separation been effected "people would have looked up to us as religious leaders and would not have accused us of acting as politicians . . .

What, then, is to be done? Can religious law be adjusted in a way that would satisfy both our modern needs and the Orthodox tradition? A few years ago, an eminent Orthodox scholar and a leader of the religious bloc, called for the convening of a *Sanhedrin* to discuss the subject and carry out reforms. The call was not heeded. The difficulty of achieving agree-

ment amongst the Orthodox themselves would prevent such a development from ever materializing. Back in the 16th century, such an attempt
was made — and failed. A group of leading rabbis in Safad proposed that
a *Sanhedrin* be called into being. All went smoothly until one rabbi in
Jerusalem refused to join them — and the plan was dead. In present-day
Israel, many more than one rabbi will be found who would condemn such
a gathering as heretical.

("Separation or Sanhedrin," APRIL 14, 1964)

It is difficult to be either objective or terribly original about theological
subjects, especially when these touch upon the very core of religion. Attitudes are usually too well-set and final to leave scope for intellectual
manoeuvering, and the two sides in such a disputation tend to argue their
respective cases on two different levels of reasoning.

. . . Dr. Louis Jacobs, whose appointment as Rabbi of the New West End
Synagogue the Chief Rabbi of Great Britain refused to confirm, speaks
for what can be termed a new trend. Advocating a rational and critical
approach to the *Torah,* Jacobs seeks a reinterpretation of Judaism which
would appeal "to the questing mind as well as to the heart." He believes
that parts of the *Torah* are not Divine but are man-made, and that reason
alone should be the final judge as to what parts of the Torah may be considered Divine. "It is now seen," he wrote in a pamphlet entitled *The Sanction
of the Mitzvot,* that "the Bible is not, as the medieval Jew thought it was,
a book dictated by God, but a collection of books which grew gradually
over the centuries and that it contains a human as well as Divine element.
This applies to the Pentateuch as well as to the rest of the Bible . . . In
modern times the Jew no longer asks, "Why did God tell us to keep certain
mitzvot?" but "Did God tell us to keep certain *mitzvot?*"

It is Jacobs's conviction that this attitude is in keeping with Orthodox
Judaism. He maintains, however, that the term "Orthodox" means "different things to different people." For him, the question is not what the
term means in other parts of the world but what it means in the United
Synagogue and in Anglo-Jewry. "If Orthodoxy means a fundamentalist attitude which is inhospitable to all modern thought and scholarly inquiry,
then we are not Orthodox and are proud not to be called Orthodox," he
declared two weeks ago at the meeting in which it was decided to establish
a new independent Orthodox congregation. A week later, conducting the
first service of the New London Synagogue, Jacobs stated that, although it
has been one great idea, Judaism "is a great idea that has expressed itself in
every age and generation in a slightly different form." He and his new con-

gregation, he said, "had to move because we believe it is more important for men to speak their mind than to mind their speech."

To such a "modernist" approach to religion the answer can be easily anticipated. In a 4,000-word statement made earlier this month Dr. Israel Brodie, the Chief Rabbi, explained why the Orthodox community was so concerned to safeguard the observance of *Torah* laws. "Those laws of the *Torah* are of Divine origin with binding authority on all who are sons of the Covenant. They are not observed for their hygienic or prudential benefits, nor even for reasons associated with the preservation of Jewish customs and national folkways. They are mandatory upon us as being Divine commands explicit and implicit in the *Torah* as interpreted by teachers whose authority is derived from the *Torah* itself . . . The *Torah,* including the Written and Oral Law, is the very basis of Jewish existence. Once undermined, as our historical experience has proved, Jewish life and tradition weakens and withers . . ."

What more is there to say? . . . One tends to agree with the editorialist of a Gentile paper, the *Daily Telegraph,* who commented that it is perfectly possible to be both intelligent and learned and yet to doubt whether unaided reason should be the final arbiter of what parts of a revealed religion should and should not be believed. Truth to tell, one cannot resist the thought that, had one been an Orthodox member of the Anglo-Jewish community, one would not have taken Jacobs's side in this dispute — if for no better reason than just because religion is not philosophy and a synagogue cannot be turned into a philosophy class for "the questing mind."

("Rabbi or Philosopher," MAY 19, 1964)

One of the reports I sent the *Jewish Chronicle* was entitled "Judaism: Extinction or Rebirth?" I give it here in full.

Exaggeration, dramatization, and extremism are sure signs of intellectual confusion, and Israel in the mid-1960s seems to have a good deal of all these. A few months ago, dramatically and quite unexpectedly, Professor Isaiah Leibovitch of the Hebrew University broke the news to us that Judaism was going to be good and dead "within one or two generations." Stressing his point, he said in an interview published in *Bat Kol,* the Bar Ilan University student newspaper, that for him this was not merely an imminent danger: "I am very much afraid that we are already past the danger point!"

Now Leibovitch is an observant Jew, though he is known to be highly critical of our religious establishment. When he speaks of Judaism, therefore, he must mean Judaism in its religious and spiritual sense rather than in the nationalist or "racial" one. This is a point of view which, coming from any source, one can easily dismiss as wrong and wrong-headed; but coming from an outspoken observant Jew it is little short of shocking.

We do not know the precise grounds on which Leibovitch bases his bleak prophecies. But the whole dismal theory that the end of Judaism is near at hand dates back to the early days of the State of Israel. As far as one can trace its origins it was first propounded by Arthur Koestler, who had spent some time in a kibbutz in pre-State days and who is a wholly assimilated Jew of Hungarian origin.

Koestler, in the concluding chapter of his book *Promise and Fulfillment,* which he wrote amidst the general atmosphere of elation following the establishment of the State, tried to analyze the implications of this event for Judaism and for Jews in general. Quite feasibly, he did this solely in an attempt to resolve his own "Jewish Problem" — and one must admit that, from his point of view at least, he managed to resolve it very conveniently and for all time!

Koestler's recipe was rather simple: the Jewish State, he argued, places every Jew outside Israel before a dilemma which will become increasingly acute: a choice between becoming a citizen of the Israeli nation and renouncing any conscious or implicit claim to separate nationhood or religion. In other words, Koestler spelled the end of Judaism in the Diaspora, both as a nationality and as a religion. Thus it was that the Jewish Problem of at least one Jew was solved: Arthur Koestler chose not to come to Israel, automatically ceasing thereby to be a Jew! Sure enough, Koestler has since kept completely aloof of everything connected with Jews, Judaism and the Jewish State: having made his choice, he is no longer troubled by those searching questions which inspired his *Thieves in the Night* and *Promise and Fulfillment.*

Whatever you may think of Koestler's theory, it at least envisages the possibility that Judaism will survive *within the Jewish State.* Leibovitch seems to reject even this possibility — and in this he has a strange ally in the person of Arnold Toynbee, himself an outspoken critic of Zionism and the Zionist State. Toynbee is convinced that the establishment of Israel means the end of Judaism everywhere and for all time. And he has a most original and ingenious piece of reasoning to prove his theory.

"Both the modern Israelis," he wrote several years ago in his book *East and West,* "and the modern Dispersion of historical Jews in the countries of the Western world are going to be dejudaised as a consequence of the establishment of the present State of Israel . . . Psychologically, a Jew is an ex-Palestinian, or a descendant of one, who is determined to return to Palestine, but has been unable to return so far; and neither the present-day Israelis nor the present-day 'Dispersion' answers to that psychological definition . . ."

Toynbee's explanation is shockingly simple: "In carrying out for themselves a territorial state on Palestinian soil, the Israelis have transformed themselves from Jews into Gentiles," he decrees, since they are already in Palestine and thus can no longer walk around with the unfulfilled and unfulfillable longing for return to Eretz Yisrael. The same is of course equally true of Diaspora Jews who now can at any time go to Israel if they want to!

Leibovitch is thus not alone in arguing that the end of Judaism is near. Whether his appraisal is correct is quite another story. One does not want to engage in prophecies, but it would probably be no less plausible than the professor's dark premonitions to say that Judaism, both in the Diaspora and in Israel, may yet experience a veritable revival, a rebirth even, the like of which it has not known for a long, long time. The visible revival in America of interest in things Jewish on the one hand, and the intellectual ferment among the youth of Israel on the other, are indeed fairly likely to result in such a spiritual revival.

THE RELIGIOUS DIVIDE

My interest in the religious divide, as in the other aspects of Israeli life with which I dealt, was largely due to the impact it was having on my fellow immigrants from countries of the Middle East and North Africa. In this particular sphere, what seemed to me to be the paramount factor in the Oriental newcomer's endeavors to attain the desired integration into Israeli society was a kind of dual pull directed by two opposed and opposing forces within that society, producing arguably detrimental effects. These two forces were, of course, those of an overwhelmingly secularized society and political establishment on the one hand and a deeply entrenched and highly institutionalized religious community on the other.

Observant, tradition-oriented immigrants from the Middle East or North Africa thus started with a marked disadvantage. The subtle but always present pressures they confronted in their daily life were intensified by what they faced in their own families and homes. If an immigrant happened to be a father, the odds were that he gradually lost all control over his children. In most cases these children—sons and daughters in their teens and barely out of high school—had to work to support their parents and their younger sisters and brothers, and what with the various influences and pressures to which they were subjected outside the home, they tended to be far more difficult to handle, and parental authority in such cases was rendered ineffective and often irrelevant. Thus, losing his authority in the home as well as his status in the community, the immigrant father can have no hope of maintaining a truly kosher household and has to watch with subdued anger while his children enthusiastically embrace the culture and norms of the secularized, "post-Jewish" society outside.

But if, as a factor in his spiritual life, the secularized society proved detrimental to the religious practices of the Oriental immigrant, Israel's institutionalized and completely politicized religious establishment cannot be said to have been of any more help here either. Of the factors responsible for this state of affairs, three strike me as crucial: the loss of the synagogue as a social-communal meeting place and institution of the first order; the increasing polarization between Orthodox and secular Jews in Israel; and the growth of political parties — religious and secular — as patrons and guardians of the religious life.

As with all other Jewries, the synagogue in Middle Eastern and North African cities was far more than a house of worship, tending as it did to absorb and to develop the social life of the Jewish community. To quote from Israel Abrahams's classic *Jewish Life in the Middle Ages* (1896), "The synagogue was not a mere place in which the Jew prayed; it was a place in which he lived; and just as life has its earnest and its frivolous moments, so the Jew in the synagogue was at times rigorously reverent, and at others quite at his ease." In more concrete terms the synagogue, besides being a house of prayer, was also a house of study and a house of assembly.

For the synagogue-going Jew from the Middle East and North Africa — rather more than for others — all this suddenly changed upon his arrival in Israel. What happened, especially in the first years of immigration, was that in addition to being physically separated from relatives, friends, and immediate surroundings, Oriental immigrants who sought houses of worship in their new neighborhoods had to content themselves with synagogues in which they tended to be and feel like perfect strangers. Even where there was a Sephardi synagogue to go to, this in no way was the cozy, friendly gathering of neighbors and relatives the immigrant had been used to and in which he could chat with friends and acquaintances in between prayers. And in those rare cases in which he could find a synagogue used by members of his own community, our newcomer found that he had a good deal of adjusting to do. A host of outside factors, influences, and pressures had in the meantime intervened to increase the confusion: the political parties ("Are you Mapai or religious?"); the virtual impossibility of separating personal piety from publicized conformism; the fact that organized religion became a state business and a subject for endless bargaining and squabbles.

Not surprisingly, these factors — and above all the politicization of religion — led many of those who used to go to synagogue to stop the practice altogether. One such immigrant, a newcomer from Baghdad, once told me that soon after he arrived in Israel he stopped going to synagogue even on Rosh Hashanah and Yom Kippur, not because of any sudden loss of belief, but because "every time I am in a synagogue here the first thing that comes to my mind is how political party functionaries and government employees seem to be running the whole 'Jewish' show." He had no confidence, he said, in the sincerity of either the one or the other when they profess faith and piety or urge the believers to prayers and donations, since their very livelihoods depended on such professions and sermonizings.

An idea of the extent of the politicization of the religious scene in Israel can be had from a brief account of the interparty row created in the early years of the state by the arrival of hundreds of thousands of immigrants from Middle Eastern and North African countries, and the hard bargains struck by the parties for dividing these newcomers into "spheres of influence" (a practice strongly reminiscent of "sharing the booty"). The high proportion of observant Jews among these immigrants gave rise to hopes among the religious parties of a coalition between the active, politically organized, and highly motivated Ashkenazi religious group and the masses of passive but religiously oriented newcomers from the Orient.

One of the ways that religious polarization affected the Oriental newcomer is adequately illustrated by the following real-life case. Salman, in his early forties, was the father of four when he came to Israel from Basra, Iraq, early in 1951 — two sons and two daughters whose ages ranged between nine and thirteen. Back in his native city, he was what in Western Jewish parlance would be termed "conservative" — observant without too much strictness, an occasional synagogue-goer, keeper of a kosher home but without restrictions on such activities as travel, using the telephone and the refrigerator, and shopping on the Sabbath. After a few valiant attempts, however, Salman stopped going to synagogue and became even more liberal about what is permitted and what is forbidden on the Sabbath. His most acutely felt loss in this respect, however, was that he and his wife, Lulu, found it easier and more natural to cease lighting Sabbath eve candles, dispense with the age-old tradition of Sabbath morning *kid-*

dush, and, finally, abandon the whole family ceremony of a Sabbath eve meal, which they both cherished and would have very much wanted to continue.

"But why?" I asked Salman, feeling a little distressed myself. "Well, it's like this," he said. "First, with the exception of my firstborn, who couldn't be accommodated in any high school in sight, all my children went to the nonreligious [state] school in the ma'bara, which meant that their outlook and attitudes became strictly secular. Mind you, even if I had been better informed about the intricacies of the educational system here, I would in any case have sent the children to a regular state school, since sending them to religious school would have resulted in the disruption of our household. The trouble, you see, is that unlike what we had in the past, in 'primitive' Basra, there is no halfway house here in matters of religious observance. It seems that you are fated to be either strictly Orthodox or totally nonobservant, a professed 'heretic.' Had we sent the children to religious schools, they would have expected us, their parents, to run a far more Orthodox household than we are able or willing to do. On the other hand, sending them to a nonreligious State school meant that we have been deprived of any feeling of religious fulfillment and identification we had had in the old country."

Salman was profoundly unhappy about the current state of polarization between Orthodox and secularized Jew. "In such a situation," he explained, "people like me and my wife, who all their lives had led an untarnished traditional Jewish existence based on the principle of 'live and let live,' cannot find their bearings. I simply refuse to be either a fanatical, strictly observant Jew or a totally secularized one who would not even spare the feelings of his observant neighbor. What is worse, I find no way of refraining from doing either and at the same time maintain a semblance of the Jewish religious tradition."

What I find noteworthy here is that the liberal, easygoing traditional Judaism observed by Salman and his fellow Oriental immigrants had no ideological classification of any kind — Orthodox, Conservative, Reform — but was the result simply of a gradual and natural process of modernization. In Israel, many of these immigrants managed to preserve this informal brand of religiosity in their households, and it is interesting to note that strictly observant Ashkenazi inhabitants of religious neighborhoods and housing projects have often complained about this phenomenon. Their most frequent complaint is that their Oriental neighbors are "not sufficiently observant" — going to synagogues but not minding TV watching on the Sabbath, sending their children to religious schools but letting them go to Saturday football matches, allowing their daughters to walk around in what the neighbors consider immodest clothes, and so on.

Meanwhile, the process of acculturation of Oriental newcomers and their children in the religious field has been as fast and as wide-ranging as that which they have undergone in other spheres of life. Many specifically eastern European religious customs and mores, which with the passage of time became for the old settlers completely identified with Jewish religious precepts and norms, were adopted by the Orientals and their rabbis without objection. Among these: the universal use of skullcaps, in and outside houses of prayer, at the dining table and away from it; burial rites, gravestones, and visitations to the dead; the religious — as against the State's — ban on bigamy; and many points of difference in the liturgy, minor matters of *kashrut* [a kosher diet], and others.

In all these spheres, the Sephardi rabbinate, like the Sephardi public as a whole, embraced the norms of the dominant group unquestioningly. This readiness seems to me to be a measure of the frailty of the Oriental newcomer's cultural power of resistance when confronted with a dynamic, aggressive, dominant culture. As such, this acceptance of foreign religious practices can be seen as merely part of the general pattern of the Oriental's attempt to make the best of a difficult, trying situation.

*T*he subject was to crop up again a few years later — by sheer accident, you might say. The time was one day in April 1967. The place: Isfahan, in northern Iran. The city was still thickly covered with snow, and the hotel in which our tightfisted Persian travel agent installed us was cold and unaccommodating. We were a group of Israeli students and scholars on a study tour organized by one of the larger Israeli universities, and, as Israelis do, one of the first things we did was to make our presence known to the city's Jewish community.

Isfahan's chief rabbi and Jewish community head duly came to the hotel. It was Sabbath eve and manifestly well after sunset, and some of us were set wondering how on earth the man had managed to make his way to the hotel on foot in such grisly weather. We did not have to wonder for very long — for as the *hakham* was bidding us good night, he asked whether he could reach us by telephone. Told that he could, he flourished an expensive fountain pen and wrote down the number. He was to telephone to confirm an appointment we had arranged with him, since we wanted to visit the synagogue and the Jewish "ghetto."

As soon as the chief rabbi left the hotel, something very much like panic overtook our group. "We seem to have had it," exclaimed one of the group's leaders, a historian and Middle East specialist. "We have no doubt unwittingly landed right into the midst of the tug-of-war between the Orthodox, Conservative, and Reform Jews of Isfahan," he added. Asked to explain, he said: "It's simple; whoever directed us to the local Jewish community gave us the phone number of the city's Reform chief rabbi, and we will no doubt be taken to task for ignoring the Orthodox chief rabbi, who probably represents the majority of Jews here. You know how sensitive these people can be."

As it transpired, the panic was totally unjustified. Isfahan's chief rabbi, the selfsame one who actually wrote on a Saturday and probably even drove his own car or took a taxi cab to the hotel, was the city's sole chief rabbi and head of the community, and that was the end of that. Not only were there no such divisions among Isfahani Jews, but it is doubtful whether even their chief rabbi had so much as heard of the three religious groupings of Jews in the Western diasporas. And if further evidence of this was needed, it came promptly on the following morning. The synagogue we went to visit — and which we could reach only by car — was a spacious old house of prayer reminiscent of hundreds of such places in dozens of Middle Eastern and North African cities and towns. Like many such synagogues, it was flanked on one side by a Muslim household, on the other by a Jewish one — and the so-called Jewish "ghetto" turned out to be no more a ghetto than any predominantly Jewish quarter in Baghdad, Cairo, Marrakesh, Tunis, or Damascus.

A minor "incident" was provoked on the threshold of the synagogue. Bent on proving a hypothesis of his, one member of the group, a newcomer from Iraq, chose to enter the synagogue without a skullcap — "just to see what happens," he explained. What happened was exactly what he said he had predicted would happen. Neither Isfahan's chief rabbi nor the *shammash* [sexton] so much as raised an eyebrow, and there was not a murmur from the congregation. It was, instead, the Israelis who made a furor, accusing the man of lack of respect and consideration for the feelings of his hosts. Obviously, it never crossed their minds that observant Jews can be quite consciously and matter-of-factly tolerant of the nonobservant, or that the process of secularization — the shift from strict Orthodoxy and observance to a less pronounced state of belief or even unbelief — can be made smoothly, privately, and without much fuss.

| ℬARBARIANS AT THE GATE

VARIETIES OF ETHNIC SNOBBISM

One early spring day in 1962 Aharon Amir asked me to take part in a symposium that he said he was recording for publication in the Hebrew quarterly *Keshet* and that was to have the general title "Ethnic Snobbism." I declined. Not that the subject was foreign to me or failed to move me. On the contrary, since coming to Israel early in 1951, I had become increasingly aware of the gravity of the ethnic problem. True, at that time I had no idea what a Sephardi or an Ashkenazi was, and I refused to believe any of the things I heard concerning "discrimination against Orientals." But I was soon to know better, though I maintained silence—both because I disliked polemics and because of the unusual complexity of the subject.

The *Keshet* symposium (which was eventually printed in the Summer 1962 issue) was, however, to prove to be something of a turning point in my own thinking on the subject, and it ultimately sparked off a controversy that lasted nearly a decade. The symposium itself—though marking a considerable improvement in the usually dismal standard of discourse that until then had plagued all discussion of the ethnic problem—contained nothing out of the ordinary. Most of the participants managed again to miss the essential point, which to me seemed to lie in the fact that the growing rift between the communities was fundamentally a cultural one, even though the dominant in-group was trying to reduce it to a socioeconomic and educational "gap" to be narrowed and finally closed through a determined attempt by society to raise the economic, social, and educational levels of the out-group.

This approach, it seemed to me then, was doubly wrong, harmful, and often dishonest. In the first place, it spelled cultural coercion against the Orientals, and their ultimate deracination and Levantinization. Second, it tended to enter the Oriental immigrant in a race that he had no hope whatever of winning.

It was not the symposium itself, however, that was to start the debate.

It was something that *Keshet* printed in its next issue in response to the symposium: a communication from a reader, occupying six whole pages and arguing flatly and with admirable candor that the solution to Israel's ethnic problems lay in the "Ashkenazization" of the Orientals (*Keshet,* Autumn 1962). The writer's name was Gideon Spiegal.

In response to this refreshingly frank proposition, *Keshet* printed in its Winter 1963 issue a five-page rejoinder by Eliahu Aghasi, an old-timer of Iraqi origin. He had served as director of the Arab department of the Histadrut for a number of years before being summarily ousted and transferred to some obscure post, presumably to deal with cultural activities among the labor federation's Oriental membership.

It was at the farewell party held by the Histadrut for its regrettably departing Arab department director that I first met Aghasi. It was one of the gloomiest and most ludicrous affairs I had ever attended: speakers sounded as though they were reciting obituaries of the poor man, and he himself gave the impression of one about to be crucified.

I saw Aghasi again shortly after the Lavon affair, which ended with Lavon's dismissal and the ouster of a number of his faithful supporters in the Histadrut. One of these was Nahum Yahalom, whom Lavon had appointed director of the Arab department during his period of entrenchment, just before he launched his crusade against Ben-Gurion and "the security establishment." With Yahalom gone, Aghasi was called to take his place, on the strict understanding that this was to be a stopgap arrangement.

Shortly afterward, when Aghasi refused to vacate his "temporary" position, he was offered the management of the newly founded Arabic Publishing House, which the Histadrut set up partly to take care of its interests in *Al-Yawm* and partly to coordinate its various publications in Arabic. From then on I was to see Aghasi almost daily.

Before submitting his piece to *Keshet,* Aghasi gave it to me to read. I found it quite interesting, and immediately after it was printed I decided to give the whole subject some publicity in a foreign language publication. In February 1962, I sent the following report to the *Jewish Observer and Middle East Review,* for which I had already been writing. It appeared in the issue dated March 1, 1963, under the heading "Strangers We Remain—New Ideas on Mixing the Communities. From a special correspondent."

Experience has shown—the report said—that, in all cases and places where Ashkenazi and Oriental Jews have met and lived together, there has not as yet emerged a type of Jew—Israeli, English or Argentinean—who is not still either Ashkenazi or Oriental, not even after the eighty years of Jewish settlement here in the Holy Land. Those who call for "mixing the communities," and who by this mean mostly "Ashkenazising" the Sephardi and Oriental communities, are engaged in a wild goose chase. There are in Israel today third- and fourth-generation *sabras* born of Ashkenazi and Oriental parents—yet they are still looked upon as Ashkenazi and Oriental.

Those, among others, are the conclusions reached by Eliahu Aghasi, a veteran Israeli of Iraqi origin, writing in *Keshet*. Aghasi was responding to an article written by Gideon Spiegal, which appeared in a previous issue of the periodical, candidly calling on the non-Ashkenazis "to assimilate"—to become "Ashkenazised."

What, asks Aghasi, is a Sephardi to do in order to attain this Ashkenazisation? Is he merely to imitate, to dissimulate, to try to be "like an Ashkenazi," or actually to be one? Above all, what is to be the yardstick for "Ashkenazism?" Who is to decide? Shall we name some sort of committee for the purpose—and if so, should its members be Ashkenazis, Sephardis, or just people who have managed to get "Ashkenazised"?

After asking these questions—then answering them, with illustrations drawn from his experiences and those of others, Aghasi arrives at the conclusion that we ought to reconcile ourselves to the fate of a nation composed of two distinctive communal groups. Instead of exhorting Israelis to get Ashkenazised, Sephardized or simply "mixed," we should merely ask them to close their ranks, to march forward, to arise, and to get on in this world. Such a course, he believes, will have the advantage of helping us to get out of the blind alley in which we find ourselves on to a path whose direction we know and which should prevent tensions and resentments.

Far from bargaining over "what to give and what to take" (as Spiegal had formulated the problem), the question is whether the Ashkenazis are at all willing to accept the Oriental Jew *qua* Oriental Jew, who cannot hope to become—at least during this generation—anything but an Oriental Jew. The reply to the Oriental Jew's plea to be accepted, Aghasi writes, has always been the same. "Having shattered his personality, the Ashkenazis proceed to ask that he be an Ashkenazi like unto themselves!"

When I wrote this summary of Aghasi's ideas, my aim was to start a serious discussion of a subject that I thought was being deplorably neglected, avoided, or just ignored. The stratagem worked. Reading the report, Spiegal went to the trouble of sending a long letter to the editor, who duly printed it in the issue dated April 5, 1963, under the heading "No Compromise on Culture: Why Westernisation?" Here is an excerpt:

> At this juncture, I cite the historical proofs, from Peter the Great to Ataturk, to show that the only possible way for an Oriental Jew is to accept what is best in European civilisation in order to contribute to the progress of Israeli society.
>
> Total imitation of European civilisation will help solve the problem of backwardness which is not only the result of economic conditions, but of an Eastern atmosphere which does not encourage study and education. I would say, by way of comparison, that the Ashkenazi Jew of Meah Sha'arim, though economically badly off, is the exact opposite here of the Oriental Jew, because he lives in an atmosphere of intensive intellectual training and exercise . . .
>
> The point is not that an Oriental Jew should become an "Ashkenazi," but rather that he should accept the good and necessary things in Western civilisation. As for the question of what to give and what to receive, I have propounded the brutal but accurate fact that at present the Oriental communities have less to give than to receive (if, of course, our assumption is that Westernisation is the order of the day). On the other hand, it is to be welcomed that Oriental Jews, while receiving the best of European civilisation, also spread their native customs and folk ways, which have a definite charm and value of their own . . .
>
> Naturally, we should always welcome Oriental representation chosen on the basis of merit. I believe, therefore, that a temporary predominance of Ashkenazi Jews is more in the true interests of the country as a whole than artificial boosting on a communal basis. Westernisation will produce a situation in which the Oriental Jews will ultimately achieve representation on the basis of genuine merit . . . Too many people admit in private what I am saying, but consider it bad form to say so in public.

Once Spiegal spoke, I took care to set the stage for a full-blown discussion of the subject. The following letter, which I sent promptly to London, appeared in the *Jewish Observer* of April 19 under the heading, "Not by Bread and Plumbing Alone," signed "Onlooker."

> Gideon Spiegal cites "historical proofs from Peter the Great to Ataturk" in order to prove his view that "total imitation of European

civilisation will help solve the problem of backwardness, which is not only the result of economic conditions but of an Eastern atmosphere which does not encourage study and education."

I am not sure that your correspondent really knows what he is talking about. Even if one accepts his thesis that non-Oriental Jews in Israel would be the right agents for "Westernising" their Oriental brethren—a thesis which is very doubtful, since the former are themselves still undergoing the inevitable process of Westernisation—one suspects that he is blissfully unaware of the enormous psychological implications of a standpoint which the Israelis have been adopting regarding this problem.

Since the subject is vexed and prejudice-ridden, I would confine myself quoting from a book by Margaret Mead, the well-known American anthropologist, which seems to me to be very apt: "As each culture," wrote Mead, "is a whole, however sorely torn at the moment—whole in the sense that it is the system by which and through which its members live—in all relationships between cultures each must be accorded dignity and value. Much of . . . the present evaluation of change within a country is conducted with explicit or implicit denial of the dignity of members of those countries which, while often the inheritors of much older traditions, have not been in the vanguard of these aspects of culture which stem from modern science . . . Phrases which divide the world into 'haves' and 'have-nots' may come to repudiate the possibility of learning anything at all, or of sharing anything at all except 'bread' with those who have so denigrated their cherished ways of life . . . [No] programme of technological development can hope to succeed in the long run if it leaves people unhappy and maladjusted."

My impression is that Israel's programme for the "Westernisation" of her Oriental Jewries has so far been leading to some very negative results—unhappiness, maladjustment, resistance to change, repudiation, and a refusal to share with the cultural "haves" anything except bread and plumbing.

The following week, in its issue dated April 26, 1963, the *Jewish Observer* carried a letter from Aghasi, under the heading "Why Should Oriental Jews Assimilate?" The letter, which I had read and "edited" before it was mailed, read in part:

Confronted by my contention that Ashkenazisation can mean nothing else but being born to two Ashkenazi parents, brought up by an

Ashkenazi family and enjoying the feeling of belonging to the Ashkenazi group, Mr. Spiegal now pleads . . . that what he really meant was Westernisation.

Now, if this means acquiring Western knowledge and techniques, then let me remind Mr. Spiegal that Oriental Jews have been doing so for the last eighty years, and even gave the West some prominent figures. It would seem, however, that merely acquiring Western knowledge and techniques is not enough in itself, and that what is really expected of the Oriental Jew in Israel is nothing short of the metamorphosis mentioned above . . .

Another way of evading the problem is the use of another ambiguous appellation. People here are rather afraid of the "Levantinisation" of Israel by those Oriental Jews who Westernise the wrong way! We therefore read in Mr. Spiegal's letter the admonition that Oriental Jews should accept only "the good and necessary things in Western civilisation," just as the Ashkenazim seem to be doing successfully. This is how our compatriots manage to keep talking about the backwardness of the Oriental Jews as a whole, and deny them, among other things, the right to hold responsible posts and be equal partners in the representative bodies of the country!

AHARON MEGGED SAYS IT ALL

While the Spiegal affair was on, another front opened by the *Jewish Observer* introduced a new and unexpected, though welcome, element into the controversy. Apparently on some lecture tour of the United Kingdom, the well-known novelist Aharon Megged was interviewed briefly by a reporter working for the weekly, and, what with one thing or other, the subject of "the cultural gap" was raised. Megged—like so many Israeli visitors abroad, who seem to believe that whatever they say about the subject of "the communities" must go unnoticed—gave vent to a "theory" of culture, literature, and literacy, and I found it unusually offensive. As a result, in reply to Megged I wrote a two-page article under the pseudonym "T. H. Babli"—the reason for not signing my full name being purely technical: I was writing regularly for the weekly on Arab and Middle Eastern culture and politics, and I and the editor, Jon Kimche, did not want non-Israeli readers to know that so critical a student of Arab politics and attitudes had such trouble himself being an Oriental in Israel.

Here are extracts from my article on Megged, printed under the heading "Stop Patronising the Oriental Jews: A Reply to Aharon Megged" in the issue dated May 17, 1963.

It is one of the ironies of history that, while the West has been steadily freeing itself from the prejudices on non-Westerners which used to bedevil it, it has fallen to the lot of the so-called Western Jews in Israel to be the last advocates of such outdated notions about "inferior" and "backward" cultures. It is, of course, doubly ironic that this deprecatory attitude towards everything not "Western" should be adopted by Jews vis-à-vis fellow Jews—and for no better reason than that the ways of the two groups happened to have parted at one juncture in their common history.

It would have been easy to dismiss these prejudices as unimportant, were it not for the far-reaching historical and practical implications which they carry with them. To start with, they are gradually but visibly creating a state of affairs where the so-called Sephardi community in Israel (which seems to include all Israelis, including sabras, who do not happen to have been born to two Ashkenazi parents) is being increasingly estranged from the dominant Eastern European culture—always, however, masquerading as *Western* culture.

In some cases, indeed, members of this deprecated community now refuse to have any truck with their cultural "superiors," and seem to have resigned themselves to a sort of perpetual separation. This, in turn, has resulted in retarding rather than accelerating that process of Westernisation which large sections of these Oriental Jews had already begun to undergo in their countries of origin. Secondly, and concurrently, this widespread and almost subconscious prejudice against Oriental Jewries has led to a good measure of self-estrangement amongst members of the dominant Ashkenazi group, since it has tended to cut them off even further from their own past and tradition and way of life. This is by no means as paradoxical as it may sound. As an Ashkenazi student of Jewish history pointed out some time ago: What the Jews of Eastern Europe in Israel really dislike about their fellow Jews from the Orient is the fact that the latter unpleasantly remind them of the social and cultural conditions prevailing only a few decades ago in their own *shtetls* and ghettoes in the Russian Pale and in Poland.

It is this unhealthy eagerness on the part of most Eastern European Jews in Israel to forget and disown their own past which has led to the prevalent sneering attitude towards the "Sephardis" and to the dangerous drift away from their own cultural background. Observers well-versed in psychology and the dark workings of the collective ego will no doubt be better placed to speak of the immense inner satisfactions to be drawn from being in a position to feel superior to the next fellow. But it is obvious, even to the layman, how gratifying it is to be in such a position.

No doubt many "Western" Israelis are genuinely distressed at the sight of so many inferior creatures living in their midst. Yet it would be no exaggeration to say that, human nature being what it is, this state of affairs has come to give these "Westerners," no matter how "backward" they are as individuals, the rare satisfaction of feeling superior to their non-Ashkenazi compatriots, no matter how "advanced" and "cultured." Having by this process convinced themselves that they are superior to their less fortunate fellow-Jews from Asia and Africa, these good-hearted and well-meaning ex-inhabitants of the *shtetl* and their descendants proceed to try to convince others. Knowing from their past experiences that they cannot easily be accepted as Westerners by Westerners, they often find no better way of gaining such acceptance than by adopting the role of "Westernisers," thus showing the whole world that not only are they not to be identified with their backward brethren from the East, but that they are actually trying to lift these Jews up to their own Western level of culture and achievement. It is no doubt this eagerness to be accepted as equals in the Western world that makes certain Israeli spokesmen overseas so outspoken and demonstrative in their pronouncements on the "cultural gap" in Israel . . .

Megged speaks as though there were in Israel only one language, literature or culture — Hebrew — whereas in fact the overwhelming majority of the population, both European and Oriental, know Hebrew only as their second or sometimes third language, and have not even a nodding acquaintance with Hebrew literature. As a matter of fact, one gets the impression that — apart from the *sabras,* who include a good proportion of Orientals — the Israelis who read Hebrew most are the backward Orientals, while the more advanced Europeans prefer English, German, French, Yiddish or their own various mother tongues. A mere glance at the list of Israeli newspapers and periodicals — and taking into account the uncommonly large number of foreign newspapers and periodicals sold in Israel — will give some idea of the essentially multi-lingual nature of the Israeli reading public.

But this is not the whole story: there are tens of thousands of Israelis, of all categories and classes and communities, who, though they may prefer to read a Hebrew paper, would never aspire to make Hebrew the language of their literary readings.

Megged allows himself to fall into another major contradiction when he implies that it is precisely the "new trend" in Israeli letters, which he claims is preoccupied with "universal human and social problems," that is "entirely alien" to the few fortunate Orientals who may be able to read Hebrew.

One should have thought the contrary was true, since one of the things which in the past proved a detriment to a wider reading public, especially amongst those who did not come from Eastern Europe, was the largely, if understandably, provincial and narrow subject matter of most of the older generation of Hebrew writers. Now that, as Megged claims, Israeli writers, playwrights and poets are "playing on universal human and social problems," the barrier should have been removed rather than strengthened between the mass of the Orientals and the few Israeli writers who represent this trend. Yet his thinking on this subject — like that of almost all "Westerners" in Israel — is so hopelessly muddled and prejudiced that he allows himself to say, in the same breath, that the new trend in Israeli literature, of which he is presumably a representative, "poses *basically Western* social and humanitarian questions." Despite this singular lack of clarity about Megged's whole thesis here, one cannot help wondering why, if the new trend is preoccupied with "*universal* human and social problems" (again quoting his own words), should the questions it poses be described as "basically Western"? Since when have the terms "universal" and "Western" become identical? And moreover, why should our universally minded writers of the new trend resign themselves to a state of affairs where they are completely cut off from "well over 60 per cent of Israel's population"?

Clearly the culture and the literature of which Megged spoke exist nowhere outside a very narrow and visibly narrowing circle of Israelis. The cultural face of Israel has already changed, and is fast being transformed in hundreds of devious, uncontrollable and invisible ways . . .

CAJOLING MICHAEL ASSAF

This rather strongly worded riposte appeared on May 17, 1963. In *Davar* of May 28, Michael Assaf — who in the past had dealt, however fleetingly, with the problem of "the communities" — published a long article under the heading "An Angry Intelligentsia," in which he took issue with Babli's reply to Megged. (Not making any attempt to hide Babli's identity, I had let Assaf know it before he wrote his article.)

Assaf's article posed a problem as far as the continuation of the debate was concerned. Not knowing English, he chose to reply to Babli in the pages of *Davar;* reluctant to write in Hebrew and suspecting that *Davar* would bide its time before publishing a rejoinder—if at all—I decided to take the only course open: I sent the *Jewish Observer* a report "From a special correspondent" in which I faithfully summarized Assaf's arguments—with the intention of writing a full-length reply to his in the same paper. The report, which appeared on June 21 under the heading "Angry Oriental Intelligentsia: A New Plea," read in part:

> "Never look back!" This is the "basic conclusion" on the inter-communal problem in Israel recently drawn by Michael Assaf, veteran Israeli writer on Arab affairs and a regular contributor to the Histadrut daily, *Davar.* His call was prompted, in the main, by the *Jewish Observer* article "Stop Patronising the Oriental Jews," by T. H. Babli. Assaf explains that, by this injunction, he means that the Ashkenazis should abstain from making any utterances on the subject of the Oriental immigrants' material or cultural past. A responsible Government or Jewish Agency official, for example, should abstain, when speaking to an Oriental Jew about his housing problems, from asking his charge why he was being so fastidious, and "Where did you reside 'back there'? . . . In a palace?"
>
> Also, "all public talk or searching writing about historical, cultural or other gaps created through the centuries (between the two communities) must cease, since such talk implies that many generations will be needed to close these gaps." Assaf, whose article is entitled "An Angry Intelligentsia," implies that the source of the educated Oriental's anger dwells in a feeling of inferiority. "It is natural," he writes, "that this intelligentsia, which came to Israel after decades of work done by the best Zionist and pioneer elements which came from Jewry's most important centres in recent generations, i.e., in Eastern Europe—it is natural that this (Oriental) intelligentsia should feel somewhat inferior."
>
> . . . Turning to the angry Oriental intelligentsia, Assaf writes that part of the trouble stems from the fact that some members of this intelligentsia fail to realise their own personal ambitions. "Had the thing occurred with a Pole, a Rumanian, etc., these would certainly not have seen in their personal disappointment a matter of communal discrimination. We therefore should not accept the call to stop patronising the Oriental Jews. The masses of Oriental Jews are needy, indeed very needy, of our concern and care . . . I have the feeling that members of the angry intelligentsia, and the extremists who were given expression in Babli's article, had in the past done nothing in their countries of origin, and are doing nothing now, in Israel, for the good of the masses of Oriental Jews . . ."

At the same time that I was writing the foregoing report, I decided to write to Assaf privately—in an attempt to persuade, cajole, or positively provoke him, for once, into revealing his full philosophy on the subject of communal interaction. Knowing of his rather low opinion of Arabs and Orientals in general, I nevertheless wanted to make sure of his beliefs before I launched on a full-scale debate with him. The result was extremely frustrating: the man was simply incapable of being drawn into such a discussion, either because he had something terrible to hide or because he never gave the matter any serious thought. A brief exchange ensued, and it tended only to give me an insight into the hopelessly confused, positively chaotic thinking on the subject by Assaf and those who think like him. In fact, his last letter seemed to me so utterly hopeless that after I wrote my reply, I put it aside and refrained from actually mailing it.

In the course of the correspondence, Assaf in one of his letters (June 18, 1963) said he showed my article on Megged to some colleagues. "Yehuda Gotthelf, for one, said 'this is an anti-Semitic article'; K. Shabtai said, 'This is a terrible article.' "

Having thus failed to make any headway with him privately, I decided to make our argument public. The following article was published in the *Jewish Observer* as the cover story of its issue dated August 2, 1963.

Michael Assaf, leading Israeli expert on Arab affairs, author of a book on the Arabs of Palestine, veteran columnist on the Histadrut's Hebrew daily, *Davar,* once wrote an article entitled "On the Oriental Quality." Among other things, the article dealt with the differences between Ashkenazi and Oriental Jews, purported to be viewed in the wider context of differences between Orient and Occident. After propounding his view of the "backwardness" of the Oriental peoples in general, Assaf asked, "What must therefore be the task of the Ingathering of the Exiles? Not only to bring [the Oriental Jews] to the soil of Israel, but also to restore to them their first exalted value. The same thing holds good with regard to all parts of the (Jewish) people who were, to their misfortune, dispersed by the hand of Fate among low-grade (*yarud*) peoples. And every Jew who is not seized by the fear of the possibility, whether it is imaginary or not, that we will not be able to prevail and to purify our [Oriental] brethren from the dross of Orientalism which attached itself to them against their will, will be held accountable for this before the guardian spirit of the nation. There is reason for the most serious anxiety . . . how to cleanse and purify these brethren—how to lift them up to the Western level of the existing

Yishuv . . ." (*Davar*, September 29, 1950. Quoted in English translation in Raphael Patai, *Israel between East and West*, p. 311.)

Nearly thirteen years later, on May 28, 1963, Assaf published a signed article in *Davar* entitled "An Angry Intelligentsia," in which he asked his Ashkenazi readers to refrain from "making any utterances on the subject of the Oriental immigrants' material or cultural past." He explained that "all talk in public and all searching writings" about the yawning cultural and historical gulf between the Ashkenazis and the Orientals is harmful in that it intensifies the feeling of inferiority from which, in his view, the Oriental intelligentsia suffers — a feeling supposed to have been engendered by a past and a culture of which no one could feel proud. His conclusion, therefore, was summed up in the slogan: "Never look back."

In other words, at the end of thirteen years of study, observation, and reflection, Assaf added exactly nothing to his knowledge of the subject. His Oriental "brethren" remain, to him, the same decrepit people he used to consider them in 1950. The dross of Orientalism, whatever that may be, continues to bedevil them, and their culture remains as "low-grade" as it was before. The only difference between 1950 and 1963 is that Assaf now asks, for various practical reasons, that the superior Ashkenazis should keep their knowledge and views about these matters to themselves. In other words, he asks them to practise dissimulation, to pretend to think what they do not really think — to be, in sum, conscious hypocrites.

Now one feels tempted to ask what has induced this sudden shift on Assaf's part from the plain, "searching" talk of thirteen years ago about the Orientals, and the paramount task of civilising them up to the so-called Western standard of the *Yishuv*, to this new-found quietism, this counsel of silence which in itself is so offensive and condescending towards Israel's Oriental communities?

As far as one can gather from the bewildering mass of woolly ideas, glaring contradictions and angry insults which constitute Assaf's latest article on the subject, the reason why he wants nothing said in public about the Orientals' backwardness and the low level of their culture stems from certain recent manifestations of the existence of an "angry" Oriental intelligentsia which, "in certain circumstances," is likely to start to look to Cairo and Baghdad . . . In the course of his article, Assaf pays me the doubtful compliment of considering my views, as expressed in the article "Stop Patronising the Oriental Jews" as representing the "extremist" wing of this intelligentsia . . .

It was as well that it was Assaf and no other who chose to enter this controversy, as I thought his was the best representative of the kind of thoughtless, cliche-ridden thesis that my article sought to expose. Indeed, his *Davar* article embodies almost all the evils there criticized: a patronizing attitude, undisguised superior airs, an unseemly eagerness for identification with everything Western, a sneering view of one's own cultural background (in this case, of the shtetl), and a strange aptitude for empty words and sloganeering.

Proceeding on the assumption that cultures are inevitably classifiable into "low grade" and "high grade," and holding his own clear views of shtetl culture, Assaf also made the strange inference that by merely mentioning the word shtetl (he actually expressed shock at Babli's use of the term!) and by denying its ex-inhabitants the Westernism of which they now so freely boast, I was deprecating the culture of the shtetl. He even misquoted me as describing the Ashkenazis as being "consumed (*akhul:* eaten!) by the low-grade culture of the shtetl."

Strange as it may sound, this in fact represented Assaf's own estimate of the shtetl and its culture, not mine. It also offers a perfect illustration of my contention that the eagerness of the dominant section of eastern Europeans in Israel to disown and forget their traditional Jewish culture of the shtetl and to identify themselves with Western culture is one of the decisive reasons why they look down on Oriental Jews, conceivably because these latter constantly remind them of a past and a culture they are so desperate to disclaim.

It is not only on deduction and conjecture that I base this contention. Indeed, it could hardly have been a coincidence that Assaf's slogan, "Never look back," originated not in the context of the Oriental Jews and their past, but precisely in a discussion of the shtetl and its culture, and of how those who come from or have their cultural roots there ought to view their old life and ways. Indeed, some months before I wrote my reply to Assaf, at a conference of the Hebrew Writers' Association, the well-known Israeli author Hayim Hazaz delivered a spirited address in which he spoke sorrowfully about the general spirit of nihilism that, he said, was creeping into Israeli society. His address made some impact, and Prime Minister Ben-Gurion, who did not share Hazaz's pessimism, invited the veteran author to a discussion.

In the course of this discussion Ben-Gurion expressed surprise and some misgivings about Hazaz's speaking "with such nostalgia and such awe about the shtetl." Ben-Gurion declared: "I know what the shtetl is. Yet I have no feeling of nostalgia for it. The best among us fled from it and settled in Palestine." Going on to describe the shtetl from which he and some of the first Zionist pioneers issued forth—a townlet "the like of which there were very few in the Diaspora"—Ben-Gurion asked Hazaz rhetorically: "But do you seriously suggest that we go back to that kind of life, to that emptiness? We ran away from there!"

Hazaz, after deploring the fact that the few kind words that he had said about the shtetl had aroused so much criticism against him, said, "I know the shtetl of the past. I never looked upon it as the perfect specimen of a community. On the contrary, I thought of the shtetl as a place where life was drab and which was to be pitied. But it had some good in it; its life was enhanced by some of the finest qualities of our people . . . From the shtetl [the first immigrants] brought with them a sense of piety, a love of the Jewish people, a love of the Torah, enthusiasm, a sense of self-dedication, a spirit of altruism . . . All that stemmed from the culture they imbibed in the shtetl . . . Nowadays, spiritual life is gone from our midst; we have no outstanding moral leaders."

At this juncture, interestingly enough, Hazaz saw fit to bring in the subject of the new immigrants. "We do not," he lamented, "possess the moral and spiritual forces required for absorbing into our midst the many settlers who came from so many different cultures, to absorb them in a way which would raise them up, or make of them a people in accordance with the great responsibility which history placed upon our generation."

It would be highly interesting to know what made Hazaz link, in so unambiguous a way, the Israelis' present derogatory attitude toward the shtetl culture with what he considered their lack of sufficient spiritual force to absorb new immigrants from other cultures. But Assaf, who had a nose for these things and seemed to be as well versed in the culture of the shtetl as he was in the dross of Orientalism, quickly took up the issue in *Davar*. Siding, somewhat predictably, with Hazaz's critics, he dismissed as totally irrelevant the shtetl and all that it stood for, and coined his now-famous slogan, "Never look back."

Thus, the slogan was neither new nor meant to apply only to Orientals. The cultural amnesia has to go all the way through: the eastern European Jew should "cleanse and purify" himself from the dross of the shtetl — exactly as the unfortunate Oriental has to be cleansed and purified from the dross of Orientalism! A better illustration of my argument can hardly be conceived.

ABBA EBAN TO THE RESCUE

In September 1962, the *Jewish Observer* carried a six-page interview with Abba Eban, minister of education and culture and president of the Weizmann Institute of Science. The title of the interview was "Israel's Education Explosion: Closing the Gap between 'The Two Nations.'" Partly in (belated) response to this interview, but also as a reaction to numerous more recent pronouncements on the subject, I wrote the following piece — after a great deal of hesitation and agonizing since education had never been my field.

The existence of a gap between the two groups of Jews in Israel cannot be denied. It is a cultural gap, an economic gap but, above all, an educational gap. Israelis talk of "the Gap," however, as if it were almost eternal and the result of "five centuries of history," as if indeed it were something that no human effort could be expected to remedy "in a short spell of time." One suspects this kind of talk has become a psychological need for those of the old *Yishuv*—which threatens to make it, through the workings of the vicious circle, precisely what they profess to fear: a real and permanent fact of Israeli life.

It is in the sphere of education, especially in primary education, that the most harm has been and is being done, and it is here that the future of inter-communal relations — if not of the whole nation — is likely to be decided. Abba Eban, when Minister of Education, depicted a grim and thoroughly disquieting picture. He said, "Some thirty per cent of the children of Oriental communities — themselves comprising over half the Jewish population of Israel — reach the end of their elementary school at the age of 14 without knowing how to read a simple Hebrew text, to write a legible letter, or to carry out the four basic arithmetical calculations. These youth, after eight years of schooling, "have only a vague idea about Israel, the Jewish people and the world surrounding them, and are often plunged in apathy and bitterness." (Interview in the *Jewish Observer*, September 21, 1962.)

What were the causes of this gap? This direct and rather difficult question was put to Eban — young, enlightened, tolerant and Cambridge-educated, a man whom no one can accuse of prejudices or preconceived notions. Well, first of all, Eban begged leave to say "what is *not* the cause of the gap." The cause, he asserted, "is not a genetic cultural difference between Western and Oriental Jews. I dismiss this not only because of a natural impulse to dismiss it, but also because history and research conclusively refute it," he said.

What then were the causes? It is here, as usual, that we are apt to become enmeshed in that mixture of historical fallacy and cultural agoraphobia which often sounds so painfully like built-in prejudice. The causes,

Eban rightly said, lay in environmental conditions. Not, however, today's conditions, nor those prevalent during the past ten, twenty, or even fifty years; they are, he said, "the result of five centuries of Jewish history. One half of our population comes from communities which since the decline of Islamic culture, have had no educational history or environment. *Their children, now in Israel, are the first generation for centuries to be educated at all.* The other half *represents European culture at its most intense creativity with the added emphasis of Jewish humanism*" (my italics).

Clearly, Eban is here engaging in exaggeration so gross it verges on willful falsification of historical facts. The average Oriental Jew from Yemen, Iraq, Syria or North Africa was surely not so totally plunged in darkness — "the *first* generation for centuries to be educated at all!" — nor could the average Jew from Eastern Europe accurately be said to represent so truly "European culture at its most intense creativity," etc. A most superficial perusal of the history of those parts of Europe to which he must be referring would have convinced Eban of the absurdity of his verdict. The assumption, on the other hand, that Oriental Jewries represented the very worst and most backward facets of Islamic culture in its darkest periods is as untenable as the claim that European Jews represented the very best and most creative in the Western cultural tradition. Here, too, a little delving into history would do European Jews a lot of good.

An illustration of the kind of hazardous pitfalls to which such historical fallacies can lead is furnished by Eban in the same interview. Despite his emphatic denial of a belief in the existence of any "genetic cultural difference" between the European and Oriental Jews, we find him declaring, *apropos* of his defence of special projects and differential courses aimed at narrowing the communal gap, that the opponents of these measures are in conflict "not with me . . . but with the nature of man."

Men, he elaborated, "are not equal in their intellectual receptivity. There are gallon-containers and half-pint jars. Our responsibility is to fill each of them up to full capacity." In defence of this perfectly right-sounding proposition, he quotes Julian Huxley: "Our idea-system must jettison the myth of equality. Human beings are not born equal in gifts and potentialities . . . 'Free but unequal' should be our slogan. Diversity of excellence, not conformist normalcy or mere adjustment, should be the aim of education."

"Free but unequal?" Perfectly all right! But poor Dr. Huxley was speaking of individual human beings, not of groups, communities or nations, as Eban was so obviously and indisputably doing! One does not pretend to know what a "genetic cultural difference" denotes precisely; but if our former Education Minister was alluding to racialist theories, then the context and full burden of his quotation from Huxley make him stand accused of holding just such theories — theories of which, by the way, Huxley is completely innocent.

As individuals, human beings may be unequal in their intellectual receptivity even at kindergarten age, but to generalise this to include whole groups of human beings can have only one meaning — racial prejudice. Far be it from me to accuse Mr. Eban of such a monstrosity; but his slip goes to show only that loose talk about "five centuries of history" would inevitably land us onto such highly perilous shores.

Call it what you will, however, almost every member of the old *Yishuv* will tell you — albeit sadly, good-heartedly and rather patronisingly — that "a problem created over five centuries cannot be solved in a year or two" — in Eban's precise words. Yet, come to think of it, what precisely is the significance of those "five centuries of history" for an Israeli-born child of six, five, or four years?

What is the exact difference between five centuries of backwardness and five decades of backwardness when it comes to the simple matter of providing decent elementary schooling for such a child? Given a sound system of primary education, with enough hours and qualified teachers, why cannot even a minimum of knowledge be given to the son of, say, a poor cobbler from Fas, even though this child may belong to "the first generation for centuries to be educated at all?"

To do Eban justice, however, one has to mention that he gives two other causes for the existing educational gap — one largely economic ("Two children may receive identical tuition. But if one goes back to a squalid home with nine children in a room, the 'equality' of his educational opportunity is purely formal and meaningless") — and the other, the prevalent educational system which insists on egalitarianism and uniform curricula for all elementary schools. "A school in Tel Aviv with Israel-born pupils and a school in Kiryat Gat with an entirely immigrant population require different treatment for at least a part of the course," Eban believes.

This, no doubt, is much nearer to the core of the education problem than mere harping on what I would call the "Myth of the Five Centuries." But here too, one can easily find loopholes; and since prospective reforms will be based on the lines of some such assumptions as are implicit in these two causes we will be well-advised to try and discover what precisely we are talking about.

To begin with, my own feeling is that too much emphasis is being placed on the question of poor and over-crowded housing and its detrimental effects on the education of our young. We do not know quite in what conditions Israelis like Eban grew up and got their schooling, but only the other day our Foreign Minister, Mrs. Golda Meir, reminisced before a *Ma'ariv* reporter about the life and fortunes of her family back in Kiev during the early years of this century — and, if she was not grossly exaggerating the poverty of the conditions in which she and her family lived in those days, one would not hesitate to assert that the gap in its pre-Israel form represented not five centuries, not even five years! Yet, to the good fortune of all of us, young Golda Mabovitch managed somehow — as did millions of other Jewish children in thousands of *shtetls,* ghettoes, villages and small towns in the Eastern European Pale, and also throughout the Moslem domain of the sons of Osman . . .

As for the inadequacy of our educational system, it can safely be said that here lie the roots of the evil. Yet there is an impression of a wholly misplaced emphasis . . . Rather than a question of five centuries of Jewish history, it is one of 15 years of Israeli history. To give one example, last year, out of the whole Oriental population of Israel, some one million strong, about 400 youngsters managed to complete their secondary education.

In 1949 — 14 years of dizzying progress ago! — the 130,000-odd Jewish community of Iraq alone produced 450 secondary school graduates. This seems to be a piece of evidence so conclusive and so damning that it can more than just speak for itself.

Take another example. There are in Israel a few schools run by Christian missions. In one of these schools, in Jaffa, two languages (Hebrew and French) are taught right from the first year of primary schooling, three (with English added) in the second year. Yet the standard of the second-year classes in Hebrew is found to be higher than that in the parallel class in a Ramat Gan school, where for the first four years at school the child learns only Hebrew! Is it any wonder then that a number of Israeli parents — good Jews not excluded — should prefer to send their children to these schools?

Such remedies as are often suggested — a longer school day in development areas; free kindergarten for immigrant children under five; special allowances in the *seker* (secondary school entrance) test; and various stipends and inducements for "children needing special care" will not only serve no real purpose but may deepen and perpetuate "the Gap."

The real need is for a healthy system based on the realities of life of the majority, not of a privileged minority; a well-trained and decently paid teacher corps, with special encouragement to those qualified teachers who are willing to work in development areas; insistence on a minimum standard of attainment by pupils before leaving primary school; and, of course, a longer school day *for all*.

These, and other changes in the same direction, will give an equal opportunity to all children to use their latent capacities to the full while still in elementary school. This, of course, will be raising rather than lowering the country's educational level. Above all, it will mark a step toward breaking that vicious circle which has so far served only to widen, deepen and perpetuate the communal gap.

("Plea for Communal Realism," by T. H. BABLI,
Jewish Observer, OCTOBER 18, 1963)

On November 1, 1963, the *Jewish Observer* printed a response by Eban, in which he lamely claimed that in quoting Huxley he was indeed referring to individuals, not to groups. He also accused me of "a flippant treatment of a grave national issue."

Hard on the heels of the Eban exchange came the clash with Ishar Harari, a member of the Knesset and veteran liberal. While in London, Harari did what many Israeli notables were in the habit of doing — namely, giving vent to all kinds of sentiments, usually extremely lacking in either subtlety or accuracy, on controversial issues that at home they usually felt constrained to leave unsaid. In the *Jewish Chronicle* of October 18, 1963, and elsewhere, Harari made a number of remarks that again led me to take up a challenge that was not really mine to take.

Writing about the white segregationists of the American South, Richard Rovere recently mused over the fact that they "aren't much given to talking." The self-satisfied bullies, he said, merely "stomp: When they do speak, they are brief." Mr. Ishar Harari, M.K., however, seems to lack that incisive subtlety without which even silence is rendered eloquent. Thus, despite his gallant attempt to be "brief" about the communal situation in Israel, he managed to say quite a lot about it during his recent brief stay in London as the guest of the British Liberal Party.

Harari is also inconsistent. In his original *Jewish Chronicle* interview he claimed that the problems arising from the emergence of "two nations" in Israel, the Ashkenazim and the Sephardim, were "exaggerated." In the same breath he decided that the problem "has no reason to exist at all," that it is, in fact, "entirely artificial." A few lines later, finally deciding that there was some such problem, Harari asserted: "There is no discrimination whatsoever. But unfortunately many Sephardim are not educated and we have to provide the means to change this."

Now it is extremely difficult to argue with Mr. Harari. Though his brevity seems eloquent enough, it lacks conciseness and intelligibility and, above all, minimal honesty. When he says, for instance, that he knows of no case where a Sephardi Jew, "who had the necessary education and qualifications," had been refused a position because he was a Sephardi — and that, "*on the contrary,*" he knew several who held positions of great responsibility — one has to believe him. But look at the flimsiness of his "proofs." To start with, the fact that Harari is unaware of any cases of discrimination does not mean that such cases do not exist. Also, the fact that he knows "several" Sephardim who hold positions of great responsibility does not mean much in itself.

We all know such Sephardim, but we also know *why* they are there. We know of the two Sephardi cabinet ministers who hold the Police and Posts portfolios; but we also know that they are there not merely because they have "the necessary education and qualifications" but because they also happen to be Sephardim. We are also aware of the existence of a handful of Sephardim who sit side by side with Harari in the Knesset; but we are sure that he himself would be the first to admit that they are there for reasons other than their possession of the same education and qualifications termed by Harari "necessary."

Those who, like Harari, hold that in Israel there is no discrimination whatever against the Orientals will no doubt argue that the above shows not only that no discrimination exists but that there is discrimination *in favour* of the Sephardim. This cannot be farther from the truth. If there are several Sephardi-Orientals who hold positions of responsibility — and who hold it not precisely because they have the right qualifications — this means merely that the exclusively Ashkenazi establishment still considers that these should be given a few such positions *qua* Sephardim.

The implications are obvious and far-reaching: for if the principle is accepted that so large a sector of the country's population must in some way get adequate representation, then the question can legitimately be asked whether those who are chosen to represent it are 1) truly representative of the Sephardi public, and 2) given a real chance to share in the running the country's affairs.

The answer in both cases is categorically in the negative.

(T. H. BABLI, *Jewish Observer*, NOVEMBER 1, 1963)

Some two months after the publication of the above, on January 10, a lengthy rejoinder was sent by Harari, who had obviously not prepared himself for a confrontation. Referring to the interview on which I had commented, Harari wrote:

The above-mentioned article was not written by me, nor was it an interview with me, but an article written by you, Sir, after an hour's conversation with me. Naturally, I can't be held responsible for the free version of part of this conversation . . .

When I spoke last year at Columbia University in New York, I was astonished at the questions I was asked; as though we in Israel had the same problems of racial discrimination as they have in the United States. I was astonished because all these questions are only a result of false reports which are being circulated, with no foundation or justification. In Israel, there exists no law of any discrimination between human beings or between the various communities. We have no closed clubs or restricted restaurants and hotels; and there exists no discrimination on the grounds of colour, origin or community. It is simply amazing that there are people who can imagine that, socially and otherwise, something of this kind does exist. The example brought by Mr. Babli, as though I was referring to Sephardi Members of the Knesset put on Ashkenazi lists, is out of place — as this is exactly what I did not refer to. All those clamouring about discrimination do not consider that the people who occupy important positions here, and who enjoy universal respect, were never appointed to these positions because they were Sephardim, and nobody thinks, even for a moment, of enquiring if they are Sephardim . . .

I repeat my conviction that there exists no discrimination between communities in Israel. And in my opinion there is no need to write about a problem which does not exist. I think that to write about a thing which does not exist only gives a false picture of the reality.

To this pitiably poor performance I wrote a very brief reply, printed in the issue dated January 31, 1964.

Ishar Harari is clearly trying to evade the issue by concentrating on largely irrelevant aspects of the controversy. His very emphases betray the weakness of his arguments. Is it true, for instance, that Sephardim who occupy important positions here "were *never* appointed to those positions because they were Sephardim," or that "nobody thinks, *even for a moment,* of enquiring if they are Sephardim?" . . . My contention is that the "education and qualifications" which Mr. Harari demands of a Sephardi have nothing to do with education, but include aspects pertaining to a person's cultural background and temperament — that, in effect, he was demanding that a Sephardi have the qualifications of an Ashkenazi . . .

YAʿACOV DORI ENTERS THE ARENA

The third Israeli of note with whom I came to verbal blows in the space of two months was General Yaʿacov Dori, Israel's first chief of staff and the president of the Technion (Israel Institute of Technology) in Haifa. As usual, the provocation was something Dori said abroad in an effort to raise funds. Thus, in his understandable eagerness to arouse the generosity of his listeners, he said that one of the greatest risks facing Israel was the fact that "the spirit which enabled the country to win two wars is not possessed by immigrants from the depressed countries . . . A large section of the population does not possess this spirit. They had come from countries in which they were depressed *and were not living as human beings.*" Further to depress his listeners, General Dori finally spelled out the ultimate damnation of this "large section of the population": "We cannot expect them to have the same spirit as those who lived in Israel or in Palestine before they came." The immediate outcome of all this was the collection of a record total of £124,320!

Now as the *Jewish Observer* was by no means widely read in Israel — or in London for that matter — I decided to bring the issue to the attention of *Jerusalem Post* readers. This is what I wrote in the column printed on January 14, 1964, under the heading "The Grimmer View":

Pessimism is notoriously catching. During the past few days, tied to bed with flu, we came across two depressingly pessimistic appraisals of this country's present state and future prospects — and we must admit that for a moment we felt greatly alarmed and dispirited. The first of these appraisals came in the form of a report in the London *Jewish Chronicle.* Under the fairly innocuous title: "Record £124,320 at Technion Dinner," we were treated to what must have been the most extraordinary interpretation of present-day Israeli society ever to be printed. The authority, the emphatic and finalistic tone, the personality of the man who drew up the appraisal — all these, combined, tended to impress. Duly impressed, we went on reading a summary of a speech by General Yaʿacov Dori, Israel's first Chief of Staff and present President of the Technion, made at a fundraising function in London on December 12, 1963.

General Dori, understandably anxious to move his distinguished listeners, chose to speak of the risks facing Israel. One of the "greatest" such risks, he said, was the fact that "the spirit which enabled the country to win two wars is not possessed by immigrants from the depressed countries." The truth, he explained, was that Israel's "secret army" during those two wars was the human factor of her people and the spirit with which they were imbued. Today, however, "a large section of the population does not possess this spirit. They had come from countries in which they were depressed and *were not living as human beings.*" Not content with letting bygones be bygones, moreover, General Dori went on to spell the virtual doom of Israeli society: "We cannot expect them to have the same spirit as those who lived in Israel or in Palestine before they came."

So much for General Dori's appraisal. The second appraisal comes from a non-Israeli, and it is no less depressing, except probably in that it can be easily dismissed as the opinion of a man who does not know anything like enough on the subject he is discussing. For Simon Raven, an English novelist and a frequent contributor to the London *Observer* and the *Spectator,* was in Israel only a few days. Yet, reading and re-reading his essay in the Summer 1963 issue of *Axle Quarterly,* we find it impossible not to be worried. For Raven seems to be a keen and sympathetic observer, and there is nothing in his essay that smacks of the kind of bias that may beset an outsider's attitude to the Jewish State. Raven indeed had the good fortune of meeting, and being shown around by, an amiable Israeli whom he calls "Moishe Yahel" — and it is from Moishe and an officer friend of his, "a Lieutenant-Colonel in the Parachute Regiment," that he acquires his impressions of Israel.

"The Attitudes of Moishe Yahel" are so varied and so impressionistically told that Raven's conclusions are not easy to summarize. One of the "basic points" he makes, however, is that, "while superficially the Israelis appear to encourage the liberal virtues of tolerance and mental freedom, there can be no doubt that the power of their faith in Jewish Israel in fact requires, as any religion does, an essential conformity." He quotes the Colonel as maintaining that he has to train his soldiers to be determined, skilful, tough and "ruthless." "Yes," said the Colonel in his precise and neutral voice, "*ruthless.*" "Unlike older and richer countries we cannot afford such luxuries as chivalry. We cannot compromise in the interest of sensitive feelings — our own or other people's. We are fighting, you see, not to preserve an extension of an empire but to keep the actual soil of our mother-country. There is therefore no room for concession or retreat." Raven agrees that the Colonel had spoken as a professional soldier: "It was to be expected that he would take the grimmer view."

Can one say the same of General Dori — to wit, that as a former professional soldier he was entitled to take "the grimmer view?" After all, General Dori must see himself as the head of an educational institution rather than the commander of determined, skilful, tough and ruthless soldiers. Coming from the president of an important institute of higher learning — which has the duty of training young Israeli men and women, both those who lived in Israel or Palestine before the establishment of the State and those who came subsequently, to be the healthy and self-fulfilling technicians and managers of the future — General Dori's remarks concerning a sizeable majority of Israel's citizens are disturbing. A while back, a Technion professor with the courage of his convictions told a reporter that, intellectually and spiritually, his students were "cobblers engaged in atomic research." If the Technion president can so casually deny the humanity of so many fellow citizens, one is no longer altogether surprised.

Dori's reply came in the form of a letter addressed to me personally, dated January 16, 1964. Excerpts:

> I have no wish to enter into a controversy with you, but I would very much like to understand what prompted your unfavourable comment on what I am alleged to have said in London last December, on the occasion of the Annual Dinner of the British Technion Society.
>
> First of all, the *Jewish Chronicle*'s report of my speech is disconnected and sketchy, and even what I am reported to have said is largely wrenched out of its context. Secondly, even on the strength of what I am reported to have said, I cannot see how I can be accused of — heaven forbid — "casually denying" the humanity of so many fellow citizens. Honestly, I doubt whether I could think of any accusation of which I could be less guilty . . .
>
> As the head of an important educational institution in Israel, my attitude to the Oriental section of the community in Israel must be largely coloured by my experience at our Institute. Only recently, we have had a remarkable illustration of what can and should be further done towards solving our educational problem. A group of 32 soldiers from several Oriental countries were selected, with the co-operation of the Defence Forces, and, while still in uniform, given an intensive six-month course to prepare them to compete for admission to the Technion. Of these, as many as 28 were successful; many of them with excellent results. I may say that this has been the most successful course of any kind which the Technion has so far run — and we are proud of it. I may add that I am particularly proud because the whole scheme was made possible by the generosity of a gentleman of Sephardi origin from the U.S. . . .

Faced with a bunch of such evasive and confused platitudes, I took my time to reply. Finally I penned this letter and mailed it on January 28. I have no record of a reply.

Dear General Dori:

Your letter of January 16 is a ponderous affair. You say that you have no wish to enter a controversy with me. The truth is that nor do I. There are certain things about which it is futile to argue, and one of these surely is prejudice. Another is cliches, and I am afraid we are by now so used to cliches and so consumed by prejudices that neither discourse nor controversy can serve any useful purpose.

But this is not the main point. The point is that your letter, despite the carefully phrased reservations, does not really constitute a denial that you had in fact said what the *Jewish Chronicle* attributed to you. Having myself written to the editor of that paper asking him if there is any possibility that you were misquoted, I now take the liberty of quoting a passage from his letter:

I have spoken to the reporter who attended the Technion Dinner. He has not kept his original shorthand notes but he is quite certain that the report we published is an accurate version of what Dori said. By way of corroboration he tells me that the *Jewish Observer*, which was also represented at the dinner, published a substantially similar version, and indeed had some correspondence on the subject without any denial having been published by Dori.

Now this, and the way you yourself relate to the subject in your letter, makes it fairly plain that your address did in fact contain the remarks attributed to you. Of course, you are perfectly entitled to your opinions. But so are others, and I thought I was only being fair in interpreting your remarks in the way I did. This is what makes the job of answering your letter a rather difficult one. For, let us face it, what is the point of your letter? Your having said what you had said, and my having said what I wanted to say — and both of our remarks having been published: What else is there to it? As I see it, there are only two possibilities open — namely, a categorical denial or a different interpretation. Yet the fact is that you cannot, or would not, deny the truth of the reports; you also, if I get you right, would not enter into discussion about my interpretation of your remarks. If I should be allowed to give an opinion, I believe there should already have been either a public denial or a public statement to the effect that a wrong and unfair interpretation was put to the remarks. I think it is due the *Post* readers, if not the public as a whole.

As to this business of the 32 lucky Orientals, I am afraid I am not in the least impressed. On the contrary, it only shows how much talent we have wasted, and how much misery we had caused waiting for the good deeds of a certain gentleman of Sephardi origin! Besides, what is so remarkable, what is more natural, in fact, about the fact that 28 out of 32 young men should pass a certain admittance exam?

I want to be completely frank with you, General Dori: It is all ultimately a question of how we treat people. If we keep considering them somewhat sub-human, and go on entertaining the monstrous thought that any human beings can ever live "not as human beings," we will in the end fail them and prevent them from advancing. On the other hand, when we have ceased having such prejudices, we will automatically cease to be struck by wonder and amazement when we discover that even Orientals can pass exams and probably do far better things besides.

Throughout history, Jews everywhere were incapacitated and discriminated against; yet they managed. It is only in Israel, ironically enough, that some Jews are being deprived of their very title to humanity. This thing must stop!

Chapter 8 | $\mathcal{G}$ENTLEFOLK AND UPSTARTS

ON NOT GETTING ALONG

*T*oward the end of 1963, the Department for Culture and Education of the Histadrut organized a public symposium on problems of intercommunal integration in Israel. One of the speakers was Michael Assaf, and he touched upon the question of political representation for the Sephardi and Oriental communities. In the course of his address, which was meant to be a reply to complaints that spokesmen of these communities made about the underrepresentation of Oriental Israelis in high places, Assaf asserted that "there can be no representation without a political struggle," the plain implication being that, in order to get the representation they wanted, these communities should organize themselves politically and enter the arena in earnest.

Knowing Assaf's critical attitude toward all political organization by Orientals, I ventured to ask him on the way out: "You maintain that adequate representation can be obtained only through political struggle. How come, then, that you and your party condemn vehemently any sign of communal organization?" The reply came promptly and without any hesitation: "But this is all part of the game, my friend!"

The incident moved me enough to pen an article on the subject. "A Game and Its Rules," after giving the bare facts, without using Assaf's name, ran as follows:

> Well, all is fair in love and war — and in politics. Our veteran Israeli, who in any public address or newspaper article — for he is, among other things, a well-known journalist — would not hesitate for one moment to label any manifestation of a communalist grouping "a cause for national discord," "incitement to hatred," or "a stab in the back of the nation," now says that it's all a game. So there we are: Every game has rules of its own, and those who are rash enough to want to participate in a game have to observe its rules. But we will leave all that to the players and the would-be players.

Meanwhile one has to content oneself with "mere" theorizing. The other day, for instance, we came across a publication called *Da'at* and styling itself "Organ of the Yemenite Jews in Israel." On its first page appears a story entitled: "D. Ben Gurion in an Interview with *Da'at:* A Positive Communal Framework Should not be Disqualified."

The emphasis, we gathered, was on the adjective "positive." But what was that, precisely? According to Ben Gurion, a positive communal framework—i.e., grouping or organisation—is one "whose aim is mutual assistance, the advancement of its members' economic and cultural conditions, and such like . . ." A "negative" communal framework, on the other hand, is one which is designed "to deepen the intercommunal division and encourage feelings of superiority or a feeling of discrimination (although I am afraid there are cases of discrimination, though these are few and insignificant)." One wonders, however, whether in a country like Israel, where "politics" plays such a decisive role and where no non-political group can ever hope to make its voice heard, Ben Gurion's counsels of moderation are really in place. The example of the various religious parties is a classic case in point. It is generally agreed that these parties have no definable political aims of their own, and that all they are striving for is the promotion of religious concepts and the safeguarding of the rights and interests of the Orthodox community in Israel.

Normally, such aims require no political framework of action. They can be attained through mutual aid and the advancement of the economic and cultural conditions of the Orthodox. They certainly do not represent a deepening of the intercommunal divisions or the intensification of feelings of superiority or discrimination. It stands to reason, therefore, that had the spokesmen and leaders of the Orthodox community had any hope of attaining their objectives outside "negative" political frameworks, they would have refrained from organizing themselves in political parties. As it is, they organise themselves politically, fight municipal and general elections, and sit in government coalitions. Ben Gurion himself, whose arguments against ethnic political groupings are really quite applicable to the religious parties, willingly admitted the latter into his successive governments.

Admittedly, two wrongs do not make a right. But is this not a case of "pull it by the tail"? Well, in Baghdad some decades ago there used to live a respected rabbi, well-known for his piety and righteous ways. One Friday evening, just after the Sabbath candles were lighted, a neighbour came to the rabbi in distress and asked what was he to do about a luckless cock which had just stumbled over the *tannour* (an oval baking oven with a small opening, used with a charcoal fire to prepare thin bread) and fallen inside it? The trouble, of course, was that the charcoal was still weakly burning. "Nothing doing," said our rabbi unhesitatingly. "To get the cock out would cause the charcoal to be stirred, and that as you know is strictly forbidden." The neighbour was helpless. "But, my revered Rabbi, the cock is yours," he pleaded. "Well," came the rabbi's considered verdict. "Hold it by the tail and pull it carefully out of the *tannour* so that the embers are not disturbed!"

Or, as the Ashkenazi saying goes, "To the rabbi, it is permissible."

The column was intended to appear on December 31, 1963, but it seems to have proved to be too much for a paper like the *Post*, in which the Histadrut still held a substantial ownership interest. The column was thus returned to me, accompanied by a note from Lea Ben Dor.

The attached raises several problems: (1) I don't think it's fair to charge a nameless "veteran Israeli" with the crassest hypocrisy without specifying who and when, etc. Besides, what did he mean? I can't see anybody making himself out a fraud by saying "it's part of the game." If he meant the Sephardim would have to take a more active part in politics before they got political positions, that still doesn't necessarily mean for communal lists—probably he meant they should work harder for Mapai. (2) The religious parties started out as independent religious-Zionist movements long before the state, like all the other parties, so the whole question of "grouping themselves in political parties" doesn't arise. They were and have remained all-encompassing "movements" which always had representation together with other "movements."

So I don't quite know what to do with this piece.

My reply, dated January 2, 1964, was sent promptly:

Dear Lea,

... (1) The difficulties raised by the piece are plainly not integral to it but have obvious other connotations. This in itself raises the question as to whether a paper with the measure of independence which the *Post* does have ought or oughtn't to let a regular columnist express his opinion reasonably, however nonconformist this might be.

(2) The question whether it is fair to charge a nameless some-

body with hypocrisy is one of trust and integrity—trust in the writer on the paper's part and his own integrity toward himself and his readers. In this case—just for your information—the veteran Israeli is Michael Assaf . . .

(3) What the man meant by saying "it's part of the game" is precisely what I imply he meant! And this raises still another problem: Is it permissible for a journalist to be so naive as to disbelieve in any manifestation of political hypocrisy on the part of Mapai—or of any political party for that matter? In my innocence (or experience if you like) I had always thought hypocrisy was the politician's daily bread.

(4) The *history* of the religious parties is of no consequence here. The important thing is that they had no political ideology and that, had life in this country—or in the Zionist movement as a whole—not been so totally politicized, no Orthodox Jew worthy of the name would have contemplated setting up shop as a political party. The Orthodox have grouped themselves in political parties to attain nonpolitical ends, having realized in their wisdom that they have no hope of achieving anything without the crudest kind of political pressure—and so, to our regret perhaps, will have to do all those groups which want to get anywhere.

. . . As I have said on a previous occasion similar to this one, it is nowhere accepted unquestioningly that the editor of a paper *has* to agree with every word printed in his publication. This seems to me to be a matter of principle, and it is to be regretted that the *Post* has not always found it possible to honour this principle.

KALMAN KATZNELSON'S VERSION

Barely three months after this "incident" another problem presented itself, this time in the form of a diatribe published under the title *The Ashkenazi Revolution*. Now the tricky dilemma in which Mapai's assorted communal lackeys and factotums found themselves had made itself felt to me on several occasions—but on none of these was it brought out so poignantly as on the occasion of the publication of that political-historical tract. I hadn't heard of the book when the call came. On the line was Yisrael Yeshayahu, the late head of the Yemenite desk of Mapai and then member of the Knesset. "Have you seen the book?" he asked after mentioning the title and the author. I said no, and he immediately offered to send me a copy, saying his department had purchased several copies and was distributing them to those interested in the subject.

I read the book — and recorded my impressions in a Marginal Column that did not make it into print. I possess no correspondence with the *Post* on the subject, and I believe the whole matter was discussed at length over the telephone with Lea Ben Dor. The title I chose for the column was "Kalman with Everything," and the date it was scheduled to appear was April 20, 1964.

Two cheers for Kalman Katznelson! He has written a book that displays almost all the virtues of good style and clear, cogent thinking. For in *The Ashkenazi Revolution* (*Ha-Mahpekha Ha-Ashkenazit*, Anakh, Tel Aviv, 1964, 256 pp.) grave and awkward questions are asked and candidly answered, sentences are finished and rounded, *t*'s are crossed, *i*'s fearlessly dotted, and conclusions are drawn that have a great deal of inner logic in them. What else does one want in a book? Yet the whole world seems to be after poor Kalman in deadly pursuit. The newspapers have written editorials condemning the book as "trash"; the Prime Minister has appealed to the people to forget all about it; David Ben Gurion has labelled its author a "chatterbox"; three distinguished Sephardo-Oriental functionaries have instituted court action; and, most scandalous of all, some petty official of the Merchants Association has instructed bookshops not to sell the book. Just like that!

Kalman's sins? Well, they are many and deadly, it would seem. First of all, citing the Bible chapter and verse, he denies the oneness of the Jewish People ("and Abram fell on his face: and God talked with him, saying, As for me, behold, my covenant is with thee, and thou shalt be a father of *many nations*" — Genesis 17:3–4), insisting that Jewry is a "commonwealth of nations" and that amongst these multitude of nations, the Ashkenazi is by far the most superior, vital and enduring. The rest, the "Sephardo-Oriental" nations of Jewry, are inferior, fatalistic and hopelessly lazy national groups whose level of civilization belongs to the twelfth century. Besides, they hate the Ashkenazim like the plague, and often vocally regret that Hitler did not "finish them off" and that Eichmann did not "work overtime." He, Kalman Katznelson, is an "Ashkenazi Nationalist" who will ever regret that, instead of setting out to build an Ashkenazi civilization based on Yiddish and thriving in the vast and green expanses of Uganda, the Zionists had decided to impose on us a dead language and bring us into this "Sephardized narrow alley" of a land.

Rather more than half of the book is taken up with subjects that have nothing to do with the Sephardo-Oriental Jewish nations. Yet the anger and the resentment provoked by it—and coming from people who have plainly not read the book in its entirety—have had to do with the offensive things the author says about the Sephardo-Orientals. Some of these passages had already been cited by the local press, and condemned outright. Closer scrutiny, however, reveals something a little familiar even about the author's more fantastic thoughts. Consider his theory regarding the current inferiority of the Sephardo-Orientals: "We [Ashkenazim] are entitled to be proud of the fact that, despite the uncomfortable climate and the fact that we have discarded our historical language, Yiddish, we still possess stupendous superiority. Clearly, there is a decisive value in heredity and environment. Superiority tends to perpetuate itself, while backwardness is also self-perpetuating . . . Cultural superiority is always related to hereditary and environmental causes that are extremely difficult to root out. In the best of circumstances, centuries will be needed to obliterate these causes" (pp. 203–205).

Now in what fundamentals does this differ from the following? "The causes [of the communal gap in Israel] lie in environmental conditions. They are the result of five centuries of Jewish history. One half of our population comes from communities which, since the decline of Islamic culture, have had no educational history or environment. Their children now in Israel are the first generation for centuries to be educated at all . . . A problem created over five centuries cannot be solved in a year or two . . . Men are not equal in their intellectual receptivity. There are gallon-containers and half-pint jars. Our responsibility is to fill each of them up to full capacity. It is no use pretending that their capacity is the same . . ." (Abba Eban, then Minister of Education, in an interview in the *Jewish Observer*, London, September 21, 1962.)

Or take this gem (Katznelson, p. 154): "Were the Ashkenazim to be removed from Israel, and were an equal number of non-Ashkenazim to replace them, the State of Israel would have been conquered by the Arab States in a matter of hours. It would have been destroyed within months, even had Nasser undertaken not to attack it but to give it protection. For a State of Israel without the Ashkenazim would have lost [her] vital control over modern time, and would have slipped back to the 15th or 16th century . . ." Now just compare with the following: "We in Israel need immigrants from countries with a high standard, because the question of our future social structure is worrying us. We have immigrants from Morocco, Libya, Persia, Egypt, and other countries with a 16th-century level. Shall we be able to elevate these immigrants up to a suitable level of civilization? If the present state of affairs continues, there will be a dangerous clash between the Ashkenazim, who will constitute an elite, and the Oriental communities of Israel. This is the most tragic thing that can befall us. We need greater equilibrium [*sic*] and immigrants from countries of a high level." (Mrs. Golda Meir addressing leaders of the Zionist Federation of Great Britain on March 8, 1964, as quoted in *Yediot Aharonot* on the following day.)

One is not, God forbid, trying to imply that this similarity — even though it sometimes verges on identity — is anything more than accidental. The analogy, however, makes it plain that Katznelson's views have roots in a standpoint which is not quite new or novel — and that what he in fact does is no more than driving this standpoint to its ultimate logical conclusion. In this he has done a certain undeniable service to all of us, if only by demonstrating the monstrosity of this standpoint, and the dangers inherent in entertaining it.

Two hearty cheers for Kalman!

Roundabout this time, what with the communal and the regional problems intensifying and the link between the two becoming increasingly evident to me, I took the opportunity of the appearance in the *Jewish Chronicle* of an article by James Parkes to write a column in which I subtly tried to establish such a link. The main interest of that column, for which I chose the title "Assorted Anachronisms" — and which was not to appear in print — is the rejection slip that I give after extracts from the text.

Just how long a span of time is 16 years? In terms of human life and history, so my dictionary says, it is just over half "a generation," which in turn is the interval between the birth of parents and that of their children — usually reckoned at about thirty years. But *Tempora mutantur, et nos mutamur in illis:* Times change, and we change with them. And so, it seems, does our estimate of the actual length of any given span of time. Indeed, speaking as Israelis living in a fast-changing society, we can justly claim that already, after just over half a generation, we have travelled so far that we are confronted by a whole assortment of nice little anachronisms. In itself, this is a natural and in many ways a desirable thing; the only trouble is that many of us refuse to see it and keep clinging to habits of thought and to concepts that have, in the meantime, become hopelessly outdated.

Take this business of "communal discrimination." Last Friday's newspapers reported that a delegation representing "the Oriental Communities' Council" of Mapam met members of the Knesset Legislation Committee and asked that it speed up the passage of a "Law Against Discrimination for *Mizzug Galuyot*—the Mixing of the Exiles." Thursday's *Post*, on the other hand, carried the equally curious report that in Dimona a committee of citizens consisting mainly of Moroccan Jews had requested the Ministry of the Interior to dissolve the Local Council which they accuse, among other things, of practising discrimination against the town's *Ashkenazi* residents. Now one is not nearly so naive as either to deny the existence of discrimination against Orientals or to take the Dimona report too seriously. Still, one could not help feeling that this whole subject of discrimination is becoming something of an anachronism.

It is a feeling that is difficult to elaborate upon or explain. Just a few days previously, there appeared in the *Jewish Chronicle* of London an article which seemed to place the whole subject, together with a few related things, into a somewhat new perspective. The article is modestly entitled "Middle East Reality" and is written by Dr. James Parkes, the distinguished Christian authority on Jewish affairs. Dr. Parkes's thesis tends to sound so far-reaching that one hesitates to express a rash opinion on it. But it is an important thesis, worthy of careful consideration by all those to whose hearts the existence and destiny of this country are near.

"Twelve years have passed since Nasser's rise to power in Egypt," Parkes reminds us, "but twelve years of change have not made any mark on his attitude to Israel." Yet there has been a fundamental change in the position of Israel *vis-à-vis* the Arab world—for in the interval "Israel has unexpectedly become statistically a Middle Eastern country, not by the growth of its Arab minority or the birth rate of its *sabras*, but by the immigration of Jews from all over the Middle East." The result has been that over 60 percent of Israel's Jewish population has never lived anywhere except in the Middle East since the beginning of recorded history, and Dr. Parkes is of the opinion that, if these figures are correct, "they change the right of Israel to exist from the abnormal basis of the special arguments which lay behind the claims of Zionism and the issue of the Balfour Declaration to the normal basis of history and tradition." For, though Herzl would have been amazed at it, and though Balfour never envisaged it, "Israel exists today in the Middle East on the absolutely normal basis that the majority of its inhabitants are Middle-Easterners and had never been anything else."

The importance of this turn of events cannot be exaggerated, Parkes believes. "The founders of Zionism, the first pioneers, the pilot planning, all were European. They meant to build up an ideal European state. Those

Middle-Eastern Jews they found in Palestine they regarded as interesting survivals, not as partners. It is, then, possible for Nasser or his successor to say: 'We were unalterably opposed to an intrusion of European colonialism into our heartlands. But what has now happened is that there has been an involuntary exchange of population within the Middle-Eastern world. That we can accept.' " Dr. Parkes concludes on a slightly anxious note: "I know there are innumerable tensions between Jews from Europe and those from Moslem countries. I find some European Jews ashamed of their Sephardi brethren and convinced that there is an unbridgeable gulf between them. But I refuse to believe that these tensions outweigh the immense value of proclaiming to the world that Israel is a Middle-Eastern country; and of announcing boldly that in helping forward its Sephardi elements, while keeping all that is of value in older ways of life, it is facing exactly the same Middle-Eastern problem as Nasser in Egypt or Ben Bella in Algeria.

Verily, sixteen years does seem to be a long span of time. It remains to be seen, however, whether they can produce such radical changes of attitudes.

This column was promptly returned to me with the following curt note from Lea Ben Dor:

Dear Nissim,

I'm afraid I think Parkes is an idiot who never understood Zionism, which predicates the right of *Jews* to be in Israel. This is practically accepting the Arab point of view that the original Zionists have *no* right to be here. One could only quote him to demolish him.

THE "LEFT-ZIONIST" ESTABLISHMENT

During the years 1963–1965 I had quite a few interesting though completely unintended clashes with a number of prominent members of the well-established, comfortably entrenched, crème de la crème "Left-Zionist" establishment intelligentsia of the land. I don't quite know how it came about—possibly through the skirmishes I had with Michael Assaf—but the general idea among these luminaries was that I was some kind of right-winger bent on attacking and defaming the Histadrut and the labor establishment as a whole. This, in addition to the seemingly inexplicable fact that someone of such low ethnic origins—who did not even speak Yiddish—had the cheek to write about problems so complex and so sensitive. *And in English!*

Something about my controversies with Assaf I have already related in a separate section. My numerous contributions to the *Jewish Observer* on the ethnic problem now started seriously to irk some of the more prominent of Mapai's publicists and ideologues. Besides Assaf—and no doubt acting on his hints and complaints—Yehuda Gotthelf, unquestionably the Histadrut's leading ideologue and soon to assume the editorship of the labor federation's daily, *Davar,* devoted one of his lengthy articles to the *Jewish Observer.* The article, which dealt mainly with the then-raging struggle for power within the ranks of Mapai between Ben-Gurion's followers and the party machine dominated by Levi Eshkol's supporters, was replete with broad though thinly concealed references to my own contributions to that weekly on the communal issue.

Anticipating a follow-up to this, I sent the *Jewish Observer* a summary of Gotthelf's rejoinder:

> Though "edited with journalistic talent," Gotthelf wrote, "[the *Jewish Observer*] is, to our sorrow, an Anglo-Saxon version of the well-known type of weekly which prefers current information and political gossip to the dissemination of opinion and basic ideas." Since, however, the weekly cannot occupy itself with the sort of scandals with which public opinion in Britain was usually preoccupied, it has lately been looking for sensations of another kind, its favourite subject being the struggle for power of the "young" of Mapai. While in it "you find almost no echo to the ideological-social controversies taking place in Israel," and while it tells you very little of the constructive work being done in town and countryside alike, the *Observer* is prolific on "the rift between the generations."
>
> . . . Lately, the *Observer* has taken on an additional task—namely, "to intensify tensions between the communities." As in the field of the struggle of the generations, so it has been with the communal question: the weekly has "informants and journalists of a special kind, who view the affairs of Israeli society from a one-sided point of view." Whereas extremely little has been printed in the weekly about the colossal efforts being made in the sphere of integration of the exiles, "you find there letters and reports by embittered correspondents caught up between an inferiority complex and one of ultra-superiority" who are never tired of speaking about discrimination against Oriental communities. Gotthelf then proceeds to tell his readers how an article by Michael Assaf in *Davar,* an article which is

"full of sincere anxiety over the question of bridging intercommunal divisions," got such a treatment in the *Jewish Observer* that the reader was bound to get the very opposite impression: "One almost reached the paradoxical conclusion that our comrade Assaf, who throughout many long years sought to bridge the yawning gap between Jews and Arabs, now has nothing else to work for but the heightening of misunderstanding between Jews and Jews."

Gotthelf's only contribution to the controversy is summed up by him as follows: "We have to double and to triple our efforts to close the existing gap [between the communities] — without affecting the spiritual heritage and the unique and positive attributes of any of the communities." The gap, he explains, has been a result of the fact that "during the past century or two the cultural life of the Jewish communities of Europe was enriched in a more intensified way than that of Jewish communities in Asia and Africa." Hence "the temporary advantage enjoyed by the Ashkenazi communities — an advantage which was felt both in the era of Zionist settlement and in the short spell since the establishment of the State."

A more serious, ideologically explosive clash with Gotthelf occurred shortly afterward, the occasion this time being a Marginal Column that I thought was quite innocuous and that I wrote after reading one of those rumbling end-of-week treatises that only Israeli and central European newspapers can publish. The title I chose for the column was "Class-War Paradox," and it appeared in the *Post* on February 11, 1964.

Rip Van Winkle is no doubt familiar to many readers: those who did not encounter him in their school books may have read Washington Irving's original story or, better still, may have met his modern equivalent in Arthur Koestler's novel *Darkness at Noon*, where, though safely locked inside one of Stalin's perfectly socialist jails somewhere in Soviet Russia, he doggedly goes on dreaming of the Socialist Fatherland, surreptitiously studying the map of the Union of Soviet Socialist Republics. We must confess that some of our political pundits, especially those on the Left, regularly remind us of old Mr. Van Winkle. Writing on such subjects as "culture," society, trade unionism, equality or progress, they remind one rather of those latter 19th-century intelligentsias with which Eastern Europe seethed and whose members knew all about text-book doctrines but remained, with a few notable exceptions, quite removed from everyday realities. The similarity is particularly striking when it comes to our present notions of socialism.

Take this business of the class war. In an article in *Al Hamishmar*

(Mapam) Mr. Yitzhak Ronkin speaks of the class war as "that essential, educational and elevating factor," and rejects out of hand the idea that its days are gone. By sheer coincidence, we have been reading a paper on this subject by Professor Eugene Kamenka, author of *The Ethical Foundations of Marxism* (Routledge, London, 1962). The article, entitled "Karl Marx and Socialism Today," appears in the latest issue of the Australian quarterly *Quadrant*. Coming directly to the point, Kamenka first describes what Socialism means — "the revolt against a society based on commerce and calculation; the fusion in a united effort and a single morality of worker and intellectual; above all, the birth of a new humanity, purified and ennobled in struggle and deprivation." The writer continues: "If Socialism means that — and I believe it does — then socialism is dead. Let us bury it before its last rites can no longer be performed with honour!"

This demise is attributed by Kamenka, among other things, to an inherent paradox. Much of Marx's serious economic work is devoted to the theme of economic rationality and to the inescapable socialization of capitalism from within. His view that the *bourgeoisie* was doomed because it was becoming an obstacle to economic development and had ceased to be its agent made Marxism intimately connected with the ideology of industrial society — "an ideology of which Marxism was in many ways the most consistent and confident expression." Thus Marxism, which professed to speak for the proletarian against the capitalist, at the same time also spoke, "far more effectively," for industrialism against merchant enterprise, for economic rationalism and efficient management against the individualistic vitality, independence and flair of the merchant-adventurer and entrepreneur.

So far, so good. But Socialism could present the struggle between economic rationalism and self-seeking individualism as a struggle between workers and capitalists "only so long as industrial enterprise was still run by men with entrepreneurial values along entrepreneurial lines." With the creation of the limited company, the spread of planning procedures, and the vast increase in the range of the calculable, however, "the lines of cleavage are no longer clear, and planning can no longer be posed as the obvious contradictory of capitalist competition. *To preach social planning thus becomes one thing, not particularly inimical to the fundamental economic structure of our society; to preach class-war becomes another.*" It is because of this that many socialists today profess to be content with the ideology of social planning "and would willingly leave the class war and the moral mystique of the movement — that once looked as though it would humanize and transform the working classes — to the museums of history."

But then this new attitude leaves socialism virtually empty of content. "It may be [Kamenka reflects in conclusion] that, as Engels believed, the development of technology . . . would produce a society in which man is a fuller and freer being than he has ever been before. But if this should prove to be so, the efforts of the socialist movement will have had nothing to do with it. The end will have been the result of a technological advance pioneered and largely carried out — I believe — by the techniques and the ideology of industrial capitalism; socialism in the West will have been one of the great moral movements of mankind that may one day inspire future moral movements in renewed days of adversity or in a new flowering of productive life; socialism in the East will have been an intermediary stage of ideological labour discipline designed to usher in the era of industrialization and capitalist plenty."

Admittedly, these are hard things to swallow for men whose life was selflessly devoted to an ideal. Socialism may die a dozen deaths before its diehard followers would even suspect the possibility. Unfortunately, however, this does not make our own Rip Van Winkles sound any the less removed from reality.

It took Gotthelf and *Davar* thirteen days to publish their reply, which, for the way it was written and the reasoned arguments advanced, must have been meant to be final and quite crushing in its effect. It began with a frontal personal snipe: "One of the *Jerusalem Post*'s regular contributors, Nissim Rejwan, is an educated and talented man. However, his allergy to the values and ideas of the labour movement prevents him from seeing things clearly and correctly. The result is that quite often, when he imagines he is assaulting bastions of intellectual conservatism, he in fact makes fun of the most modern and progressive in order to perpetuate the old and the outworn."

The title Gotthelf chose for his rejoinder was "Rip Van Winkle," and he gave a selective and highly artful summary of the things I had written in my comment. One of the arguments he used in refutation of Kamenka's view was that whereas no political party anywhere dares call itself a capitalist party, the world is full of parties that call themselves socialist — conclusive proof that socialism remains "legal tender!" Another argument was that the majority of Israelis continue to vote for socialist parties. Toward the end Gotthelf declares his astonishment at the fact that "a contributor to an Israeli paper" does not seem to have heard of "democratic socialism."

Another establishment luminary, Shlomo Grodzenski, a prolific scribbler with high pretensions, chose to take his time, getting his belated revenge seven long years after the controversy erupted with his *Davar* colleagues. I had met Grodzenski when he called one day, soon after the appearance of my column, asking to borrow my copy of *Quadrant*—and somehow "invited himself" to coffee, which he duly got one early evening at our home. I now have no doubt that the visit was arranged with the approval of all-powerful Gotthelf, and also out of a wish to see what sort of strange animal that Rejwan was and whether he actually possessed a copy of that outlandish Australian quarterly.

My second encounter with Grodzenski came when he worked for the American Jewish Committee's Israel office, serving briefly as editor of their short-lived Hebrew quarterly, *Amot*. During the mid-1960s, when the periodical started publication, I still had great respect for the American Jewish Committee as that rarity—an American Jewish organization that remained fairly independent of the official Zionist establishment. As the man chosen by the committee to edit its Hebrew periodical, and also because of the impression he was able to make on me as a thinking person, I extended my esteem to Grodzenski himself, and agreed to contribute two or three articles on intellectual and political trends in the Arab world. During his editorship, too, there erupted in the pages of *Amot* a controversy in which Assaf, Aghasi, and Shimon Ballas engaged—among others—but in which I took no part, since Ballas's stand was virtually identical to mine.

Upon leaving *Amot* and the American Jewish Committee, Grodzenski went back to work for *Davar*, to which he contributed what in Israel are called *publicistika* pieces—usually lengthy polemics and casuistries that were then in fashion and that rendered the Friday issues of *Davar* and certain other dailies virtually unreadable. One of these efforts in *publicistika*, a fairly well-written and well-argued piece full of long-preserved venom, appeared in the June 4, 1971, issue of the paper. The occasion, allegedly, was the rise of the Black Panther movement: a group of frustrated young men, most of whom had come to Israel with their parents when they were small children, attended Israeli schools, spent three years in military service, fought in at least one of Israel's wars—but still failed to make any headway in life and found themselves dragging behind them all the weight of the "backwardness," the deprivations, and the assorted disadvantages visited on their parents.

The article I am referring to was the second in a series on the Black Panthers, and in it Grodzenski managed to launch—anonymously of course —one of the most vicious attacks ever directed at me by an establishment intellectual. But, then, Grodzenski was a special kind of intellectual: one, he wrote, who "had always been interested in the typology of Jewish as-similation everywhere." He was thus interested in "a certain type of Sep-hardi half-, third-, and fourth-intellectual," one of whom he happened to have met some time before. "He is a journalist. Having been in Israel for years, he has yet to learn to write in Hebrew. Even things of his that appear in Hebrew newspapers are translated from the English original."

At this point Grodzenski struck what he thought was a well-aimed blow. "His mother tongue was Arabic," he laments. "Was it harder for him to learn Hebrew than it was to learn English?" There were other such gems. For one, he ridiculed the fact that our journalist had taken him, Grodzenski, for "a genuine American Jew," and it was to this Ameri-can Jew that he had confided "his low opinion of these Jews of the East-ern European *shtetl.*" This reminded him, so he wrote, of Negro anti-Semitism, about which "I thought for many years and had a theory to explain it." To put it briefly, his theory was that anti-Semitism was a source for solidarity — "the source for this one solidarity — between the oppressed Negro and his white oppressor." He did not enlarge on this thesis — which was a pity, because I still fail to make the connection.

In fact, Grodzenski did hail from the United States, and since he was the editor of a periodical sponsored by an independent American Jewish organization, one felt justified in assuming that he was "a genuine Ameri-can Jew" rather than the usual run of provincial Israeli publicist.

There were, to be sure, many other clever claims and inventions in Grodzenski's learned diatribe. The identity of the journalist whose work he quoted was so easily recognizable that I still wonder how the paper's editor allowed a piece so libelous to be published. For a few days following its publication, in fact, friends who read *Davar* kept drawing my atten-tion to the article — one of them, a lawyer, offering to take up the case in court. I firmly declined; I refrained even from mentioning this to the edi-tor, Hanna Semer, whom I had known from meetings of the newspaper editors' committee.

Thinking of it now, from the perspective of a quarter of a century, I cannot help wondering whether Grodzenski ever asked himself why he kept all that venom to himself for over seven years. After all, throughout those years I never stopped providing the likes of him ample reasons for venting their anger. Week in, week out, I said something objectionable, something to raise Grodzenski's blood pressure. Or so it seems. Now, however, with some hindsight and after considering the man's general frame of mind and the pettiness of his sentiments, I rather tend to think that his long wait had something to do with the fact that by that time I had virtually ceased to feature in the Israeli press. Also, he may have thought that a person so down was virtually a dead horse, which he could kick at leisure.

Here I must add, however, that in one respect at least Grodzenski was right. I was indeed rather more than sympathetic to the Black Panthers and their tactics, which I thought furnished an excellent example of "collective bargaining by riots."

THE BLACK PANTHERS: A PARTISAN VIEW

As a matter of fact, at the request of the editors of a little-known short-lived English-language periodical called *Lillit,* I contributed an article to which was given the title "Israel's Eastern Jews: A Partisan View." It was largely a defense of the Black Panther organization and its objectives, and I signed it "Maimon Ben Hammu" — not because I didn't want the writer's identity known, but simply because I wanted readers to think its author was a genuine "Moroccan," Ben Hammu being a typically Moroccan-sounding family name used by the country's Jews. The article was published in the August 1971 issue of the magazine. A few short excerpts:

> "Give a dog a bad name and you can hang him. After he has been hanged you can accuse him more than ever. We do not listen to the murderer's evidence against his victim." Thus Simone Weil. At the Labour Party Convention early last April, a number of delegates "representing" the Oriental Jews of Israel tried to convince the party's Steering Committee to adopt resolutions calling for granting more educational facilities to their communities, a minimal quota of their members in top political and administrative positions, and a third in the party's various representative bodies. Not only were these modest proposals rejected out of hand; they never were submitted to the convention for voting, and the irony of it was that a number of veteran Uncle Toms — such as Police Minister Shlomo Hillel and Deputy Labour Party Secretary-General Mordechai Ben Porath (both of Iraqi origin) — were themselves against putting the proposals to the vote . . .
>
> But it may be deemed uncharitable to criticize these gentlemen, who after all are where they are only because they have virtually renounced their communal affiliation. They are there in exchange for services rendered to the Party, not to their alleged electors among the Oriental communities. The official position was well and clearly stated by Finance Minister Pin-

has Sapir. Robust, candid, and totally convinced of what he was saying, Mr. Sapir told delegates: "Anyone who believes that poverty can be eliminated by issuing bigger social welfare benefits is making a mistake. You get rid of poverty by giving people education, qualifications for employment, decent jobs, and the possibility of acquiring a decent home to live in." "I am ready to state," he added, "that part of the existing problem of poverty derives from the failure, or sometimes even the unwillingness of individuals to exploit the opportunities available."

While one can have no quarrel with the first part of Mr. Sapir's statement, one must be a complete fool not to see the horrible implications of the second. For what Mr. Sapir is saying here is simply that the Orientals are "no good." They were offered opportunities but, either out of failure or unwillingness, refused to seize them. They were offered jobs but failed to show the proper qualifications; they were offered educational facilities but have proved too lazy, backward or dumb to utilize them; and they were offered houses but, since they came from backward countries where people were just not used to such amenities, they turned these houses into slums. They have, in short, with their own hands created the conditions of poverty under which they now live—and all Mr. Sapir is asking is just to be given enough time to solve the problem: to give the children of these people education, qualifications, decent jobs and decent places to live in. Contemplating Mr. Sapir's statements, in fact, one would think that the powers-that-be in Israel have had no share whatever in the present mess.

This is as it should be—and as it has always been in similar situations. No oppressor or exploiter has ever been heard condemning himself or his system; the blame has invariably been placed at the doors of the oppressed and the deprived. That this is unjustified—that it is merely the device used by the master, whether he be heartless and reactionary or merciful and liberal—is a truism which hardly needs elaboration. Still, I want to take this opportunity to relate my experience in this field.

I was born in one of the larger cities of Morocco in 1942 of an old Jewish family of small merchants and middlemen and went to the local Jewish school, the Alliance. Just before sitting for my *Brevet* examinations, my parents decided to immigrate to France. The institution of a national government after independence, and the tensions created by the establishment of the State of Israel, along with the subsequent mass immigration of Moroccan Jews to the new state, made things rather difficult, and my father, who was still in his late thirties, finally decided to take me, my mother and two younger sisters to search for new opportunities in Paris.

At the same time, of course, there was a fairly massive movement of

Jews to Israel, but my parents—for reasons which I was considered too young to have any say in—preferred France. We had a year of hardship in our new home, but in the end we settled down to a fairly decent economic existence, and I and my two younger sisters did fairly well in school, I at the *lycée,* they at their primary school. After I obtained my secondary-school certificate, I took a few years off to help my father with his small business, and in 1965 we were sufficiently well-established for me to be permitted to pursue my studies. I then joined the Sorbonne, taking courses in sociology and French language and literature. When the days of crisis and tension came in May 1967, I wanted to go to Israel as a volunteer—but I had barely had the time to make arrangements before June 5 and the sweeping military victory which it brought Israel . . . In the summer of 1968, taking advantage of a generous Jewish Agency offer to come and complete my studies at one of Israel's universities, I came to the country under the Oded programme, which offered grants to participants to support them through their studies. In my particular case, I have therefore no personal complaints to make, and if I feel affinity with the Black Panther movement, it is only because, after almost three years of observation and reflection, I have come to the conclusion that nothing—but literally nothing—except action, massive political and organizational action on the part of the Orientals themselves, will ever be able to rescue the Middle Eastern element (and with it Israel as a whole) from the intolerable socio-economic situation in which they have all landed. Call it Black Power, Oriental Power, or whatever you please, it remains a fact that only their own power will emancipate Israeli Orientals from their present deplorable situation. From men like Mr. Sapir and his Oriental party functionaries and vote-contractors, nothing better than mere tokenism will ever come.

But to return to Mr. Sapir and his arguments. During the first weeks of my stay in Israel, a year or so after the Six-Day War, I was making a tour of some towns and immigrant centers in the south of the country, where most of the North African immigrants are concentrated. One day, when I was in company with a fellow Oded student who happened to have been one of my classmates at the Alliance school in Morocco, we suddenly came across two young men whom we thought we knew. It took us only a few seconds to realize that they were none other than our old classmates Albert and Elie (now Abraham and Eliahu). Our friends' families left Morocco two years before ours did. It was almost dark when we met, and Albert and Elie were going to the local cafe to play their usual game of cards. They were decently dressed, and we soon seemed to regain the old familiarity. Yet I could not help noticing a shade of embarrassment, along with apprehension, bitterness and perhaps a little envy in them. I was soon to discover the reason: having told them about our fortunes (my companion was studying to become an electrical engineer), they had to start to tell us about theirs. It was a painful experience. Albert was working as an unskilled labourer at a local textile factory, while Elie was an agricultural worker. Neither of them dared invite us to visit their homes, and neither I nor my companion had the heart to ask them. "You two have been lucky," Albert finally let out. "You went to France and became men with diplomas and a future; we came here and this is the result!" Here I should perhaps add that Albert and Elie came from exactly the same background, economic, social, and educational, from which I and my companion hailed. The sole difference was that their parents decided to come to the Jewish State while ours took us to France, to the Diaspora.

So much for Mr. Sapir and his convenient arguments. Even he, perhaps, will not maintain that Albert or Elie were unwilling to exploit the opportunities given them in Israel. The exact opposite is true; from the very beginning, the Israeli-European power structure never spared any opportunity to label, denigrate, insult and finally drive the Moroccan immigration to the bottom of the socio-cultural and economic ladder. Since meeting my old classmates I have spoken to many Israelis on this subject. One of them—a middle-aged lady who came with her husband from England in 1950—told me that on board the ship which brought them to Israel there were "masses" of immigrants from North African countries. Yet she and her husband, together with all the Europeans on board, were cautioned against mixing with "the Moroccans," who in turn were not allowed to come up. "They are animals," one Jewish Agency emissary told this lady with undisguised disgust . . .

About three years ago, Jacob Talmon, Professor of Modern History at the Hebrew University, wrote that it was a stroke of "good fortune" that the Oriental Jews in Israel did not succeed in setting up political organizations of their own. Coming from a well-known historian, this view is nothing short of shocking, but it is shared by the Eastern European establishment in Israel, though probably for reasons other than those which motivated Talmon. After all, it was this same famous professor who, in a television programme not long ago, declared that he saw in Israel "a direct continuation of the culture and society of the Jews of Eastern Europe"— apparently oblivious of the very existence of an Israeli majority that had little if anything to do with that culture and that society.

However that may be, it is my conviction that the failure of the Oriental Jew in Israel to organize ethnically, culturally *and* politically may yet prove to have been something of a misfortune for Israeli society as a whole and its body politic. Political organization, the power this organization brings in its wake, and the position of influence which such power bestows on its holders — these would have given the Middle Eastern element in Israel some much-needed self-esteem and pride; they would have given its members a feeling of belonging and identification which they do not now have; and would finally have made their true integration and participation possible and meaningful. In the absence of all this, we find the Middle Eastern element disorganized, marginalized, disgruntled and virtually disenfranchised. And as anyone who has observed these things would know, it is of such colourless, listless, leaderless and powerless masses that the stuff of discontent, disaffection and political chaos is made.

Chapter 9 | ꟑSRAEL'S COMMUNAL PROBLEM

Steven Schwartzschild, whom I first met at an American Jewish Congress dialogue in Rehovot, asked if I wanted to write on the communal problem for *Judaism*, which he edited. I did, and the article appeared in the Winter 1967 issue of the quarterly under the title "The Two Israels: A Study in Europeocentrism."

THE MELTING POT FALLACY

There she lies, the great Melting Pot—listen: Can't you hear the roaring and the bubbling? There gapes her mouth—the harbor where a thousand mammoth feeders come from the end of the world to pour in their human freight. Ah, what a stirring and seething? Celt and Latin, Slav and Teuton, Greek and Syrian—black and yellow—
Jew and Gentile—
Yes, East and West, North and South, the palm and the pine, the pole and the equator, the crescent and the cross—how the great Alchemist melts and fuses them with his purging flame! Here shall they all unite to build the Republic of Man and the Kingdom of God . . .

These are the glowing terms in which Israel Zangwill made Paul, hero of his play *The Melting Pot*, depict the American scene fifty-eight years ago. The irony of it, however, was that not only did the Melting Pot never really "happen," but that Zangwill himself, writing only eight years after his play was first performed, found himself obliged to admit: "It was vain for Paul to declare that there should be neither Jew nor Greek. Nature will return even if driven out with a pitchfork, still more if driven out with a dogma."
Israel Zangwill is now dead, his play deservedly forgotten, and the purging flames of the great Melting Pot not only failed to fuse Jew and Greek, Celt and Latin, Slav and Teuton together into a new, homogeneous race of men, but—as Nathan Glazer and Patrick Moynihan point out in

Beyond the Melting Pot—it is now generally considered "a good thing" that the process of fusion did not work. In this article it will be argued that the Israeli concept of the Pressure Cooker—denoting the process of "mixing the exiles"—has about as much validity as had Zangwill's idea of the Melting Pot; that the slogan *mizzug galuyot* has proven in a very important sense to be a boomerang; and that the sooner these anachronisms are cast away, the better will be the prospects for a healthy and harmonious Israel society.

It is often argued that the American experience during the past 150 years differs fundamentally from that of the State of Israel—that the difference between Greek and Jew is far greater and more basic than that between, say, a Polish Jew and a Yemenite coreligionist. For the purposes of this article, however, we take as our point of departure the assumption that, at least as far as identifiable cultural traits are concerned, the gap separating the Arabic Jew from an Arabic Moslem or Christian—or a modern American Jew from his non-Jewish compatriot—is not wider than the one yawning between an Eastern European Jew and a South Arabian Jew. This assumption is not as arbitrary as it may sound. The influence of home environment on the formation of that complex or those norms and attitudes constituting the code of conduct of individual and group alike is a truism of the social sciences. The family is the smallest social unit and the primary agency for transmitting these norms and attitudes. "As soon as the child has free motion and begins to pull, tear, pry, meddle and prowl, the parents begin to define the situation through speech and other signs and pressures . . . His wishes and activities begin to be inhibited, and gradually . . . the growing member learns the code of his society" (W. I. Thomas in *The Unadjusted Girl*, quoted in Coser and Rosenberg, *Sociological Theory*, New York, 1964, p. 235).

To those not familiar with the work done, and still being done, in Israel in the sphere of *mizzug galuyot*, "mixing the exiles," all this may sound like belaboring the obvious. But if it be true, as it was once said, that the ultimate revolution is the assertion of common sense, this is especially apt in the case of Israel, where—to borrow Zangwill's metaphor—pitchfork and dogma worked hand in hand to produce a state of communal polarization and an educational gap that threaten the very life of the body social. The trouble has been that, for close on two decades, those who preached the dogma have also been those who wielded the pitchfork, and—armed with typical Slavonic tenacity and a blissful ignorance of the relevant facts— the wielding of the latter was matched only by the blind adherence to the former.

There is one point which would better be cleared up at this stage. The dogma of *mizzug galuyot* ordinarily referred to the fusion of the various communities to produce the Republic of Man and the Kingdom of God on earth; yet what its proponents actually sought to accomplish was something even less credible — and certainly less *creditable:* the fusing — "absorption" and "assimilation" would be better terms — was to be one-sided. It was not meant to involve the already existing dominant culture, the secular post-Haskalah culture of the Eastern European leadership. The process of fusion or assimilation involved only newcomers who belonged to certain "unfortunate," "backward" Jewish communities, mainly those hailing from the countries of the Middle East and North Africa. It was these who were supposed to be assimilated, selectively and one by one, *into* the dominant culture; the latter was to remain intact, an example and a model to be aspired to and emulated. To make another analogy with the American experience: It would never have crossed the mind of Zangwill's Paul to include the white Anglo-Saxon Protestant group with those which his Melting Pot was supposed to fuse into a single American nationality. He could not possibly have done so, since the WASPs *were* America.

There is no lack of material to illustrate this Israeli approach to the subject of immigrant absorption. Israeli publicists and opinion leaders now tend to be more careful when they treat the subject in public; but ten or fifteen years ago these views were expressed freely and without inhibition. Both Raphael Patai, in his book *Israel between East and West,* and Abraham Shumsky, in his *Clash of Cultures in Israel,* supply a wealth of such material. One example would suffice. Writing in the Eastern European Zionist Establishment's leading daily organ, *Davar,* Michael Assaf, Mapai's expert on Arab affairs and for years now the Chairman of the Israel Journalists Association, wrote in that paper's issue of September 29, 1950:

What must therefore be the task of the Ingathering of the Exiles? Not only to bring them [the Oriental Jews] to the soil of Israel, but also to restore them to their first exalted value. The same thing holds good with regard to all parts of the [Jewish] people who were, to their misfortune, dispersed by the hand of Fate among low-grade [*yarud*] peoples.

And every Jew who is not seized by the fear of the possibility, whether it is imaginary or not, that we will not be able to prevail and to purify our brethren from the dross of Orientalism which attached itself to them against their will, will be held accountable for this before the guardian spirit of the nation.

There is reason for the most serious anxiety . . . how to cleanse and purify these brethren—how to lift them up to the Western level of the existing *Yishuv* . . .

(Quoted in Raphael Patai, *Israel between East and West*, New York, 1953, p. 311)

This was the dogma, as propounded by a leading spokesman of the Establishment. Outside newspaper offices, in immigrant camps, in kibbutzim and, above all, in the schools, the pitchfork was being wielded with equal force and conviction. The declared goal of "remolding" the Oriental was pursued with a vigor and a self-assurance that in retrospect seem truly staggering. Moreover, side by side with the cleansing and the purifying, and as a perfectly logical outcome of the great fear with which "every Jew" was seized lest the low-grade culture of the Orientals gain a foothold in Israeli society, other precautions were taken. Using a variety of threadbare excuses and rationalizations, the dominant group practiced a systematic policy of exclusion and incapacitation, a policy which did not leave unaffected even the country's institutions of higher learning. When, in 1964, a spokesman of the Sephardi Community Council in Jerusalem described this operation as "cultural genocide," this gave rise to a great deal of shock and angry protest. The whole question, of course, is in reality one of sheer semantics.

That this culture-cleansing approach still prevails, after eighteen years of patent failure, can be verified on a variety of levels and in several spheres. The goal of "lifting the Orientals up to our own Western level"—implying, of course, that until this has been accomplished, the Oriental cannot be accepted or treated as an equal—is in fact still in vogue among the cultural establishment. Recently, this has been given ample proof by the utterances of two prominent Israelis who, in temperament and vocation, are quite different, though they hail roughly from the same cultural milieu—the world of the Eastern European Jewish *shtetl* at the turn of the century.

David Ben-Gurion, Israel's first Prime Minister and the man who remained at the helm throughout the State's first 15 years of existence, told a *Look* magazine editor, Robert Moskin, not long ago: "[Jews] from Morocco have no education. Their customs are those of Arabs. They love their wives, but they beat them . . . Maybe in the third generation something will appear from the Oriental Jews that is a little different. But I don't see it yet. The Moroccan Jew took a lot from the Moroccan Arabs. The culture of Morocco I would not like to have here. And I don't see what contribution present Persians have to make" (*Look*, New York, October 5, 1965). As this issue of *Look* reached Israel at the height of the electoral campaign for the Sixth Knesset, Ben-Gurion's opponents hastened to make political capital out of his reported remarks. The usual denial came promptly—at one stage the claim being made that the meeting between Moskin and Ben-Gurion never took place! However, Ben-Gurion never either gave a satisfactory explanation of what he did say to Moskin or managed to persuade *Look* even to publish his own disclaimer. As a matter of fact, Moskin privately affirmed the truth of the statement and expressed readiness to testify in court if asked to do so. A few months later, Mr. Ben-Gurion told Eric Rouleau, of the Paris daily *Le Monde:* "We do not want Israelis to become Arabs. We are in duty bound to fight against the spirit of the Levant, which corrupts individuals and societies, and preserve the authentic Jewish values as they crystallized in the Diaspora" (*Le Monde,* Paris, March 9, 1966).

THE EUROPEOCENTRIC SYNDROME

Needless to say, Mr. Ben-Gurion did not take the trouble—no member of the ruling elite in Israel ever does, though they all freely speak of the same values—of explaining precisely what he meant by "authentic Jewish values as they crystallized in the Diaspora," nor did he make it clear what Diaspora he had in mind and whether he considers Morocco, Persia and other Oriental countries in which Jews lived for thousands of years part of that Diaspora. It is obvious, however, that these authentic Jewish values have little if anything to do with what most of us commoners would usually understand the term to denote—namely, Jewish religion, Jewish traditions and Jewish culture and way of life as they were developed by observant Jews in post-Exilic times. (In an interview with a *Jewish Chronicle* reporter shortly before the *Le Monde* interview took place, Mrs. Paula Ben-Gurion was asked whether she bought meat at a *kosher* shop. "Yes," came the prompt reply. "But at home I make it *trefa*" [*The Jewish Chronicle,* London, Rosh Hashanah issue, 1965].)

Our suspicion is that the authentic Jewish values which Mr. Ben-Gurion is so eager to preserve have just about nothing to do with Jewish values and Jewish culture as, say, a Yemenite, Moroccan, Persian or Iraqi Jew would understand the term. This suspicion is greatly strengthened by another highly respectable, and, in the circumstances somewhat unexpected, source. Mr. Haim Hazaz, who, after the Nobel Prize Laureate S. Y. Agnon, is considered Israel's leading novelist and man of letters, was recently interviewed by the mass-circulation Israeli evening paper *Ma'ariv*. In the course of this interview, printed in the last Rosh Hashanah special issue of the paper, Mr. Hazaz asked his interviewer rhetorically: "And who are we? One people? Decidedly not! We are communities, communities! . . . We stand on the edge of a precipice in so far as Levantinism is concerned." And then, in the same breath: "We must try and bring European culture to the Oriental communities. We cannot afford to become an Oriental people. I feel great resentment at such a development. We had to travel a road of 2,000 years to become a European Jewish cultural division, and now it is impossible to turn the wheel backwards and accept the culture of Yemen, of Morocco, or of Iraq."

What makes Hazaz's utterances especially difficult to understand is that of all the Hebrew writers of his generation he was the only one to take a special interest in the Yemenite community about which he wrote two famous novels. Moreover, his own estimate of "the Ashkenazim" is anything but flattering. The following is taken from the first page of his novel *Hayoshevet Baganim* (*Mori Sa'id*, in Ben Halpern's translation, New York, 1956):

There are the Ashkenazim, libertines and free-thinkers, hold-faced twisters, quarrelsome and contentious, high-handed and base, befuddling the world with their tongue-wagging, mastering public affairs like charity-warders, spending their money like bankrupts, all the earth's in their hand and everything theirs, nor may the rest of God's creatures lift their heads before them.

Again, Hazaz refrained from defining his terms; but it is quite obvious that when he spoke of "European Jewish culture" what he had in mind was approximately the same sorts of wares denoted by Mr. Ben-Gurion's "authentic Jewish values" — namely, that body of religious unbelief and political activism which inspired the thoughts and activities of the *shtetl* followers of the European Haskalah movement of the last century. However, those who read Hazaz's interview through to the end will become aware of a central historical factor which accounts for much that has gone on in the sphere of immigrant absorption in Israel. In reply to his interviewer's query as to how he came to write his books about the Jews of Yemen, Hazaz admitted:

Listen! We the Jews of Eastern Europe had thought, in our innocence, that the Jews who lived in Greater Russia . . . that it was these Jews who constituted the Jewish People, and no one else besides. True, we had known that Jews were to be found in Germany; but as far as we were concerned this was a Jewry whose relevance was fast disappearing as a result of Reform and assimilation which greedily ate into its body. We also knew that there were Jews in France, England, and overseas. *But Oriental Jews!* We simply forgot that such a thing existed!

The Israeli dogma that the Jewries of the Middle East and North Africa have to be "absorbed," and that this absorption amounts to nothing less than bringing European culture to them, rests on the assumption that there exists in Israel a fairly well-defined "native" culture to which these immigrants have to adapt and into which they can and have to be fused. But is there, was there ever, such a culture — and, if it did exist, was it capable of "absorbing" such a mass of people with so many deep-rooted cultures of their own, and, what is more, outnumbering the bearers of the native culture?

ESTABLISHMENT SOCIOLOGISTS TOE THE LINE

Here we feel we must turn to the social scientist for guidance, both as to what has happened so far and what ought to be done henceforth. Unfortunately, however, the famous dictum that a people gets the government it deserves seems quite applicable in this field. In the same way as the WASP establishment in the United States almost always managed to get the sociologists it deserved — and asked for — so also the Israeli establishment: of all those Israeli students of society who took due note of what was going on, the only ones who prevailed were those who accepted the assumptions underlying the official line. These were sociologists who unquestioningly adopted the dogma of the Pressure Cooker, educationists who in the face of all the recent findings of the social sciences drew up school curricula modeled exclusively on European patterns of thought and behavior, and psychologists who eagerly applied Europeocentric tests and measures to non-Europeans — and duly found them wanting in all kinds of "right" cultural attributes (such as the power for "abstract thought").

In his remarkable study of the decline and fall of the white Anglo-Saxon Protestant establishment in America, Prof. E. Digby Baltzell shows how the leading social scientists of the day "tended to sympathize with the various forms of racialist thinking, were often anti-Semitic, and were strong supporters of immigration restriction. They were evolutionists who were convinced that the Anglo-Saxon millionaires who ruled the nation in their day were the 'fittest' men in the world" (*The Protestant Establishment: Aristocracy and Caste in America,* New York, 1956, p. 98).

A similar process, though less pronounced, was at work in Israel in the heyday of mass immigration, and it cannot safely be said to have disappeared altogether. The scope of this article allows for only two illustrations. Professor S. N. Eisenstadt is a sociologist of very good standing — and not only in Israel — who has been Chairman of the Department of Sociology, at the Hebrew University, for a good many years. His interest in the problems of immigrant absorption dates back to pre-State days, and he is the author of a number of books and papers on the subject. His book *The Absorption of Immigrants: A Comparative Study Based Mainly on the Jewish Community in Palestine and the State of Israel* (London, 1955) makes a rather good first impression and a good start. In its first parts Eisenstadt points out that indices ordinarily used to measure the process of acculturation are all inadequate, mainly because they were constructed as indices of full assimilation, which seldom or never takes place. Immigrant groups are not usually dispersed throughout the social structure of the receiving country, Eisenstadt points out, but tend to congregate in one part of it, where they maintain some degree of separate identity. There thus arises a pluralistic society, the various parts of which are different both in ethnic origin and social class. Whether an immigrant is able to adjust satisfactorily depends on what his desires and expectations are, and on how well these can be met in his new country.

The relevance of all this to the subject of immigrant acculturation in Israel is self-evident enough. However, when Eisenstadt deals with the Israeli situation, we find little if any trace of it, and, as Professor William Petersen remarks, the book thus proves "a disappointment." The fact is that Eisenstadt more or less accepts the prevalent official thesis:

1. that the core of the Israeli nation is the Hebrew-Zionist tradition;
2. that the adaptation of other groups can, therefore, be indicated by measuring the degree to which they have accepted this tradition;
3. that the range of cultural differences among the various sectors of the Israeli population is less wide than might appear on the surface, and that the prospects of achieving a homogeneous nation are good.

Petersen examines these three assumptions one by one, and it is highly instructive to follow the lines of his argument. With regard to Eisenstadt's thesis that the core of Israeli culture is the Hebrew-Zionist tradition, Petersen's impression is that the Israeli sociologist "consistently overstates the present strength of the Zionist tradition," and that "he certainly contributes to the building of its legend by exaggerating the heroic aspects of the pioneer settlements. Thus, in his discussion of the motives for Jewish emigration, he contrasts the 'economic or other satisfactions' sought by those Jews who went from Eastern Europe to America with the 'social and cultural aspirations' that motivated those who went to Palestine . . ."

Concerning Eisenstadt's indices of absorption, Petersen refers to one of them — whether or not children go to public schools, a practice which for the new Middle Eastern immigrants is a new and often disagreeable experience. "But," Petersen comments, "if he had also asked whether the children go to *cheder,* the traditional Jewish religious school, then the secularized West Europeans and Zionists would have scored lowest." Again, Eisenstadt's findings reveal that, in contrast to Middle Eastern immigrants, who adapt less readily in part because they hold on to their traditional norms, Serbian and Bulgarian Jews fit into Israeli society without difficulty. This, Eisenstadt points out, is in part because the latter's "lack of traditional, nonformal Jewish identification [makes] this process much easier for them." Prof. Petersen continues:

Thus pious Orthodox Jews, "returning" to Israel after long exile, are welcomed with the request to shed some of their "less assimilable" Jewishness. It is a measure of Eisenstadt's partisanship that he appears to have no inkling of how strange this looks to the outsider.
 (W. Petersen, *The Politics of Population,* New York, 1965, pp. 220–226)

Our second illustration is of much more recent date. Writing last year in the British journal *New Society,* under the title "Pregnancy — East and West," Dr. Esther Goshen-Gottstein, Lecturer in Clinical Psychology, Hadassah Medical School, the Hebrew University, offers a summary of an inquiry conducted into "the difference of attitudes to first pregnancy between Oriental . . . and Western women living in Israel." The inquiry involved 160 Jewish women from East and West living next to each other and going to the same pre-natal clinics.

The original hypothesis of Goshen-Gottstein's inquiry set out to test the assumption "that the attitudes of women to their first pregnancy are mainly determined by their ethnic origin." The statistical evaluation of the data suggests, however, that the socio-economic class to which the women belong "might be equally decisive." Goshen-Gottstein is aware, however, that all this "is largely a play on words, since class and country of origin are in our case closely associated." (Presumably realizing how strange such a blunt statement of the facts would appear to an outsider, Dr. Goshen-Gottstein hastens to make the somewhat unverifiable and certainly irrelevant assertion that this close association between class and ethnic group is due to the fact that "it was mainly the backward elements from certain Oriental communities that came to Israel, while the upper strata remained behind or immigrated to other countries.")

In addition to such unsupported statements, Goshen-Gottstein's brief study turns out to be replete with cross-cultural evaluations based on patently Europeocentric value judgments. Here is an example:

On the other hand, women having a more satisfying partner-relationship, such as Western women do . . . tend to look forward to the child for its own sake and not for what they personally can get through it. Though both Orientals and Westerners may be motherly, the woman living in a modern marriage will tend to give child-centered reasons for wanting her first child—unlike Oriental women for whom the child often represents an avenue of compensation for the husband's lack of attention.

(*New Society*, London, August 25, 1966)

This implicit acceptance on Goshen-Gottstein's part of certain Western attitudes regarding an ideal type of family relationship inevitably led her to classify certain attitudes and behavior of the pregnant Oriental woman as "selfish," "self-centered" and "narcissistic"—terms which, as a reader pointed out in a subsequent issue, are "neither neutral nor cross-cultural," but merely betray a lack of understanding of Middle Eastern traditional societies and a typical Europeocentric approach to the subject. As the writer of the said reader's letter wrote: "Cross-cultural comparisons are different from cross-cultural measurements; the writer proposed to do the first but ended inadequately doing the second" (*New Society*, September 8, 1966).

A PHILOSOPHY PROFESSOR'S VERSION

However, if the sociologist's approach constitutes an index, albeit inadequate, of the general climate of opinion, then a certain amount of progress in this field can be said to have been made in recent years. For the first time in Israel's history a gathering took place in Jerusalem last autumn in which sociologists of the Hebrew University discussed and compared notes on the subject of *mizzug galuyot*. The symposium, held on the University campus on October 25–26, was convened at the initiative of Professor Nathan Rotenstreich, the Rector, and Professor S. N. Eisenstadt. Considering that it came after over eighteen years of study and observation in a field so crucial to the country's future, the results and findings of the symposium were modest enough, and the whole enterprise could not fail to remind one of the famous definition of a sociologist as a fellow who spends $100,000 to find his way to a house of ill-repute. Two of the findings are directly relevant to our discussion.

First, expansive talk by members of the veteran *Yishuv* about the great sacrifices they have made in order to bring the new immigrants to Israel and to integrate them into their own ranks represents the exact opposite of what has actually taken place. In a paper based on the findings of official and semi-official research bodies, the economist Dr. Ruth Melul-Klinov demonstrated that, far from suffering any privations or making any economic sacrifices, the veteran settlers benefited greatly — as individuals and collectively — from the sudden appearance on the stage of so much non-competitive man-power, which made possible for them an upward social and economic mobility of unprecedented scope and rate.

Second, Europeocentric cultural monolithism which the education authorities imposed on Israeli schools has not only failed in achieving its objective but produced the opposite result: instead of helping fuse the various communities, it actually caused a widening of the communal gap. In this connection, two of the sociologists were quite outspoken. Dr. Judith Shuval deplored the fact that the school curricula placed undue emphasis on European culture and the Ashkenazi environment, ignoring the background and culture of the non-Europeans — and she demanded that these curricula be revised in keeping with the present composition of the population. Dr. Haim Adler, of the University's School of Education, revealed that at the conclusion of the first eight years of schooling, differences between children of Europeans and those of Middle Easterners become more pronounced than they are when the children first enter the school.

The overall picture which emerged from the two-day discussions was one of failure and frustration. Everybody admitted that something very important had gone wrong in the so-called mixing of exiles. With regard to the future, however, opinions differed as to the best line to be adopted, though implicitly everyone agreed that the Establishment's attempt to recreate the Middle Eastern immigrants and their children in its own peculiar image of Europeans has failed dismally. Division crystallized in the end over the question: Pluralism or "Individual Absorption"?

About pluralism, reservations were sounded from important quarters. Eisenstadt, for instance, asserted that we speak of pluralism but do not really know what *kind* of pluralism we want—a statement which strikes one as startling coming from so esteemed a social scientist. The substance of his approach to the problem was that the policy of *mizzug galuyot* brought negative results. It failed as soon as the country's institutions woke up to the fact that, along with their meager luggage, the Oriental immigrants brought with them their own cultural traits and peculiarities. At this point, he added, social scientists started talking of a pluralist rather than a culturally homogeneous society. He rejected both of these solutions and suggested a third way: a fruitful encounter between the veteran society and the immigrant groups, each preserving the core of its own cultural traditions. In propounding this thesis, Eisenstadt used the word "transformation"—neither fusion nor pluralism, he said, but the transformation of Israeli society into something new.

It is interesting to note that real opposition to pluralism came from the only non-sociologist who took an active part in the proceedings. Prof. Nathan Rotenstreich is a philosopher by training, though he has written a good deal about a variety of other subjects and is also active in the Mapai splinter group, Min Hayesod. Speaking in a bewildering mixture of ancient Zionist cliches and transcendental Kantian concepts, Rotenstreich implicitly rejected the whole cultural-sociological approach to the problem by assuring his audience that the mixing of the exiles failed because "the veteran society . . . ceased to be founded on the idea of the discharging of duties." Not because immigrants from the Middle East and North Africa were of a different socio-cultural make from the veteran European settlers, but because these latter failed to be better citizens, more conscious and conscientious Zionists, firmer believers in voluntary work and willing to make more sacrifices! The assumption underlying this line of argument can hardly be other than the time-honored one of the Eastern European establishment, namely, that the Orientals "have no culture" worthy of the name.

There is, of course, no way of verifying the validity of Rotenstreich's diagnosis, since the veteran society behaved not according to any philosophical concepts and abstractions, but in accordance with better-known norms of mortal human behavior. What is clear, however, is that Rotenstreich's thesis implies a denial of the most elementary findings of the social sciences of the last fifty years. It was only to be expected, therefore, that he should have so vehemently proclaimed his rejection of pluralism and his insistence on the fiction of "individual absorption."

It hardly needs pointing out that "individual absorption" is just another name for cultural monolithism. The procedure is quite simple: the veteran, "absorbing" society agrees to admit into its ranks certain "qualified" members of the newcomer groups — but one by one, and in accordance with its own, inevitably ethnocentric idea of what these "qualifications" ought to be. In even simpler terms, this means that a member of the outgroup, in order to be "absorbed" into the dominant culture, has to shed his cultural identity and disown his own group before he qualifies for admittance. Needless to say, our man would by then have become a total social and cultural wreck. The most popular expression of such admittance is when a Moroccan, Iraqi or Yemenite is told something like this: "Why, I would never have taken you for a Moroccan (Iraqi, Yemenite). You look and behave virtually like one of us!"

The truth is that the idea of "individual assimilation" is based on yet another fallacy — namely, the theory of social individualism. This theory teaches, in effect, that society is made up of isolated individuals who depend mainly upon their own talents for the positions they achieve in society. This is at best an unsubstantiated theory. In the case of Israel, it is a total fiction: both economically and politically the structure of Israeli society is clearly influenced by ethnic-communal factors. In other words, Israel is a society where the rights, attainments and privileges of an individual rest largely on the status achieved by the group to which he belongs, and ultimately by the power it controls and can wield.

PLURALISM VERSUS A CASTE-LIKE SYSTEM

One final point: As in other instances of inter-group conflict, the case for "individual assimilation" in Israel is normally supported by talk about the need for "maintaining standards," preserving the modern character of the country and its high technical quality in the face of the quantitative superiority of her neighbors, and so on. This, again, is nothing but the traditional ethnocentric reaction on the part of the dominant group to any serious threat from outsiders. As an American social scientist put it in another context, the argument about standards is "as often a rationalization of prejudice as a concern for quality" (David Danzig, "The Meaning of Negro Strategy," *Commentary*, New York, February 1964).

Thus, when Rotenstreich proclaims—as he did at the concluding session of the sociologists' symposium—that "the only human being" he recognizes is "the individual human being," this may be accepted somewhat indulgently as an abstract statement of some philosophical proposition. When he makes the statement in a sociological context—and specifically in the context of immigrant absorption in Israel—one has to take it in dead seriousness, with all the practical social implications of the doctrine. After all, his approach and his views are entirely typical of the official line in *mizzug galuyot*. Sociologically speaking, this point was settled a long time ago. (For detailed discussions on this subject, see the work of Georg Simmel [1858-1918] and Emile Durkheim [1858-1917]. Also quoted in Coser and Rosenberg, *Sociological Theory*, pp. 6-8.)

What, then, can or should be done? Individual assimilation, with its concomitant manifestations of cultural monolithism and social inequality, has proved a near-disaster—and remains the surest road to the development of the kind of Levantine society which all Israelis profess to abhor.

There is, on the other hand, a certain appeal in Eisenstadt's formulation, envisaging the "transformation" of Israeli society into something new, presumably a synthesis of the cultures of the various groups. It is, however, extremely difficult to translate this vision into anything like concrete terms—especially when Eisenstadt has taken care to warn us from the very beginning that he is not inclined toward pluralism, that in fact he does not know what kind of pluralism we want. In all probability, indeed, the "transformation" to which he refers would never actually occur, since it will presumably be greatly restricted by the actions of the dominant group—whose approach to this problem is best illustrated by the question its representatives constantly ask: "And what, pray, are these Oriental cultural traits which ought to be preserved?"

Historically, we can trace four categories of long-term solutions to the kind of problem posed by the prevalent state of inter-group relations in Israel: destruction of the weaker group; formation on the part of the stronger group of one or more caste-like strata above the weaker group; social and biological integration; and democratic pluralism.

With the first type of solution, we are not concerned here. It is very much to be feared, however, that what has actually been taking place in Israel in this sphere is a combination of the second and third types of solution, with the scales weighed in favor of the former, i.e., the creation of a caste-like social system through which the weaker groups are permanently kept at bay. In this connection the first thing to be borne in mind is that the formation by the dominant group of caste-like strata is a self-accelerating and self-perpetuating process. In Israel it is further helped by several factors: over-institutionalization; ingrained suspicion of out-groups; ethnic intolerance born of past persecution and frustration; an educational system with a structure allowing for very little mobility for members of the out-group; and, not least, the concentration of too much social control and economic power in the hands of the Government. Leonard J. Fein calls Israel a "state-society" ("Ideology and Politics in Israel," *Judaism,* Summer 1966). "It is assumed," Fein writes of the Israeli system, "that the shape of the society and the policies of the government are inseparable, and that any social problems are naturally the concern of government."

To have an idea of just how this process works, we may turn to the experiences of other societies. The point of forming caste-like strata above the weaker groups is that these are in the end confined to performing the menial tasks in the society and are denied many of the rewards that go to the upper-caste groups. This happened centuries ago in India, when invaders from the northwest conquered the aboriginal residents. It has happened in South Africa, where the white men occupy strata above the non-whites. And it has happened to some extent in the United States, where the whites have occupied the top strata, with the descendants of African slaves below them, and with other non-white people generally having fewer privileges and less power than the white group.

As has been indicated, in Israel this process is accompanied — and to some extent also tempered — by the prevalence of another type of solution, namely, integration. Integration, however, can be one-sided — in the sense that members of the weaker groups are integrated *into* rather than *with* the dominant group. Besides, it is by definition almost a very long process. In Brazil, for instance, the present fusion of racial and cultural groups (Indian, Portuguese and Negro) is the result of four centuries of intermarriage and miscegenation.

There is no gainsaying the fact that the ultimate aim of Israeli society is integration; on this point few Israelis seem to differ. However, integration by itself is a neutral concept, especially when it is taken to mean biological fusion. Integration can take place even in a system of slavery, as when in the early years of slavery white slave-owners in America took Negro women as concubines. It can also proceed in a caste-like system of society, where it can have little, if any, effect on the system. The question to be asked is, therefore: In what sort of system can integration be attained most smoothly and with the least tension and culture conflict? The answer seems to lie in the fourth type of the solutions listed above, i.e., democratic pluralism.

"Democratic pluralism" has been defined as the state in which the various groups in a society "settle down to an amicable coexistence, each group keeping its culture fairly intact and intermarrying little or not at all with other groups." A condition of democratic pluralism may be said to exist if equal respect and equal opportunities and privileges are accorded to all groups. This has been the situation in Switzerland, with its French, German and Italian cantons, and in Canada, where the French and the English share the country. A state of democratic pluralism can also be said to prevail in a country like Lebanon, where Moslems and Christians, in their various denominations, each get their allotted share of "the national pie."

There is a sense in which it would be true to say that some such condition of pluralism must obtain in Israel *before* the stage can be set for genuine integration. It is a pity, and not a little surprising, that some Israelis should feel somewhat bewildered about the prospect of a pluralist society. In the circumstances, such a development offers the only alternative to Levantinization — or something far worse.

| $\mathcal{F}$REEDOM OF SPEECH,
ISRAEL STYLE

DAVID HAKHAM'S REBELLION

$\mathcal{W}$riting about the specific liberties that compose the freedom enjoyed under the British parliamentary system, Professor Michael Oakeshott stresses three particular ones: freedom of speech, freedom of association, and freedom of private property. Whereas he considers the first to be vital, he thinks that it has been so overstressed that excessive emphasis on this one liberty may conceal the loss of others.

The major part of mankind, he explains, has nothing to say. The extraordinary emphasis on freedom of speech, therefore, may be supposed to be "the work of a small vocal section of our society and, in part, represents a legitimate self-interest."

Nor is this an interest incapable of abuse. It is thus wrong to suppose that "so long as our freedom to speak is not impaired we have lost nothing of importance." Indeed, however secure a man's right to speak his thoughts, he may find that some other right that seems more important to him has been lost: if, for instance, his house is compulsorily purchased or if he is forced to join a trade union in order to take a job.

Moreover, Oakeshott asserts, there is a great danger in one of the usual lines of defense of free speech — namely, that it is the only way of reaching "the truth." This is because truth seekers are likely to think that they have reached their goal and so to oppress further free speech as being redundant, any opposition to them being perforce based on "error." The truth, he writes, is that the real rationale for the right to speak freely is the belief that politics is not concerned with this sort of "truth" at all, its real goal being simply peace, tranquility, and the conventional "decencies of conduct among men."

$\mathcal{I}$ did not know David Hakham personally, but his case was to play quite a part in my final break with the establishment. Hakham was one of those "primitive Zionists" who, though they had been the backbone of the movement in Iraq and played a decisive role in the liquidation of the Jewish community there, were ignored and abandoned as soon as they came to Israel. Unlike many of his colleagues, however, Hakham had the guts to try his luck in Israeli politics, and in 1963 he became the subject of a minor scandal within Mapai.

In its dealings with new immigrants, Mapai, which had ruled the country almost uncontested since the establishment of the State, was high-handed, condescending, and parochial—and even in the best of cases, rather paternalistic and domineering. It did not tolerate ideas that conflicted with its own anachronistic mixture of institutionalized socialism and exclusivistic Jewish nationalism. Its luminaries had never—or hardly ever—been aware of the existence of any brand of Zionist, or even Jew, other than the eastern European, Yiddish-speaking, Second or Third Aliyah type. The enormous power the party wielded through the country's only two real employers—the government and the Histadrut—was used with great skill and advantage as leverage to make newcomers conform. The leaders of its so-called ethnic departments, or desks, were never allowed to be anything more than "vote contractors" who also acted as *mukhtars* (heads of local neighborhoods) or notables, doling out little benefits and bread crumbs to favored members of their respective ethnic groupings.

David Hakham was born in Basra, Iraq, in 1920 and finished his secondary schooling there. At twenty-two, he was one of the founders of the Halutz Movement, and subsequently he organized its defense section, known as the *Shurah*. He was arrested and sentenced to imprisonment, but eventually managed to make his way to Israel, where he settled in Beersheba. Joining Mapai and acting as its representative in the town for about ten years, he became, in a relatively short time, deputy mayor.

However, when the mayor, a Mapai member himself, was forced to resign and Hakham subsequently—and rather naturally—offered his candidacy, the Mapai headquarters in Tel Aviv started to waver. In those days it was unthinkable to allow an "Iraqi" to become mayor even of a small development town like Beersheba. Sensing foul play, Hakham resorted to similar tactics and openly defied the party machine—also known simply as the Machine—thus thwarting Mapai's attempt to reconstitute the local council so that he would not have a chance of being named mayor. But the Machine was not used to such defiance, not from "new immigrants" anyway, and certainly not from Orientals. To assert itself, therefore, the Machine hastened to expel Hakham from the party.

One hot day in August 1963, I attended a meeting in Ramat Gan at which Hakham spoke. The meeting was organized by a predominantly Iraqi group with the name *Ahva* (Brotherhood) and was held in Beit Ha-Ezrah. Although it was a well-advertised public meeting, there were no photographers to "immortalize" the event, and the few reporters present, looking rather desultory and unimpressed, with the exception of the one representing one of the two evening papers, quietly made their way to the door and out.

The keyword at that gathering was *tzedek* (justice). Many of the speakers took care to disclaim any purely communal motivation. If this was a communal organization, one speaker argued, what would you call a list of 120 Knesset candidates, only two or three of whom were non-Ashkenazis? Wasn't *that* a communal list? No, Ahva was not a communal movement; it was a movement seeking tzedek and equitable integration between the communities. In those days spokesmen for the Ashkenazi establishment were still able to frighten people with the word "communal" — and as one cabinet minister had said in Beersheba that same week, a communal list was "a stab in the back of the nation."

Sitting there and listening to the speakers, I wondered about the question, simple in itself, but cruel and damning in its implications: what had brought these people to their far-reaching decision? What accumulation of disillusionment, resentment, hurt pride, and sheer anger had led to this state of things? Some of the speakers spoke about their credentials, and a glance at these may help answer these questions.

I have already described the background of David Hakham. One of the founders of Ahva was Abraham Avisar, then thirty-two years old, eager, bespectacled, eminently the intellectual type, and radiating no small amount of enthusiasm and sincerity. I imagined him in 1951, coming to Israel at the age of twenty after finishing his secondary schooling and a spell in the Halutz Movement, eagerly and willingly serving his two and a half years in the army.

One also could picture the great shock that awaited him and many others of his generation of Iraqi Jews — the shock of finding out that he was not a simple Jew among other Jews, but some nameless "Oriental" among "Westerners," a man who was to be "raised" to the standards of his new society, to be "cleansed and purified," as one Israeli publicist put it at the time, "from the dross of Orientalism." The political scene, too, must have offered Avisar very little comfort indeed. The 1951 parliamentary elections found the new politically conscious immigrant from Baghdad rather bewildered. For, having had a largely textbook notion of democracy, he could not help watching the democratic process being abused and distorted by the unscrupulous vote hunters and vote contractors of the party machines.

Another spokesman of the movement was Robert Haim, a forty-two-year-old immigrant from Egypt and seven years in Israel. At one point the all-powerful Mapai had decided to put Haim at the head of its list of candidates for the town of Ashdod, but for some reason he was subsequently asked to surrender his seat as chairman of the town's local council. Unlike Avisar, Haim knew what it was like to work for a party. He implied that those who bind and loose at the party's headquarters in Tel Aviv thought that he, as a new immigrant, ought not to have any real say. "However," he said, "it was we who built Ashdod, and it should be we who ought to continue to manage the town's affairs, not the Tel Aviv HQ of this party or that." Much the same argument was submitted by David Hakham, who now found himself heading an independent list and contesting the election with Mapai, whose list was headed by Eliahu Nawi.

The catch, however, was that Nawi himself was also an "Iraqi"—and what did he have that Hakham didn't? It would have been funny were it not so saddening, but the truth of the matter—as one Mapai luminary actually put it at a meeting of the party's central committee—was that Nawi was only three or four when his family came to Palestine, and Hakham was already in his early twenties, and never mind that he had been the moving spirit of the Zionist movement in his native city of Basra!

The gathering at Beit Ha-Ezrah moved me enough to devote a Marginal Column to the subject. It created a good deal of fuss because in it I attacked Mapai's party machine for deciding to oust Hakham from the party, and I also expressed regret that I was not a resident of Beersheba "and thus unable to share in [Hakham's] great and creative act of defiance."

The column, to which I gave the title "The Machine" but which finally appeared under a far less subtle heading ("Non-Ashkenazi Justice"), was printed as is—no changes, no cuts, no complaints—on August 13, 1963. The same morning I received a phone call from Mark Segal, who was then the paper's political reporter and close to Mapai's Secretary-General Reuben Barkat. Segal expressed amazement and some shock, asking how dare I, editor of the establishment's Arabic-language daily, attack the ruling party in such unambiguous terms. I didn't know what to say, and dismissed him by saying something about this being a free country.

The following day, the *Post* actually carried an editorial on the subject. The writer made an interesting analogy between the movements calling for an equitable share of political power for the Oriental communities in

Israel and those advocating equality for women in society. Lea Ben Dor, who most probably wrote that particular leader, also sent me a letter, dated August 14. It read in part:

Dear Nissim:

Your column on the communal lists went into Tuesday's paper without my having read it, owing to a series of misunderstandings.

You will have noticed that to some extent we disavowed it in today's editorial which, I suppose, represents about my own point of view. This isn't a normal procedure.

I'm perfectly in agreement with your general approach, even if it is not that of the paper: it is a signed column. On the other hand, I cannot understand anybody who's known this paper so long quite casually introducing so many snide remarks and such devastating adjectives as "the rotten (Party) machine in Tel Aviv." We are not averse to pointing out what makes a machine rotten, but this adjective, standing by itself unsupported, about Mapai is obviously incompatible with the general line of the paper. The charges you level against this machine would have told their own story without that word.

All this, of course, is apart from the fact that you've made crusading heroes out of a couple of people whose records for integrity leave a lot to be desired.

You know that I'm always anxious for you to write on Israeli rather than on purely Arab internal affairs, but I think you must also keep in mind the general aim, attitude and style of the paper.

Jerusalem, August 18, 1963
Dear Lea:

. . . I agree with you that one should turn to local topics rather than confine oneself to Arab affairs. These days, indeed, [Mapai's alleged operator] Netser holds more horrible fascination to me than does Nasser . . . As for the *Post*, I venture to think that it will do itself honour to seek to give expression to some of the voices now emanating from the Other Israel—the Israel of the future. The *Post* cannot be a narrowly communal newspaper in the tradition, say, of *Davar*.

However, in an attempt to pacify the editors, I managed to write the following week's column, which I dispatched from Netanya, where I was spending a short holiday. Excerpts:

"Well," retorted our interlocutor, an upright and tolerant fellow in his early sixties and a son of the Third *Aliya*. "You do surprise me! Don't you know what a political party is? Such are the ways of all parties!"

"But that is how things are," exclaimed with visible impatience another friend of ours, a middle-aged Baghdadi Jew, whom, though he has been in the country more than 12 years, I shall call a new immigrant. "This is political reality!"

The identity of the two men's concept of democracy was no coincidence. After all, neither of our two friends had known what representative democratic government was really like. Neither had, in his country of origin, had the experience of belonging to a political party, and neither had actually taken part in anything even remotely like democratic elections — except perhaps local elections to their respective community councils.

And this, it occurred to us, was a historical fact of the first importance for our political life. After all, the overwhelming majority of the population comes either from the Eastern European Pale, as our Third Aliya friend does, or from the lands of the Arab Orient — and neither of these regions had in the past, or has recently, had the least taste of liberal democratic rule as the term is understood in the West.

Of course, there is one big difference. While our Iraqi immigrant was here only 12 years or so, our Third *Aliya* friend has been out of Russia for over four decades, and, it may be argued, it is in those 28 intervening years that his attitude to politics was formed and developed. But does the idea of government embodied in this attitude really differ from the one which our other friend brought with him from Baghdad 12 years ago? We can only judge from the scanty evidence at our disposal about the actual behaviour of the parties which he and his comrades had established and still lead — those vote-hunting machines which, it would appear, have been playing havoc with the political education of the new Israelis . . .

Now the question is: do the functionaries of these parties realize the extent of the harm they have been doing to the nation as a whole, or are they merely acting innocently and according to their best lights — according, that is, to an idea of democratic government than which they know no better and which is the only one they know? Be that as it may — and since this is the parties' idea of both civic education and immigrant integration — can anyone be expected to take with anything but extreme scepticism the current righteous declarations casting doubts on the integrity of this or that political dissenter or opponent? . . .

("Misplaced Righteousness," AUGUST 20, 1963)

My original column and the editorial that appeared in the paper the following day moved my friend Jacqueline Kahanoff to write a letter to the editor, which appeared on August 19, entitled "Ambivalence to Newcomers." Excerpts:

Sir,

I wish to thank *The Jerusalem Post* for the public service it performed in printing Nissim Rejwan's latest Marginal Column, "Non-Ashkenazi Justice." This title rings too sharp, but perhaps by now the Oriental and Sephardic communities in this country have heard so much about what the veteran community thinks of those it calls its "Oriental brethren" that many of their members can no longer identify with the veterans as they had once hoped to. Honestly, many of us don't quite know where we stand, and I suggest that the ambivalent feelings the veteran community expresses towards new immigrants awakes a similar ambivalence of the new immigrants towards the *vatikim* (old-timers) and their children.

The *Post*'s editorial entitled "Ashdod Touchstone" mentioned the *Yishuv* being "swamped" by new immigrants; this expression strikes me as odd when applying to Jews coming to Israel with a different feeling of belonging here than new immigrants may have towards the United States and Canada. Incidentally, even a group as indigenous as the French Canadian is still fighting for recognition . . .

Perhaps Sephardic parties are roughly the equivalent of feminist movements and women's organizations? These manifestations of some sections of public opinion may help to bring about a better kind of representation for the deprived sectors of our population in our existing parties. Mrs. Idelson reminds women they represent half the population, and, ironically, another half takes up the cue. There are at least two ways of cutting up a lemon . . .

RIFT WITH THE *POST*

Though the Hakham incident—like the Katznelson affair that preceded it—marked no serious rift with the *Post*, things started to be a little tense, and for the first time memoranda explaining why a certain column could not possibly be carried by "a paper like ours" started coming. Following are excerpts from the few rejected Marginal Columns I managed to preserve.

Of all those countless thousands of words written in criticism of Hannah Arendt's *Eichmann in Jerusalem,* few have seemed as searching and as illuminating as those written recently to the editor of the *Sunday Times* of London, commenting on Professor Hugh Trevor-Roper's review of the book, which appeared on October 13. The letter is signed by Paul Senft, who writes that, as a Jew, he asks himself why Arendt's "penetrating intelligence fails so utterly?" And his reply is that Miss Arendt "seems to know nothing of the two motivations, the two conceptions, which governed the situation of the Jews when the Holocaust had overtaken them: There was religious communal leadership perpetuating their past, and Zionist political leadership exhorting them to a new future."

Between these two motivations, Senft maintains, the Jews "were a people with no present reality of their own." The remarkable thing was that, however different the ideas and attitudes of the religious and political leaders may have been, "both had accepted catastrophe as in the logic of a historical destiny — God's wrath once more descending on the Children of Israel [for] straying into foreign realms of assimilation, and the chosen people were once more paying in agony." Thus lost between religion and politics, the Jewish masses proved most docile — "a people who had long lost their identity and were equally alienated from the organized existence of either." It was because of this loss of identity that the Jewish masses followed their own leaders "neither with a sense of a spiritual mission nor with that of a national selfhood." To be sure, where sparks of either of these existed there were singular deeds of heroism; but generally speaking these masses accepted their fate in silence: "Blank existence does not ignite resistance." . . .

Where the effects of the same kind of process — though under circumstances a thousand times less extreme — can more easily and accurately be discerned is in the life of other, immeasurably less unfortunate Jewish communities elsewhere. It is a source of unending wonder, for example, to ponder upon the passivity and docility with which long-established Jewish communities in the Orient let themselves be dissolved, liquidated communally, and finally herded out of their age-old homes in, say, the Yemen or Iraq. Here, without doubt, was discernible that same spiritual schism, that seemingly aimless wandering between a religious communal leadership perpetuating their past and a Zionist political leadership enjoining them to a new future in a national home of their own. In the case of Iraqi Jewry, at least, it is possible to say that, without this momentary "loss of identity," this vacillation between a fast-disappearing traditional religious motivation and an emergent, dynamic political leadership exemplified in the young Halutz movement and in the work then being done toward the establishment of the Jewish State, the voluntary and startlingly rapid liquidation of the Jewish community would hardly have been accomplished.

("Jews in Mid-Ocean," NOVEMBER 1963)

"One generation passeth away, and another generation cometh: But the earth abideth for ever." We have always found Ecclesiastes' ripe reflections on the generations of man rather more civilized and appealing than the fiery concept in Numbers of the Desert Generation. In fact, with its implicit assumption that the present should be sacrificed for the sake of the future, one could not help reflecting how much in common this concept has with the readiness of the Bolshevists in Russia to sacrifice one generation for the sake of some future one yet unborn. The idea, moreover, is peculiarly arrogant, rather uncharitable, and fallacious. For once you have reconciled yourself to the assumption that a whole generation of human beings may or ought to be sacrificed for the sake of some doubtful textbook ideal—in such cases always disguised as "the future"—you are likely never to be able to stop. The temptation to pass the curse from one generation on to another would then be too great—if only because, as little really changes, the ideal is likely to prove increasingly remote and inaccessible . . .

It may, of course, be argued that, to the extent that each generation tends to consider it its duty to work for a better future, every generation is in reality a desert generation. This, however, is something quite different from what we were taught to understand by the term. According to this reading of it, at least, no second-generation Israeli—and a kibbutz-born one least of all!—could reasonably belong to the "wilderness" category of Israeli Jew. Even the God of Moses, who saw fit to decree that their carcasses "shall fall in this wilderness," confined His wrath to those who were "twenty years old and upward." As to the little ones, He mercifully decided "them will I bring in, and they shall know the land which ye have despised."

These are fairly precise, if rather severe, words to utter. No such clarity can be claimed by those in our midst who had sought to apply the same principle to a later generation of Jews.

("The Desert Fallacy," FEBRUARY 1964)

For a number of years which one would not care to remember, we Israelis have been going around with one nice little chip of wood on our shoulders, which for lack of a better term may be called "the Arab Menace." Now there is something always unattractive about people with long-standing grievances, but in this particular case the drawback was more than just aesthetic. Wittingly or unwittingly, we have allowed our grievance to place us in the pretty uncomfortable position of appearing always at variance with the Arabs and their many aspirations — or at least what the majority of them consider to be their aspirations . . .

The situation is of course greatly accentuated by the way our grievance is translated into an impossibly fastidious attitude to Cairo. When we speak of Egyptian President Nasser's "democracy," for instance, we manage to forget everything we know about Egyptian history and political tradition and become dreamy perfectionists. Arab Socialism? It either does not exist or is in some sinister way connected with a worldwide Communist plot. We also manage to appear as the supporters of the medieval regime of the Imam in Yemen, of the British presence in South Arabia, and of the chauvinistic though conveniently anti-Nasserist Baʿth Party — all in the name of the Arab Menace.

Another, and perhaps greater, disability from which we suffer as a result of carrying this permanent chip on our shoulders has been our apparent failure to see the other fellow's own grievance. In an important and carefully worded interview which he gave to the London *Observer* early this month, Nasser was asked whether, in saying that war with Israel was inevitable, "this means you regard attack from Israel as inevitable but [that] you do not intend to attack yourself?" Nasser's reply was admittedly very cagey ("the Arabs will not accept the *status quo* over Palestine at all . . ."); but he made it quite plain right away that by rejecting the *status quo* he was referring to the refugee problem. "The *status quo* is impossible," he said. "Palestinians were driven out of their homes, their land and their nation."

Now no matter what we in Israel may think of the refugee problem, we will not be able to go on ignoring its existence. The refugees' case as put forward by Nasser . . . is plainly unacceptable as it stands. But the opposing case — which is that, for us, the refugee problem had long since been solved through an exchange of populations whereby we received the Jews of the Arab countries and the refugees moved to these countries where they ought to feel more at home and "in their element" — is bound to seem equally untenable, at least to outsiders . . .

("A Chip on the Shoulder," JULY 1964)

Diary entry

August 1, 1964

The conversation had taken several turns—the Israeli press, apartheid, the London *Times,* the future of African culture; but in the end The Question had to come. "And what do you think of Israel's future relations with the Arab states?" There were five of us: two South Africans of European origin, an English-speaking African intellectual, and two Israeli journalists. One of the South Africans, who had earlier declared that he was "obsessed" by the racial question in his country, hastened to add: "When, in brief, would Israel become a part of the Middle East?" We felt tired and bored, and being at a loss for an adequate answer, we tried to conduct the discussion in such a way as to break up the question into its various components. Shall we start, we ventured, by considering the socio-cultural structure of present-day Israel and try to envisage what it will be like in 10, 20, or 30 years' time?

Then the difficulty arose as to how it was possible to indulge in predictions of this nature when dealing with a country of immigration. Our non-Israeli friends expressed the conviction that no large-scale immigration from the Soviet Union would be allowed for at least two decades, and that one could therefore safely proceed on the assumption that no significant change in the country's demographic or cultural structure would take place during that space of time. But in what way was this likely to affect the future status of Israel in the area? We ventured that as the ideal of a full and really effective cultural amalgamation of the various communities was proving daily more elusive, and as a new leadership must emerge in which the native-born and the non-European population are adequately represented, a process will eventually be started through which, on the one hand, the Arabs may become less suspicious and frightened of Israel and, on the other, the Israelis may start discovering a common language with the Arabs. Such a process may conceivably lead to the setting up of some sort of Middle Eastern federation in which Israel would find her proper place.

"The question is," said our anti-apartheid South African, "what would *precede* such a consummation?" It was obvious that he was not quite convinced that Israel's full integration into the Middle Eastern landscape was possible without much bloodshed and tragedy. "That," came the reply from various directions, "may entirely depend on Nasser's political maturity and foresight—or lack of them." Should he persist in his bellicose mood and try to make good his old threats to push Israel into the sea, he will not only court disaster but may considerably delay the setting in of that same natural process through which Israel can be peacefully integrated into the area. If, on the other hand, Nasser or any other powerful Arab leader of the day should have enough insight and imagination to look 20 years ahead he would give up all hope of destroying Israel, tacitly accept her as she now stands, or even go so far as to formalize this acceptance by actually concluding peace with her. Such a course of action would, it was observed, be the best guarantee for Israel's becoming an integral part of the Middle East.

But do we really and sincerely want Israel to be an integral part of the Middle East? Here the second Israeli in the company wanted to say something. He was young, of very advanced views, and rather left-inclined. He still was far more liberal-minded than we thought, and would not really care if his little Israeli-born granddaughter could speak Arabic. "But," he added gravely, "*I* came here to live as a Jew!" There was a pause, and everybody seemed to be saying, "Why, *but of course!*" "As a European Jew," our Polish-born friend hastened to add, anticipating the objection. Pressed a little further, however, he admitted that what he had in mind was not merely to live as a European *Jew* but in reality *as a European*—"as people live in Paris, Warsaw, Brussels." From then on it was no longer a matter of how Israel should be integrated into the Middle East, but of what sort of a country the two sections of the Israeli population, the Europeans and the non-Europeans, would want to live in.

Not that there was lack of understanding for our European-born Israeli host. After all, culture is a very serious matter indeed, and one does not expect people to discard their age-old cultural patterns overnight. Moreover, our friend being a non-observant Jew, it was only natural that he should not be content with wanting to live just "as a Jew"—whatever that may mean exactly in the present context. Yet his insistence that he came here to live as a European Jew—or simply as a European—could not fail to set us wondering. To start with, what are those of us who did not come from Paris, Warsaw, Brussels, or Prague really doing here? What kind of life we have come to lead here? Have we come to live as Asian, North African, or

"Arab" Jews? Have we come here—those of us, at least, who, like our host, are non-observant—simply to live as Asians, North Africans, or "Arabs"? And if so, how is this wish to be reconciled with that of our Polish-born friend, who came here to live as a European?

It seemed an unanswerable question. Our own feeling was that we had come here to live as no one in particular, neither European nor non-European, but as Jews living together—and that unless we can rediscover the meaning of Jewishness, it is difficult to see how we can live together at all.

SEARCHING FOR A NEW APPROACH

It was roundabout this time, mid-1964, that I decided to give expression to an idea I had contemplated for some time—i.e., that there was a close link between the communal problem and the failure of the Eastern European Zionist establishment to resolve it, on the one hand, and Israel's continuing conflict with and estrangement from the world surrounding it, on the other. Thus, in a long paper I wrote, and for which I chose the title "Israel and Her Neighbours: Notes for a New Approach," I devoted a few pages to this particular aspect of the subject. After analyzing the influences and the ideas that I claimed had shaped the attitude of Israel to the Arab world and to the Pan-Arab nationalist movement, I wrote:

Israelis are of course right in telling Arab nationalists that the Middle East can never be comprehended in exclusively Arab terms. But, then, nor could any of the countries of the region, taken separately. If we exclude the Arab Peninsula, we find that there is not a single Middle Eastern country that can be comprehended in exclusively Arab or any other ethnic terms. Moreover, in a pluralistic Middle East, where Asia, Europe and Africa, Islam, Judaism and Christianity interact freely, the Israelis, too, will be called upon to cease viewing their country in exclusively Jewish terms. Naturally, it will take a good deal of reciprocation on the part of her neighbours to make official Israel proceed in such a novel and revolutionary direction.

Such a new approach to the problems of the area may well work, and at the same time they may be augmented on a deeper cultural level. For there is an additional factor at work here—namely, the introduction into the homogeneous, overwhelmingly Eastern European society of Israel of an important new element following the mass immigration of Jews from

the countries of the Middle East and North Africa. . . . For the temperament of these Middle Easterners, their background, their long experience
of living side by side with Arabs, and their fundamentally different type
of reaction to the non-Jewish world are bound to leave their imprint on
future Israeli-Arab relations. (Another aspect of this question is the position of the so-called "Arab Jews" in Israel. To these Jews, the classic Zionist
approach to the Arab question is totally foreign. The cosmic opposition
which this approach draws between "Jew" and "Arab" places the Middle
Eastern Jew in a pretty intolerable position, in that he seems to conform to
the Eastern European Zionist concept of neither Jew nor Arab. This condemns the Arabic-speaking Jew to a marginal sort of existence culturally,
since the combination in him of both Jewishness and Arabness marks him
as the odd man out.)

The fact is that Israel has now become largely a Middle Eastern country in population as well as in geography. In 1948, the Jewish population
of the area that was to become the State of Israel numbered less than
650,000. Eighteen years later this population has grown more than three-
fold. The majority of the additions hailed from countries of the Middle
East and North Africa, and the result has been that somewhat over half
of Israel's present Jewish population is Middle Eastern, while of the remaining Jewish groups, an increasing number are "technically" Middle
Eastern, having been born in the country, though of European extraction. (Israel's non-Jewish citizens — Moslem, Christian and Druze — constituted about 13 per cent of the total population before the considerable
additions which came with the territorial changes resulting from the Six-
Day War.)

Demographically at least, but to a certain extent culturally too, this development should suffice to answer the Arabs' standing argument against
Israel as an alien creation, a bastion of the West, and a "cancer" in the body
of the Arab world. An additional, if somewhat accidental, consideration
in this connection is that this development was brought about largely by
Arab action which, by making life intolerable for Jewries as old and as
deeply rooted in their countries as those of Yemen, Iraq and Syria, was
instrumental in the mass immigration of these Jewries to Israel.

From a purely "legalistic" point of view, too, this development changes
the right of Israel to exist in the Middle East from the somewhat dubi-
ous basis of the Balfour Declaration and the special claims of the Zionists
to the perfectly normal basis of history, tradition, culture and demogra-
phy. To quote James Parkes, "Israel exists today in the Middle East on
the absolutely normal basis that the majority of its inhabitants are Middle

Easterners and never have been anything else." The fact, moreover, that these Jews are now concentrated in the single area of Israel is the result of local migration and cannot affect their character as Middle Easterners.

Naturally there is nothing automatic or deterministic about these things. The picture is especially confused where the attitude of the Middle Eastern element to the Arabs is concerned. In general discussions in Israel about the country's future relations with its neighbours, it is often argued that far from being better inclined toward the Arabs, the Orientals in Israel are actually more "anti-Arab" than their European compatriots. There is an element of truth in this observation, at least on the surface and as far as these Orientals' initial reactions are concerned. During their first years in Israel, immigrants from the countries of the Middle East and North Africa were bound to feel a good deal of resentment, both at being victimized in their lands of birth and as a result of the hardships they were to face in Israel. Not unexpectedly, many of them tended to vent their anger and their resentment on "the Arabs."

More significantly, coming to a society whose whole set of attitudes, mores and sentiments were strongly slanted in favour of European ways and which was openly contemptuous of the East and its ways, and in which the most observable prestige criterion was affinity to Europe, it was only too understandable to see these immigrants going out of their way to dissociate themselves from their origins and culture, often knowing no better way than to channel their resentments and hatreds toward their former compatriots. But this was bound to be a passing phase, and as far as one can see there is now reason to believe that these "Arab Jews" are gaining enough self-esteem and self-confidence, and discovering enough new things about themselves and their new surroundings, to have a more balanced view of their situation.

Such a development can open up endless new vistas. For one thing, the prevalent image of the Arab as just another version of the European anti-Semite — only a bit worse — is bound to disappear. This depiction of the Arab as a wild, murderously inclined neighbour (an image which, to be fair, has partly been a product of the Arabs' own indiscriminate propaganda and threats) has done much to distort the general picture, and a more sober, historical view of the Arabs will be of decisive importance if relations between Israel and the Arab countries are to be normalized.

For another, the Israelis themselves will gain considerably from having a closer, more realistic look at their own habitat. The founders of Zionism set out to build a model European state, having scarcely been aware of the existence, let alone the status, of Middle Eastern Jewries. It is therefore probably not quite easy for the present leadership of Israel, itself almost exclusively Eastern European by birth and background, to resign itself to the idea of an increasingly Middle Eastern Israel. This no doubt partly accounts for the fact that no serious attempt has ever been made by Israel to present the new realities even as arguments to balance and counter the Arabs' classic propaganda claims against Israel as an alien element and an intrusion. This is a great pity. For in order to make the Arabs accept Israel, it is essential that her present political and cultural elite should do so first.

Needless to say, the Arabs will themselves have their own share of common sense to contribute. First and foremost they will have to realize that they cannot possibly have it both ways. For the ultimate irony of the present situation—i.e., Israel's virtual transformation into a Middle Eastern country—is that it was created by the Arabs themselves. They would not accept the establishment of a Jewish state in Palestine on the basis of its having unique historical claims. They insisted that the claims of the natural majority, the Arabs, were paramount. Then by the work of their own hands they turned Israel into a state where the natural majority demands an independent state of its own. This majority—the Middle Eastern Jews and those born in Palestine—has never known or lived in any other area but the Middle East, and now lives in that part of the Middle East which the Arabs themselves have determined it should live in: This the Arabs will one day have to grasp.

For in their long and fruitful life together, Judaism and Arabic Islam have demonstrated beyond all conceivable doubt that there is sufficient cultural and spiritual common ground between them to make such coexistence possible, desirable and useful. Fundamentally, there exists no opposition between the Jewish tradition and the Arab-Moslem tradition. Indeed, the vision of Israel as an exclusive Jewish state, the view that her integration into the Middle East and its culture spells "assimilation," that the prevailing hostility of the Arabs to Israel amounts to "anti-Semitism," that Arab threats imply murder and pogroms à la the Christian West— these are all largely the products of the collective historical experiences of those in Israel who continue to shape her policies and set her cultural tone.

Despite outward signs to the contrary, there are indications that Israel's neighbours are gradually freeing themselves from the narrow nationalistic view of the Middle East as an "Arab" area. They do, however, seem to insist on viewing it as a non-Western area, especially in the cultural sense of the term. In this sense, a stubbornly "Western" and ethnically exclusivist Israel will probably continue to be considered an alien creation and a legacy of Europe's cultural intrusion in the area. It would probably be no exaggeration to say that this question of identity will remain the crucial one in any appraisal of Israel's future relations with her neighbours and ultimately her whole position in the Middle East. Dr. Charles Malik, leading Lebanese thinker and a former foreign minister, has a few very pertinent things to say on this subject. Pointing out that to establish a state is one thing, to ensure its continued existence another, Malik asserts that "entirely different moral qualities" are required for this latter task. In the struggle for establishment, he writes, "you treat the others as alien forces, to be crushed or pushed back or at least prevented from encroaching upon you; your relation to them is external, summary, destructive, negative; under no circumstances can you allow internal, positive intercourse with them on a basis of equality. But in the struggle for enduring existence you must come to terms with them; you must take their existence positively into account; your idea must be softened and modulated and trimmed to accommodate their idea; you must enter into an interacting relationship with them, based on mutual respect and trust. Whether the leadership and the ethos of Israel are adequate to the requirements of existence, of course only the future can disclose."

These words were written in 1948; yet Dr. Malik's last question remains largely unanswered. To be sure, Israel has proved conclusively that she can ensure her continued existence, at least for the foreseeable future, by the efficiency, brilliance and valor of her defense forces. But to quote Dr. Malik once more, "history has not known an instance of a nation at permanent enmity with its immediate world."

Fundamentally, the Israeli-Arab conflict is a cultural rather than a political one.

This article I sent, I think, to the London monthly *Encounter,* at its own request, since it was planning a special issue devoted to Israel and the Israeli-Arab conflict. For reasons best known to the editors, however, the article was returned to me, accompanied by a letter of apology from the editor of the special issue, whose name I forget.

| THE MYSTERY OF EDUCATION

GENESIS OF A GAP

Of all the controversial issues with which I somehow felt bound to deal in my writings, education was the most sensitive — at least judging from the often violent reactions that came from the powers that be. The way that my involvement in this aspect of the communal-cultural controversy started and then deepened became manifest in the articles I wrote on the subject in the *Jerusalem Post*. What really made me take up this thorny subject was the way the education authorities were trying to come to grips with what came to be known as "the communal gap." My first attempt to come to grips with the problem:

> In the past, listening to the endless, sometimes distinctly self-satisfied chatter about The Huge Gap or reading of the results of the Ministry of Education exams and of how, year after year, the percentage of failure among children of the Oriental communities was very high, I had always suspected that something was basically, disastrously wrong with the educational system itself. It was only this month, however, that I had the opportunity of having a good look at how to open, widen and perpetuate an educational gap — and my thoughts and sympathies on this New Year's Eve must go to all those parents who, like myself, have the otherwise exciting experience of sending their first-born to their first year at school. I am, of course, referring mainly to those mothers and fathers who have more than one child to rear, whose jobs or domestic chores do not allow them to devote much time to their children's education, or who did not have the advantage of having any education themselves.
>
> In particular, I am thinking of parents who either do not know or do not care to remember the principles of algebra — or have no time to attend a special course in that particular subject. For myself, I have really no cause for complaint: Rony's mother happens to have an excellent memory for

such things, and we hope that, with a little luck, our child will eventually get the help he — or rather his teacher — needs in order for him to learn simple arithmetic . . .

One can already hear the usual objections — that for "backward children," or for those children whose parents happen to be "backward" or over-reproductive or just plain ignorant, there are all sorts of special arrangements, such as the extra hour, the longer day, the club and the 10 percent "allowance" for children of the Oriental communities upon their sitting for the Ministry of Education exams. The answer to all these objections is simple and not far to seek: a country does not base its educational system on the capacities of the privileged and then try to make allowances for the majority.

In other words, why make a rule of an exception and then proceed in panic, and when it is almost too late, to make exceptions for what actually is the norm? Why not build an educational system that would take full cognizance of the demographic and human factors *as they actually are?* As to the "10 per cent allowance," it hardly needs emphasizing that it is an insult both to the children and to their parents — not to speak of its absurdity from the purely pedagogical point of view . . .

It is more reasonable, more human and more natural that, taking all factors into account, our school system should be totally "self-supporting" and in no wise dependent on the hypothetical help of a hypothetically educated parent having the money, the time or the inclination to provide such help. If this is not accepted, the educational gap will always be with us, allowing our education authorities the privilege of occasionally making an "exception" here and there and permitting them to express their regret for this yawning gulf.

("Genesis of a Gap," SEPTEMBER 17, 1963)

This was followed by a number of other tries. A few are given here:

Determined to learn something about the workings of our educational system "at the source," I spent an hour or so the other day poring over the 78 questions of the annual *seker* test. I found the experience fascinating and rewarding: I enriched my Hebrew vocabulary by several words and thought that the test itself was, on the whole, well and rather intelligently composed — though I could not help commiserating with the children, who complained that it was "unusually difficult."

It is, however, with another problem that I found myself grappling and for the solution of which I found no clue. The problem, important to all societies but probably crucial in a land of immigration, is how far do material and environmental conditions affect the educational progress of a child? Our education authorities are of the opinion that such conditions are all-important, and that it is due to these — poverty, overcrowding, uneducated parents — that the percentage of failures amongst primary-school children of the Oriental communities has been so high in recent years. There are, on the other hand, those who point out that the authorities tend to exaggerate the effect of these factors, and that too much emphasis on poverty and overcrowding sometimes serves to cover up poor teaching and a faulty system of elementary education.

This landed me in a blind alley, and I decided to consult authorities in the field. Trying to assess the degree to which "intellectual performance is related to . . . characteristics of the home such as socio-economic level or material possessions," C. M. Fleming of the University of London's Institute of Education writes in his book *The Social Psychology of Education:*

Sweeping statements have sometimes been made to the effect that of course the brighter children come from the more prosperous homes; and teachers have often been tempted to advise against continuance of secondary education because of a low level of income. While poverty does result in a dangerous lowering of the level of nutrition, there is . . . reason to believe that the variations which occur from home to home are related to intrinsic characteristics such as attitude and point of view rather than to extrinsic attributes such as prosperity or possessions. When homes are classified according to the occupational level of the parents (or according to any other purely socio-economic criterion) it is found that many dull children come from the A group and many bright children from the groups classified as C or D.

Fleming also refutes the proposition that the intellectual activities, practical skills and social interests of a pupil are decisively determined by the qualities of his parents. ("Jim's father can't spell. He will never do any better." "Margaret's mother is very poor. Too much must not be expected of her." And so on.) The likeness of children to parents, Fleming implies, is no tenet of educational psychology. It has, however, "provided a theoretical justification for caste distinctions and class distinctions for more centuries than are recorded. It has been used as an argument for excluding entrance to certain professions and as an excuse for the shepherding of some into their fathers' occupations. Children have been threatened with the temperamental fate of their fathers and (less often) they have been encouraged to believe in their own potentialities as members of superior groups."

If this shows anything, it shows that we should resist the temptation to use this as a handy alibi for our own failings and start looking for remedies elsewhere. After all, it is nowhere written that the sins of the fathers must be visited upon the children.

("No Handy Alibi," NOVEMBER 12, 1963)

With a few variations, it is almost always the same topic: little Danny is a problem. Whenever Israeli parents get together, it is about some little Danny that they worry: Why can't Danny read? Why (supposing he is doing well at school) is he so undisciplined, so lacking in respect for his elders, so careless about his language, and generally so *unheedful* of what his parents tell him? The trouble is not confined to any specific class or group of classes, communities, religions or cultural groups. Whether the parents come from Berlin or Casablanca, London or Baghdad, the complaint is the same: children are not what they used to be . . .

The trouble with Danny originates in three basic assumptions which for some time have been informing his elders' attitudes to him and to his education. The first is that there exists a child's world that is autonomous and must be left to the children to govern; that adults are there only to help with this government; and that the authority that tells the individual child what to do and what not to do rests entirely with the child's group itself. Thus, by being emancipated from the authority of adults, the child in a sense is banished from the world of grown-ups. He is either thrown back upon himself or handed over to the tyranny of his own group, against which he can neither rebel nor reason, and from which he cannot escape to any other world.

Danny's reaction to this particular brand of pressure tends, often enough, to be either complete conformism or some species of juvenile delinquency, and is frequently a mixture of both. At school, moreover, the situation confronting him is no less perplexing. For — and here we come to our second basic assumption — under the influence of modern psychology, pedagogy has developed into a science of teaching in general, in such a way as to be wholly emancipated from the actual material being taught. The result is that, since the teacher does not need to be trained in his own subject, it frequently happens that he is literally just one hour ahead of his class in knowledge. This in turn means that Danny is actually left to his own devices, but also that the legitimate source of a teacher's authority as the person who knows more and can do more than oneself is no longer effective.

This pernicious role which pedagogy is playing in the troubles besetting Danny would not, however, have been possible were it not for a certain modern theory about learning, which itself is the logical application of the third of our basic assumptions. This is that you can know and understand only that which you have done yourself, and its application to education has been as primitive as it is obvious: to substitute doing for learning. According to this theory, a teacher should not pass on "dead knowledge" but, instead, should constantly demonstrate how it is produced. Closely connected with this theory is the view that a child's characteristic activity lies in play; learning in the old sense, by forcing a child into an attitude of passivity, compels him to give up his natural initiative . . .

Though these reflections were written in a somewhat different context (see "The Crisis in Education," in Hannah Arendt's *Between Past and Future*, Meridian, New York), it has complete relevance to Danny's seemingly inexplicable ways. Writing of the educational crisis in America, Arendt asserts that this crisis "results from the recognition of the destructiveness of these three basic assumptions and a desperate attempt to reform the entire education system."

("The Trouble with Danny," JANUARY 28, 1964)

The gist of a press conference held in Tel Aviv last Thursday, in which the Minister of Education and Culture took part, was that following the introduction of certain new measures in primary education, the bright pupil "will forge ahead much faster"; the average child will "also learn faster"; and the slowest group will progress at its own pace but, in the long run, will also "make great strides forward." This state of near perfection in our primary schools we are promised in about three years' time, when the so-called "Beersheba experiment" has been extended to all the three top grades of these schools. As is well known, the Beersheba plan envisages the division of pupils in the sixth, seventh and eighth grades — i.e., those aged between 11 and 13 — into three groups: advanced, average and slow. The division, which is made on the strength of the pupil's standard in Hebrew, English and mathematics, is based on the same principle as the English system of "streaming," and it can give our education authorities no great comfort to learn that, even as their press conference was proceeding, this system was being effectively demolished in London.

This act of demolition has been performed by a British educationalist, Dr. J. W. B. Douglass, who since the first week of March 1956, has been systematically following the fortunes of some 5,000 children, all born within the same week, and publishing progress reports on his unique follow-up study. His third report, published last week, is entitled "The Home and School: A Study of Ability and Attainment in the Primary School" and deals with the children's primary schooling between 1951 and 1957. The chapter devoted to "streaming," which a *Guardian* writer believes "is going to be quoted for the next half-century," demonstrates how educational selection can in effect be social selection, and shows how education decisions can be "simple self-fulfilling prophecies."

Opponents of "streaming" have for a long time maintained that middle-class children get into the top streams because they have learnt at home to use words precisely. Once in the top stream, they get better verbal training, maintain their superiority and do better still in future tests. Working-class children, on the other hand, find themselves in the lower streams because of lack of stimulation at home — and are then further deprived by getting a relatively inferior schooling. As Douglass comments, "This is an extreme statement of the social bias that might be implicit in early selection by ability."

Now it hardly needs pointing out that, like the working-class children of Britain, many Israeli children begin with the handicaps of a poorer physical and cultural environment and — like them — their disadvantages tend to be intensified. If they live in poor areas, they go to schools with a low record of success; those who are least cared for will find themselves in the "slow group"; their school performance will tend to conform to their classification . . ."

("Obliging Forecasts," FEBRUARY 18, 1964)

"What would Bacon say to our school system?" This improbable question was recently put to Israeli pupils sitting for the *bagrut* (matriculation) English examination. In case you are wondering how a harassed Israeli pupil should know what Francis Bacon would say to our school system, the answer is, as indicated in the exam paper: through a careful reading of his well-known, elegantly phrased but scarcely helpful 600-word essay "Of Studies." "Reading maketh a full man; conference a ready man; and writing an exact man . . . Histories make men wise; poets, witty; the mathematics, subtle; natural philosophy, deep; moral, grave; logic and rhetoric, able to contend: *'Abeunt studia in mores'* " — and such general pedagogical gems. In what way this can qualify a pupil to know what the Viscount St. Albans would say to our school system is something which only our English examiners seem to know.

Abeunt studia in mores [Studies form character], indeed; but one may well ask, Bacon or no Bacon, what role is English supposed to play in our pupil's life? Judging by the standard set by the exam papers at our disposal, the answer must be pretty upsetting. One, we hope exceptional, paper deserves careful scrutiny. It has to do with appreciation, and it sets the pupil an "Unseen Passage" (meaning material not included in the curriculum) on the Finnish secondary school which he is asked to read carefully and then to answer the questions that follow. The paper sets a time limit of 45 minutes to read the passage carefully, translate the "key words" into Hebrew or Arabic, and answer the questions "in English."

I must confess that it took me rather more than that time to decide that what I was holding was a genuine document and not some practical joke. And the question which I would like to ask now is: How does an educationalist who is as inept as the author of the above exam paper become a responsible employee of our Ministry of Education?

("Bacon to the Rescue," APRIL 8, 1964)

DEBATING *HAKBATZAH*

I have spent a good deal of time during the past few months trying to learn something about the workings of our educational system. I must report, however, that the more I have read and seen and heard, the more I find myself helpless and even mystified. The mystery seems to grow deeper and deeper with the weeks, and last week, deciding to trace the subject back to its origins, I found that what would normally seem the simplest of questions are in reality the most difficult of all. To take just one example: *Who, precisely, is responsible for making all those fateful decisions concerning the education of Israel's children? How — and on the strength of what —* are these decisions made? But no! It is simply no use. The questions are far from simple. A simpler one would be, perhaps: What *are* these decisions? What, indeed, are the facts of a given educational situation? In vain does one try to find answers.

Lest the reader start wondering what the fuss is all about, however, I will hasten to furnish a concrete example. Six months ago, 41,000 Israeli boys and girls sat for the *seker;* some three months later, the Minister of Education announced in a press conference in Tel Aviv, on February 13, that in about three years' time the so-called "Beersheba experiment" (wherein pupils in the sixth, seventh and eighth forms of primary school are divided into "advanced," "average" and "slow" groups and taught accordingly) would be extended to all primary schools in Israel. There was no suggestion whatever that (a) the plan had any "retroactive" bearing on the status of pupils in these classes elsewhere, or (b) that it was in any way linked up with the *seker* test held as long as three months previously. Yet if we are to believe our own eyes and take seriously what the education ministry's spokesmen say, this was precisely what happened.

The facts of the case, as far as can be verified, are as follows. On the strength of some apparently confusing statement made by the minister himself, two newspapers came out with the news recently that only 29 percent of those who sat for the latest *seker* had passed the test. No one seemed to have become unduly excited; but the spokesman of the ministry, who does not seem to have yet learned the great advantage of silence in these cases, hastened to issue a denial. First of all, in case you are interested in the genesis of the misunderstanding, the spokesman was there to help you: The origin of the newspapers' "misleading reports," he volunteered, was that their reporters had confused the word "sat" — which the minister actually used — with the word "passed." For what the minister actually said was that 29 percent of all the pupils had *sat for*, not *passed*, the *seker*.

Clearly, this was further confusion. For how could it be that only 29 per cent of the 41,000 pupils had sat for the test when in reality, and by definition, 100 percent of them had sat for it? The spokesman, apparently totally unaware of the implications of what he was saying, was again ready with an explanation. For "purposes of research," he said, the 41,000 pupils who sat for the *seker* at the conclusion of the past school years were placed in four categories: the "advanced," who made up 29 per cent of the total; the "average," totaling 23 per cent; the "below average," who composed 38 per cent; and those whose attainments were "below the minimum" and who made up the remaining 10 per cent. Thus, the spokesman continued, the minister of education did not speak of the number of pupils who had passed the *seker*, but only of the numbers of those who sat for it "and their classification into four groups."

But at what stage, precisely, had the pupils been so classified "for the purposes of research"? On the strength of what had the classification been carried out? And how was it that the minister had chosen to equate the 29 percent "advanced" pupils with those who sat for the test? The confusion is further increased by what the ministry's spokesman had to say further. "The number of pupils who pass the [*seker*] test is determined by the Ministry of Education policy," he said in an interview which he himself afterwards circulated. "[The ministry] fixes a certain number of questions which have to be answered in order to pass the test." His ministry, we are further told by the spokesman, "had fixed two standards [for the test] — one, which is higher, for children of the old *Yishuv* and those of European extraction, and another for the newcomers and for those born in Afro-Asian countries."

Again one is plagued by questions. Who? Why? When? How? *What?* Well, one fact at least we can now boast of knowing: Not 29 but 38.2 percent of those who sat for the *seker* last October passed. But what difference does it make, one way or the other, when — as we are so disarmingly told by its spokesman — the results of the *seker* are predetermined by the ministry itself?

("The Mystery of Education," APRIL 29, 1964)

When does a lofty social ideal become narrow "dogma"? When is a first principle not at all a principle but some derided "cliche"? I could not help asking myself these questions and many equally bewildering ones of a similar nature when reading and rereading the other day the report of an interview given to a *'Al Hamishmar* reporter by Mr. Zalman Aranne, the minister of education and culture. After listening attentively to a set of six very clear, relevant and well-organized questions, we are told, the minister chose to give an "overall answer" preceded by some "general remarks." "There is," the minister started, "no field in which cliches reign so supreme as that of education. Every walk of the country's life has undergone a revolution — but education is still governed by pedagogic, social and party patterns. In this sphere people go on advocating dogmas that stand in opposition to reality."

Coming closer to the point, Mr. Aranne continued: "Here [in education] people make judgements. Experiments and research projects are rejected when they are not in keeping with a certain point of view. And what is most regrettable and worrying of all is that this dogmatism comes precisely from young educationalists. Education is by nature conservative, and I would have understood, and even forgiven, had this attitude been common among old and veteran educationalists. But young ones?" As the interview — or rather the monologue — progresses, we get some idea of the nature of that dogmatism and those cliches which seem to cause our minister so much dismay and bewilderment. The targets, it transpires, are those who oppose the ministry's new policy of *hakbatzah*, or streaming, and the allegedly outdated dogmas and worn-out cliches which these opponents were being accused of holding are none other than the elementary principle of equality of opportunity and the same education for all.

For it is this elementary principle, embodied in the Declaration of Independence, that the policy of streaming has come to negate . . . Indeed, in seeking to justify his new policy, Mr. Aranne claims that "the egalitarianism which was followed until now was no good, and experience has shown that it has failed." Yet when speaking of the streaming experiment, the minister does admit (1) that it has not yet been concluded, and (2) that "it is not so bad if we discard some of its negative aspects." The effects of these so-called negative aspects will be eased, we are promised, by the highly "flexible" use which the ministry will make of the new policy, as well as by other special measures, including the posting of good teachers in the "slow" classes.

The trouble with all these apologetics is, of course, that the ministry, even with the best will in the world, is not likely to be able to control the situation or prevent malpractice. Once the principle of the same schooling for all is discarded, no amount of flexibility or special measures can prevent the development which Aranne's young, cliche-ridden dogmatists seem to fear most—viz., communal segregation in Israeli schools. As though to lend force to these fears and forebodings, the minister himself let the cat out of the bag. In addition to all its merits, he declares, the system of streaming "will create greater opportunities for the advanced pupils." If we fail to furnish these opportunities, he continues, "we are likely to be faced with a state of communal homogeneity in many schools, since parents will not agree to see their children prevented from making progress because of the high percentage of slow pupils." Instead, these parents "would start sending their children to other schools."

Who are these parents whose possible actions the minister fears so? And who are the "slow" children whose percentage is so high in schools? The answers are not far to seek: "The latest *seker* test has proved that a large section of the children of Israelis hailing from Islamic countries belongs to the slow group," the minister tells his interviewer. It is obvious that those who have it in them to influence the Ministry of Education and transfer their children to other schools do not belong to this group of Israelis. And the crucial question now is: Can we afford to let the grocers and the clerks of Solel Boneh, of Kiryat Shmonah, Dimona and Beersheba dictate our educational policies by threatening to transfer their children to other schools? Yet even this would perhaps have been tolerable were it not for the astounding amount of prejudice governing not only these fat grocers and petty clerks but also a good many of the teachers. Here, too, one can take a clue from the interview in question. Seasoning his sentences with Russian and Yiddish words, Mr. Aranne asked his interlocutor: "I hope you at least know Yiddish; otherwise I would altogether despair of you!"

("Streaming into Despair," MAY 12, 1964, NOT PUBLISHED)

The Israeli elementary schools are, in the opinion of the people of Israel, basic and necessary parts of our democracy. I am convinced that they must, and I hope that they do, provide equal opportunity for every child. This means that those at the bottom can compete through education for life's prizes with those at the top. All that is needed is brains, a will to do hard work, and plenty of ambition. This basic belief in the democratic functioning of our schools is only partly true. The book on which this article is based—*Who Shall Be Educated?* by W. Lloyd Warner, Robert J. Havighurst, and Martin B. Loeb (Harper & Bros., New York, 1944)— describes how our schools, functioning in a society with basic inequalities, facilitate the rise of a few from lower to higher levels but continue to serve the social system by keeping down many people who try for higher places. The teacher, the school principal, the school board, as well as the pupils themselves, play their roles to hold people in their places in our social structure.

If the Israeli faith in the school system as a democratic force is to become less fictional, we must examine the relevant facts and determine what distorts this picture . . . The Israeli school reflects the socio-economic order in everything that it does: in what it teaches, whom it teaches, who does the teaching, who does the hiring and firing of the teachers, and what the children learn in and out of the classroom. The curricula of our secondary schools provide early pathways to success and failure; they operate in a different way on the several class levels; and they are used in a different way by the children of the higher and lower levels. It is apparent that the secondary school curriculum is a mechanism which helps perpetuate our class order.

The most significant feature of our status order is the emphasis placed on the social elevators which take the more fortunate up to the heights and drop the less fortunate to the basement. The chapter on social mobility tells how Israelis use such powerful forces as money, talent, beauty, sex and education to climb from the lower social levels to those higher.

The place of the Oriental in our society in many respects is like that of a member of the lower classes. He has many of the same penalties applied to him and is prevented from enjoying many of the same opportunities as the latter. But there are profound differences between Orientals and lower-class Ashkenazim which have fundamental consequences for the kind of education provided for them. A whole chapter in this book is devoted to an analysis of how the education of Orientals works in our caste system. Because Israelis are deeply concerned about increasing the quality and quantity of democratic thought and action, in the final chapter a set of principles is stated as a foundation for the betterment of educational methods. Concrete proposals are then offered which we believe are necessary for the advancement of democratic education.

("The Challenge of Unequal Opportunity,"
JUNE 30, 1964, NOT PUBLISHED)

Chapter 12

THE DEBATE INTENSIFIES

MAPAI STRIKES BACK

The higher one's view of the human potential, the more one is liable to dislike school and the educational system as they actually stand. This is true in all the civilized world and wherever children are sent to school. The fact that the resultant discussion, heat, and often anger serve very little purpose does not seem to affect the situation: theory keeps piling on theory and argument on argument, sometimes with little regard to the facts. As Martin Mayer, an American who has written a remarkable book on the process of education in his country, put it so well: "Changes are hurled and slogans coined," he wrote, "and cliches stand upon the ground in rows like death's heads in a looted graveyard" (*The Schools,* 1961).

One trouble, of course, is that although we all take an intense interest in the schooling of the young, very few of us know much about the actual process of education. Another difficulty is that, despite all the nice theories and the elaborate philosophies, teachers and children, parents and administrators, critics and professors all alike refuse to behave in that neat statistical manner which can make a commentary really valid — naughtily, and rather irritatingly, insisting on behaving like all other mortal human beings. This places all concerned in a pretty unenviable position. The other day, for instance, discussing the subject with a high official of our Ministry of Education, we were told that there are pupils now in their eighth or seventh year of schooling whose standard of achievement is as low as that of the fifth or even the fourth year, and that this alone would be enough justification for the ministry's decision to introduce *hakbatzah* (streaming).

Who let these pupils reach the seventh and eighth forms when they ought to be in the fourth or fifth? Who plans the schools? Who determines the curriculum? Who trains and appoints the teachers? Who makes it possible for pupils to go up from one form to another, and on the strength of what? Finally, does not this argument in favour of *hakbatzah* in reality constitute an eloquent indictment of the whole elementary-school system as well as those in charge of it? Our layman's queries and questionings had no end. The heat, the anger, the sorrow, the bitterness were almost tangible.

Not that our interlocutor was entirely at a loss for answers and counter-arguments. Children did not grow up in a vacuum, the argument ran. Backward environment, poor surroundings, the absence of a "cultural atmosphere," the ignorance of parents or their refusal to help with the education of their children, the lack of an educational tradition among certain communities — all these factors have a share in the responsibility, we were told. Pressed further, the high official cited other, more "objective" difficulties having to do with the educational authorities rather than the unfortunate parents and the poor surroundings and the humble homes. Training and supplying better and adequately paid teachers means more funds and more manpower, it was pointed out. A longer school day? Well, that is a budgetary problem, besides having to do with the availability of more teachers and better school accommodations. But the ministry was trying and trying yet again.

Truth to tell, we were not convinced. We thought that a great wrong was being perpetrated, that the sins of the fathers were being heartlessly visited upon the children, and that if the ministry put its mind to it, funds could be found, teachers trained and paid better, and accommodation provided. Above all, our layman's instinct kept telling us that in introducing *hakbatzah*, the ministry was putting the cart before the horse. Instead of effecting overall reform of a plainly faulty system, resort was being had to all sorts of ineffectual, dangerous, and ultimately extremely harmful devices. Back home, rather perplexed and somewhat dispirited, we picked up a battered paperback edition of Alfred North Whitehead's *The Aims of Education*. "When one considers in its length and in its breadth," this remarkable philosopher and educator wrote almost forty years ago, "the importance of this question of the education of a nation's young, the broken lives, the defeated hopes, the national failures, which result from the frivolous inertia with which it is treated, it is difficult to restrain within oneself a savage rage."

Reading this gave us some wry solace.

("The Savage Rage," JUNE 16, 1964)

Three weeks later, responding to a letter I received privately from a reader, I sent this column in. Though it was duly printed, the editors made certain changes and "amendments" that they thought would soften the tone, though they preserved the title I gave the piece, "Why Climb Mountains?"

On the day the column appeared, July 7, 1964, I called Lurie to protest what I considered a distortion of my style and presentation. This was followed by a lengthy letter.

July 7, 1964
Dear Ted,

. . . The dismemberment of the luckless column was such that, believe it or not, it became far more bitter, pointed and vicious than it was before the operation was undergone . . .

So that I am now being blamed for saying things which I did not *quite* say. I don't know who made these cuts, and I don't care either, but I am sure that the editor was not aware of what he or she was doing. We have to face it, Ted: all public office is fatiguing and full of headaches — and editing a daily is public office. Therefore, if a paper wants to print serious stuff and serious ideas about serious matters of national importance, then it should see to it that the stuff is tackled in a workmanlike, unhurried and leisurely manner rather than read at midnight or thereabouts, after one had written a leader and seen to a hundred small and nerve-racking little things. I send my columns early enough in the week for them to be considered at length and carefully — and for me to be contacted in case there are hitches.

And now I would like to come to the main point of our conversation — namely, my writing on education. Now, I am a fairly reasonable fellow, and I would readily see a point when it is honestly and straightforwardly made. I would, for instance, immediately stop writing about education in the *Post* if I am told (1) that my uncompromising tone injures certain people and institutions, and (2) that the *Post* is in no position to antagonize same. Your suggestion, on the other hand, that because I am a complete ignoramus about education I should stop writing about the subject is untenable on many, many counts. To begin with, education is not quite chemistry or medicine or engineering or even economics. Your military reporter is not, as far as I know, an ex-general or even a graduate of a military college. But why go far? I gather that in a few months you are going to have an education department — to be run by your present parliamentary correspondent. Can you say in fairness that he is a trained expert on education? He will, of course, undergo some apprenticeship — get to places and see things and hear opinions — but then that is what I have been trying to do. Let us be frank about this, Ted. I suspect that it is only those who can please the king — i.e., conform to the ministry's ideas and methods — who will ever be allegedly knowledgeable about matters educational, at least in the eyes of the ministry. The rest will *always* be ignoramuses — or ignorami. This is how it is about education — and not only in Israel, though here it is rather more so than elsewhere. The subject is such, ignorance of it is so complete, feelings about it run so high, that the same man can be at once and at the same time a fine expert on education and a complete ignoramus — depending on which side of the fence we stand on.

As I tried to explain to you over the telephone, however, the subject of *hakbatzah* is in one valid sense not at all "education" — and that you can be a total ignoramus about education *and* have the right to fight it tooth and nail. *Hakbatzah* is a social problem which concerns the sociologist more than it does the pedagogue. Mr. Aranne, I know, has gathered some signatures: 1,900 teachers and principals were asked if they opposed *hakbatzah,* and very few of them turned out to do so. Here, I concede, one should know something about the workings of the educational system to solve the mystery. Well, I happen to know this much: As far as teachers are concerned, it is infinitely easier to teach a so-called homogeneous class than a mixed one, and if the teacher is — as many of our elementary school teachers unfortunately are — concerned more with her private affairs than by education and knows hardly a thing about teaching, then it takes no unusual knowledge of the subject to guess why Aranne's teachers voted for *hakbatzah*. It takes real pedagogues to teach mixed groups, and they are mostly improvised teachers! As to the principals, it may be heartless to say this, but they get more pay if they have more classes, and *hakbatzah* is going to mean more classes. Aranne also boasts that *the parents,* too, are for *hakbatzah.* I leave it to you to decide *what* parents are for *hakbatzah;* it is plainly those who have been weeping over the lowering of the standard of their children's schooling by being taught together with the "slow ones" and who, as Aranne himself once said in so many words, threatened transferring their children to other schools if no solution would be found to this problem. Well, now that Aranne *has* found a solution how could these parents possibly oppose *hakbatzah?* As for the parents of the slow ones, I maintain that they are either too inarticulate to express an opinion or do not care enough.

No, the question of *hakbatzah* is not such a pedagogic mystery. It is not even an educational subject, strictly speaking. It is a social and communal subject, and no Israeli who cares about the future of this country and who also knows the dangers inherent in the system will ever support it. You ask who is against. Well, everybody who has ever written about it! You say quote me some. Well, *you* quote me a single one favouring it! I am aware that the minister is now, or has already, organized some support for it, precisely to balance the wave of attacks the policy has faced. I am sure he will sell you some, and I think it is proper to buy. But for heaven's sake give the other side a chance to state its point. I shall go even further and say that this is one of the rare occasions where a paper like the *Post* ought to adopt a cause and hammer it day and night. It is a worthy cause, a just and useful one, and a newspaper can only gain in stature by adopting such causes. Failing this, at least give both the pros and cons. Your solution — that Rejwan should no longer write about something of which he knows absolutely nothing — is no solution at all. For one thing, it is not at all *true:* as I told you, I know no more about Egypt or Syria than I do about one or two aspects of education in Israel . . .

I wrote this letter not knowing what Lurie was going through in the aftermath of my column. For, as I was told later, early on the same morning on which the column appeared, Lurie was awakened from his sleep. The night before, as on almost every working night, he had gone to bed very late and, in the normal course of events, would have gone on sleeping until about ten that morning. But the call was urgent and the caller a man of consequence. Zalman Aranne was calling to say he wanted to see Lurie in his office at the ministry immediately.

Lurie must have known the reason for the call and the summons. For sometime previously, Aranne had been hinting — to put it rather mildly — at his displeasure with what a certain Nissim Rejwan was writing about his education policies, especially insofar as these affected the chances of children of Oriental newcomers. Apart from subjects that could be described as purely pedagogical, such as the level of English taught and the new teaching methods in mathematics, my criticism of Aranne's policies had concentrated on two main devices introduced during his long service as minister of education — namely, school streaming (*hakbatzah*) and what was meant to constitute reverse discrimination in favor of Oriental children taking the *seker* examinations at the conclusion of their elementary schooling. The device consisted of a discount in marks, so that all Oriental children were allowed to pass the exams and move on to high school even if they attained lower marks than the regulations demanded, whereas their Ashkenazi peers had to get the marks specified by the system.

But besides those columns on education that aroused the ire of Aranne and his senior staff, the *Jerusalem Post* had another set of troubles with the party of whose old guard Aranne was a prominent member. Following Ben-Gurion's "resignation" from the premiership in the autumn of 1963, he and a group of his followers — mainly Moshe Dayan and Shimon Peres — formed a new political party, which contested the elections scheduled for late 1965. That party, Rafi, was a fierce critic of the government that Levi Eshkol succeeded Ben-Gurion in heading, and the all-powerful Mapai used to be highly sensitive about which of its members and camp followers were in open or secret sympathy with the new party. Both Ted Lurie and his second in command, Lea Ben-Dor, were suspects, although aside from the latter's lifelong admiration for Dayan, and Lurie's old association with Peres, the paper treaded very carefully so as not to anger the real bosses.

As far as I was concerned, from what I gathered about Rafi's foreign and security policies I rather preferred the Eshkol crowd. I remember a fierce attack that Rafi's weekly, *Mabat Hadash (New Outlook)*, carried in one of its early issues against Eshkol's repeated calls for peace with the Arab states. The writer, whom I couldn't identify and who I thought wrote under a pseudonym, took Eshkol to task for seeking to make peace with the Arabs when — among other "outstanding" issues — Jerusalem was still divided! Although I did not put much store by Eshkol's calls, I found this piece of reasoning against Arab-Israeli peace outrageous.

But even before this "discovery," I was completely out of sympathy for the men who made up Rafi's leadership. Early in the proceedings, when they were busy forming their new party, Teddy Kollek called me on the phone and suggested to me that I join the group. Kollek, who had been director-general of the prime minister's office at the time I was offered the editorship of *Al Yawm*, must have known that I did not belong to Mapai or to any other political party. He must also have read my columns in the *Post* and known what I thought on a number of issues. He was, however, no doubt under the impression that any critic of the establishment would be willing to be a founding member of the new party. I thought he was a little shocked, not to say disappointed, by my declining the offer on the spot.

Aranne knew better than to identify me as a secret Rafi man working for Mapai's downfall. Instead, he bluntly accused Lurie of using me and my strong views about his educational policies as a means of undermining the Eshkol government and indirectly aiding and abetting Rafi. The occasion for Lurie's summons that morning was my column titled "Why Climb Mountains?" which was occasioned — as I said in the opening paragraph — by a letter I had received from a reader in Bat Yam and that gave me the shock of my life. The reader, who had a distinctly central European name but who asked to remain anonymous, opened his letter with a kind word or two about my articles in the *Post*, adding, however — with no prior warning of any kind — that after reading "The Savage Rage," my latest column on education in Israel: "I am all for your becoming Minister of Education."

In those days I used to write in the lordly "we," a habit that I think I had picked from the *New Yorker*. In the column that so angered Aranne, I went on to quote from my Bat Yam fan: "And, infinitely embarrassing though it is for us to mention this, he did not seem to be joking: 'Everybody,' he went on, 'is busy plastering over the educational structure because they can't seem to realize that it is a faulty foundation that is to blame. Let us hope that part of this structure does not cave in some day and hurt us. Please keep it up . . .' This made extremely depressing reading and, instead of 'keeping it up,' we decided then and there not to touch the subject of education any more. It was no use. It would seem that if you read the papers, and have a sense of responsibility and some remnants of public spirit, then the only way for you not to write about education is either to be dead or give up in utter despair . . ."

And so on. The subject of the article, however, was English and the matriculation (*bagrut*) exams in English. Aranne's fury — for that is what it was — centered on this last sentence, and he accused Lurie and the *Post* of being secret followers of Rafi and of using my preoccupation with the subject of education simply as another way to fight Mapai and the Eshkol government. I will presently relate how the interview between Aranne and Lurie affected my relations with the *Jerusalem Post* and ultimately led me to stop writing for them altogether. Here I want to tell the story of how Mapai and the Labour establishment in those days had an almost uncontested power over the *Post*.

Relations between the *Post* and its editors on the one hand, and between Mapai and the Labour establishment on the other, remained tense and rather unhappy throughout 1964 and 1965, although Lurie and Ben-Dor tried their best to appease the powers that be and went out of their way to appear neutral in what seemed to be a naked and sometimes even an equal struggle for power. Mapai's secretary-general at that time was Reuben Barkat, who had been ousted from the directorship of the Histadrut's Political and Arab departments in the early 1960s, when Pinchas Lavon suspected him of undermining his position and siding with Ben-Gurion in the notorious Lavon Affair. Generally speaking, the leadership of Mapai in those days consisted of men who were wise in the ways of politics and political infighting, and there was, of course, no question of taking a drastic step against any of the men suspected of supporting Rafi or being guilty of other kinds of misdemeanors, before the 1965 parliamentary elections were held and the results known. After all, it was Rafi's first election campaign, and no one was sure, especially because nobody seemed to know exactly how many votes — and whose — the Grand Old Man (Ben-Gurion) would muster.

As it turned out, the elections proved something of a disappointment for Rafi, and the glorious political machine in Mapai's headquarters in Hayarkon Street emerged victorious — proving again the thesis that he who holds the reins of power and the sources of funds tends to prevail. As soon as the results were made known and a new coalition government was formed, leaving Rafi lamely in the opposition, the time was deemed to have arrived to settle a few outstanding accounts.

In September 1964, I arranged to see Lurie when we were staying with my wife's family in Jerusalem for the weekend. It was a Friday evening, and Lurie chose to see me at his office when nobody except the sentry was there. He wanted to have my opinion or advice on a personal matter: he was being pressed to resign and did not know quite how to respond. At that time I was more or less in the same boat and could offer no useful counsel, though in the course of our long chat, Lurie said to me in all seriousness, "Be Mapai and you will be offered to replace me as editor." He made it clear, however, that, after consulting with a few friends and thinking the matter over at length, he had decided to stick it out and wait for the storm to pass. He quoted with approval the gist of the advice given him by his friends — something to the effect that it would be better to wait and see — "and who knows what may happen next?"

He did, and so did Lea Ben-Dor, and eighteen months or so afterward something did happen, something so big and crucial that even Rafi, together with the hated Herut and the Liberals (then aligned in Gahal), was invited to join a "national unity government," the better to face what was presented as the mortal danger of an Egyptian attack.

Following the resounding victory that Israel achieved in the six days of war in June 1967, there prevailed an air of complete national reconciliation. Everybody suddenly fell in love with everybody else. Levi Eshkol, although said to be bitter at the thought that since he was no longer minister of defense, credit for the six-day victory had been snatched from him by Moshe Dayan, a man whom Eshkol had said some quite unflattering things about only a few short months previously, gave a festive public address in which he announced that there were no more rifts in the nation. If I remember well, Eshkol said something to the effect that all those problems—such as the struggle between Right and Left, rich and poor, Ashkenazim and Sephardim—were now dead and gone, and the nation again united as one man.

*T*he column that had so enraged Aranne was, of course, not the first that I was to devote to the education system and its failures. Nor was the *Post* usually too eager to publish these laments on what I perceived as the disastrous results the system was bound to have on the future of the younger generation of Oriental immigrants. What might have been the first such outburst, which was never published, I titled "Sympathetic Attitudes." It was meant to appear in the *Post* on April 4, 1961, and I give it here in full.

Being possessed of a great passion for the exact quotation and having little use for précis and paraphrase, we have always experienced a certain amount of frustration when reading newspaper accounts of Knesset debates. Naturally, the frustration becomes acuter when the subject is of special interest to us, and recently, when the Knesset finally got down to debating Minister of Education Zalman Aranne's report on the work of his ministry, one felt sorry one was not there to hear for oneself. The following day, however, under the heading "Aranne warns against educational conservatism," we read in this paper a brief account of the reply the minister gave at the conclusion of the Knesset debate on his ministry's budget.

Our curiosity only deepened, however. "He was especially sharp," the good reporter wrote, "in replying to the attacks of Mrs. Ruth Hektin (Ahdut Ha'avoda) and Mrs. Emma Talmi (Mapam). He declared that they were both 'prisoners of their own cliches' in their criticism of the ministry's experiment with homogeneous classes set up in Hebrew, mathematics and English in the top three grades of elementary school." Especially sharp—and to *two* ladies! What could the minister have possibly said? Reading an account in *Ma'ariv* a few hours later only deepened the mystery. "Mr. Aranne," we read, "rejected this argumentation [of Mrs. Hektin and Mrs. Talmi] in extremely harsh terms—so much so that he often had to stop short in the middle so as not to lapse, as he himself put it, into unparliamentary expressions and adjectives."

Well, there was nothing to do about it but to obtain the appropriate Knesset minutes, we decided. But while we were awaiting the minutes, Mr. Aranne came to our rescue with a letter to *Ma'ariv*, signed by himself. The letter purported to be a correction. After citing the paper's correspondent's description quoted above, the minister provided the exact words uttered by him as recorded in the Knesset minutes. These were: "Out of *Ahavat Yisrael* [love of Israel], and perhaps out of a sympathetic attitude to the Daughters of Israel, I don't want to state how I would define this argumentation (that is to say, of Knesset Members R. Hektin and E. Talmi)."

Now, one really does not pretend to know what, precisely, is "parliamentary language"—and in what way, exactly, it differs from ordinary human parlance. But to us it seems obvious that instead of correcting the impression the report in *Ma'ariv* was liable to make, Mr. Aranne has managed merely to harden it. Whether this was his intention, one of course cannot tell. But just consider: what terrible things would the minister have said in describing "this argumentation" had he not been guided by *Ahavat Yisrael* and sheer sympathy for the Daughters of Israel, whom apparently he did not want to insult just because they belong to the same sex as the two lady members of the House?

Really, one can hardly believe one's eyes. A friend of ours, one of the good Daughters of Israel to whom Mr. Aranne has displayed so much charity, suggested that Jewish women all over the world start writing letters to the minister of education, thanking him for sparing their reputation in this gentlemanly manner, and for his sympathetic and considerate attitude to their kind. Well they might! For ourself, we would just like to know what Mr. Aranne's reaction would be if someone were to say, in or out of the Knesset, something like the following: "Out of *Ahavat Yisrael*, or perhaps out of a sympathetic attitude to the males of Israel, I don't want to state how I would define the manner in which Mr. Aranne has replied to his two lady critics."

But God forbid that anyone should be so charitable to the males of Israel!

1965, THE WATERSHED

It never rains but it pours. In addition to all the problems that my ouster from the editorship of *Al Yawm* created for me and for the household, another fight was brewing, this time with the *Jerusalem Post*. For with the onset of 1965, there was no mistaking where my old passion for definitions was leading me. A series of five articles published in the spring of that year in the *Jewish Observer*, under the general title "Israel in the Middle East," could be said to constitute a first serious attempt to grapple with some of the basic ideological problems surrounding all three of my public preoccupations—the ethnic problem, the status of the Arabs in Israel, and the Arab-Israeli conflict.

The first article, dealing with how Zionists regarded—and defined—Arabs and Arabism, had the title "The Doctrine That Failed." In it I tried to show that the Zionists themselves were among the most consistent advocates of Arab nationalism and Pan-Arabism, and cited Ben-Gurion and some of his pronouncements on the subject.

In the second I wrote briefly about Muslim-Jewish relations in the past and tried to show how anti-Semitism had neither historical nor cultural roots in Arabic Islam.

The third part of my dissertation was devoted to a discussion of Israel's place in the Middle East. In it I argued against those Israeli leaders who proclaimed almost daily that Israel was culturally a part of Europe, though situated in the Middle East.

The fourth installment had the title "Forward from Pan-Arabism," and its thesis was that there was already a tendency in the Arab world away from the unrealistic tenets of political Arab nationalism and Pan-Arabism.

And in the fifth and concluding article, "Israel: A Bold Look Ahead," I tried indirectly to show that Israel ought to be much less guided by Pan-Jewish concepts and should accept that, geographically and culturally, it is a Middle Eastern country. The article also contained a passage contesting the thesis that Israel's integration into the Middle East spelled "assimilation," as this term was understood by Jews in the Christian West.

I wrote the *Jewish Observer* series shortly after returning from a three-month stay in London: I had replaced Jon Kimche as editor of the weekly for a few weeks while he was on a leave of absence. I sent it to Kimche sometime in January 1965, and in that same month there began what seemed to be a final break between me and the establishment. Trouble had been brewing for some time. The timing and form of the rupture had to do with the newly appointed advisor to the prime minister on Arab affairs—a man with a long record of work for the Israeli security authorities (a euphemism for the secret services known in Israel as the Shin Bet). Using all the wiles and devious ways of his profession, Shmuel Toledano tried—and managed without much difficulty—to accomplish what his predecessor, Rehav'am Amir, had apparently refused to do. I recorded my first encounter with him in a piece I intended to publish—but didn't—shortly after leaving my job as editor of *Al Yawm*.

"It's altogether foolish to speak of *Israeli* Arabs," said the high-ranking official with a tone of finality. "They belong to another nationality."

"Another nationality than which?" My reaction came almost involuntarily, and except for what seemed to be a genuine look of shock in his ever wide-open eyes, the official did not respond. I then realized how ill advised my question was. A question like that, coming from a man holding the sort of position I held, could have been interpreted in either one of two ways—as being incredibly stupid or needlessly provocative.

Yet the question was legitimate. Like most of Israel's fundamental problems, that of the Arabs' precise status as citizens of the state has never been faced squarely by the government, the Zionist parties, or the Arabs themselves. There has been, to be sure, much talk about "equality," "integration," "loyalty to the state," "preservation of the [Arabs'] national culture," and so on. But what seems to me the cardinal problem—the place an "Arab" in a "Jewish" state—has never got the treatment it deserves.

Thus, though it was obvious from the beginning that I could not see eye to eye with the high-ranking official on the intricate issue of nationality, I still sought an opportunity to discuss the subject with a man whose approach was radical enough to declare "Israeli Arab" a contradiction in terms. It never crossed my mind that the issue was one of those that were simply not to be discussed—that, in other words, the statement that an *Israeli* Arab "belongs to another nationality" was something in the nature of an unquestionable truism.

At the time of my meeting with Toledano, in December 1965, I was only beginning to grasp the depth of the dilemma posed by any serious treatment of the problem of the Arabs of Israel. But that realization didn't come all at once. For a considerable time the Eastern European Zionist establishment's attitude to the Arabs had been striking me as part and parcel of its attitude to everything non-Western. At about that time I remember telling a minor establishment figure, "Many of our troubles will end when this state decides to treat as full human beings first its Oriental citizens, then its Arab inhabitants, and finally its Arab neighbours—in that order."

The last quarter of 1965 was a time of hope in Israel. The general elections had just been held: the "moderate" Mapai-Ahdut Ha'avodah alignment led, and Ben-Gurion and Dayan's group, Rafi, received far less support that it had expected and thus had to remain out in the cold. Levi Eshkol, a man of a moderate, congenial temperament, was to continue at the premiership, his authority now much reinforced by an overwhelming and clear-cut mandate against his bitterest opponents, Ben Gurion and his group. Living up to his public image, Eshkol gave an interview to the Histadrut daily, *Davar,* on the morrow of his party's victory, and in it he declared that "a new era" was at hand in the government's policy toward Israel's Arab inhabitants: from now on the Arabs would be granted complete equality.

Coming from a man of Eshkol's reputation, and coinciding with a political constellation that was assumed to give the prime minister a free hand in the treatment of more basic issues, the interview struck me as something more than the usual run of double-talk and rhetoric to which we had been accustomed. Something, I thought, was at long last "moving" — something worthy of serious attention and, perhaps, cultivation. It was then that I decided to submit my questions to the prime minister — questions that eventually led to that fateful meeting with Toledano, when I, for the first time in my fifteen years in Israel, got a clear and honest definition of the place of a non-Jew there.

Eshkol's *Davar* interview was published early in November. On the 29th of that month, the prime minister was to be the guest of a committee of daily-newspaper editors at a luncheon given in the PM's honor every year on the anniversary of the adoption by the United Nations General Assembly of the Palestine partition plan on November 29, 1947. Editors' written questions were to be submitted two or three weeks ahead. These were my three:

1. A former high government official [the reference was to Shimon Peres, former deputy minister of defense and one of Ben-Gurion's most trusted assistants and disciples] has just revealed that General de Gaulle had at various occasions during Ben-Gurion's rule offered to mediate between Israel and her Arab neighbors, and that Ben-Gurion had declined the offer in each case. Would the government go on declining such offers should a third party make them?

2. In your interview in *Davar* you spoke about a new era for the Arabs of Israel and said they would from now on be granted complete equality. What measures are being taken, or contemplated, to see to it that such full equality is attained?

3. Will Arab citizens be allowed to purchase homes in Carmiel, the new development town currently being built?

Eshkol ignored the questions — all three of them. No doubt one of his aides never submitted them to him or considered them irrelevant — or too embarrassing. What is certain is that they were referred to Toledano to see what sort of weird animal was editing an Arabic daily for which he, Toledano, was nominally responsible. This was made clear to me at our meeting, when Toledano asked what on earth was I talking about. "Carmiel is being built with Jewish money on Keren Kayemet (Jewish National Fund) land. How could we permit Arabs to build or purchase homes there?" It was at this same point that Toledano was to stress the logical contradiction in the expression "Israeli Arab."

ERIC ROULEAU AND DAVID LAZAR

Eric Rouleau, then *Le Monde*'s Arab affairs editor, came to Israel for a fairly extended visit sometime in October or November 1965. He was accompanied by his wife, Rosy, and he called one day asking to have a talk with me. Rachel and I decided to invite the couple for dinner — and being our naive selves, we also decided to invite Shmuel Toledano and his wife. It was a Saturday night, and most of the time was spent in a conversation conducted largely between Rouleau and Toledano, the latter trying his best to sound "liberal" and "different," as usual, in his approach to the intricate business of dealing with Israel's Arab citizens.

As far as "work" was concerned, Rouleau thus had no chance of having the chat he wanted with me. Moreover, although I met him again — probably at Rashid Hussein's place in Ramat Gan — we again had no chance of talking. He was interested in an in-depth chat on the ethnic problem in Israel rather than in what I thought about the position of Israel's Arabs. And so, finally, by way of compensating him for the interview he never got, I gave him an offprint of my 1964 article in *Midstream*, "Israel's Communal Controversy," telling him it contained practically all I had to say on the subject.

More than three months later, Rouleau sent me cuttings of a series of articles he had written for *Le Monde;* one attributed to me a remark to the effect that when the Eastern European Zionist establishment spoke of "educating" the Orientals, what it really meant was to "Westernize" them. Although he did not refer to my *Midstream* article, Rouleau had the decency to imply that he was quoting from something I had *written.*

Rouleau's articles were received with the usual outcry in Israel — pro-Arab, anti-Israeli, a nonentity of Egyptian origin, but above all, "a self-hating Jew." Somehow my name got embroiled in the ludicrous fracas. David Lazar, literary editor of *Ma'ariv*, belonged to that generation of Polish Jewish scribblers, liberally dubbed "publicists," who, with little of substance to say but with a great deal of space to fill, had their way with words. Lazar attacked Rouleau viciously and made what he must have considered "hay" of others whose pronouncements he cited. When my turn came, however, he was far more "friendly" and circumspect, but by no means less vicious. After telling an old tale about a rabbi and his assistants, he added that Rouleau, too, had assistants "whom he names and— to our great sorrow—the majority of whom are Orientals."

So far, so good. But then this:

By the way, we are quite surprised at our friend Mr. Nissim Rejwan, editor of the Arabic-language daily *Al Yawm*—an educated Jewish immigrant from Iraq and a talented journalist—for the modest "stratum" he contributed to the libel-ridden construction built by Rouleau by saying that, when Israelis speak about providing education to the Oriental communities, what they actually have in mind is to turn these people into Westerners. What does Mr. Rejwan actually mean? When teaching Yemenite or Moroccan children the poems of Bialik or Tchernichovsky, or reading together with them the stories of Peretz and Agnon, would that be considered "Western" education and thus a danger to these children? And what does our friend Rejwan suggest they should be taught? The epic poems of Imru el-Qais [Imru al-Qays] or the *Koran?* Would that be the right education?

Lazar then came up with this typical piece of prose: "Okay, from now on we give up Shakespeare and Beethoven, Oestrach [David Oistrakh] and Yehudi Menuhin. We broadcast only the songs of the great Egyptian singer Um Kulthum and belly-dancing music."

Lazar's diatribe was instantly put to use by those of the establishment who already had made up their minds to get rid of me, and I knew that I had to do something to defend myself. But I was reluctant to engage in such a vulgar-toned discussion, and in the end scrapped the letter that I had written to the editor of *Ma'ariv*, especially since the paper printed two other letters criticizing Lazar. In my letter I placed the whole controversy in context and explained to what specific pronouncements my remark had referred. I also cited statements by Yizhar Harari and then–finance minister Pinhas Sapir: they had clearly implied that what was lacking in Orientals was not "education" but some other unspecified qualities necessary for taking one's rightful place in a country said to be part and parcel of Europe and Western civilization.

A few days after Lazar's article was published, I was asked to see Toledano for a chat. I interrupted a short holiday and met him at a Tel Aviv cafe, and after a good deal of beating about the bush, he said something to the effect that the Histadrut had announced that it would cease subsidizing *Al Yawm* if the editor was not replaced—and that if I were to insist on remaining in the job, the paper would then have to be closed!

*W*hen, sometime in the late seventies, things came to a head in the leadership of the so-called Council of the Sephardi Community in Jerusalem, David Siton, the executive director, wrote a letter to the editor of *Ha'aretz*. In that letter Siton sought to explain the background of the rift between him and Elie Eliachar, who had just been eased out of his decades-old presidency of the council. The central point in the letter was that the constitution of the council spoke about promoting the cause of the Sephardi-Orientals in Israel, but made no mention whatever of the Palestinians or the Arabs or peace between Israel and the Arab world. This being so, Siton added, Eliachar was not acting properly in choosing to head the newly established Committee for Peace with the Palestinians—a left-wing organization whose leading lights were the likes of Uri Avneri, Lova Eliav, and Matityahu Peled. Siton stopped short of accusing the organization of anti-Zionism, a charge that had come from some other quarters and that had led these four luminaries to go to court to protest that they were indeed good Zionists—a protestation that the court duly accepted, exonerating the four from the terrible libel.

Siton's letter to *Ha'aretz* was remarkably revealing—and it reminded me of those bleak days following my ouster from the editorship of *Al Yawm*, when I briefly worked for the council part-time. My very first encounter with the council and with the concept of "Sephardim" came some time in 1951, when one Saturday morning I decided to go to a small meeting in the old Beit Ha'am on Jaffa Street in Jerusalem to listen to a talk by Eliachar. It was electioneering time, shortly after the mass immigration of Jews from Iraq and other Middle Eastern countries had reached its peak. I listened carefully to what Eliachar had to say, and left the meeting murmuring to myself that I would never, never allow my budding interest in the country's ethnic-cultural problems to lead me to indulge in the kind of special pleading and narrow "communalism" that Eliachar had evinced.

What had started to worry me then was not whether a number of Sephardi functionaries obtained seats in the Knesset, but the intensive process of acculturation going on in the country's huge *ma'barot* and immigrant reception camps. In a gesture of lame protest against this state of affairs, my vote in those elections went not to the Sephardi list but to Agudat Yisrael because of its stubborn—and, I believe, largely successful—opposition to the conscription of immigrant girls from Yemen for army service. I felt at that time—and I believe that I would feel so again in the unlikely event of the same circumstances obtaining—that this was an issue of far deeper significance than having two, three, or four Knesset members whose platform called merely for "equal treatment" and "an equal share" of the national pie. What most interested me was how human beings were being manipulated—and how, accordingly, the process of immigrant "absorption" ought to be conducted. Agudat Yisrael's argument concerning the conscription of girl immigrants—namely, that young women who had led fairly protected lives within religious or traditional families should not just be recruited into a service and a way of life that amounted to a veritable upheaval—was fully convincing. Having followed the platforms of the various parties and groups, I failed to find anything as worthy of support as that particular part of the Aguda's program.

| $\mathcal{S}$TEPPING ON "VERY

DELICATE GROUND"

AL YAWM AND AFTER

$\mathcal{S}$ometime in the mid-1960s, during the controversy I
helped initiate in the pages of the *Jewish Observer*,
and in which Elie Eliachar, the president of the Sephardi Council of Jerusalem, took part, Eliachar called me one day in my office to say that he
wanted to have a word with me. At the meeting, he said he planned to
publish a periodical dealing mainly with the communal problem in Israel,
and he offered me the editorship.

A few months after, a meeting was arranged with David Siton, director
of the council and editor of its Hebrew monthly, *Ba-Ma'rakhah*. Siton
repeated Eliachar's offer, but refrained from entering into details; I said I
would think about it. And there the matter rested.

Curiously, though rather typically, as soon as I had finished with *Al
Yawm*, the attitude of the Sephardi Council and Siton toward me changed
—and so did their proposal. Vagueness verging on confusion surrounded
what had seemed to me to be a very earnest project. Eliachar, on his return, tended to concentrate on the council's English-language publication, *Israel's Oriental Problem*, and Siton made no sign whatever of wanting or intending ever to relinquish his editorship of *Ba-Ma'rakhah*. I, on
my part, continued to be the easygoing, easily cajoled person I believe I
always was and have been.

They offered a revised proposal, I accepted, and at a meeting with
Eliachar and Siton in the former's Jerusalem flat on Ramban Street, the
shabby deal was closed: I would do the monthly bulletin in English—
single-handed, of course, except for the actual printing—and contribute
one or two articles to *Ba-Ma'rakhah* each month. My pay: a flat 700 Israeli
pounds a month, no social benefits whatsoever, no medical insurance participation, no holidays, nothing. I should add that this sum was something
like half of my net monthly salary at *Al Yawm*, not including expenses and
such extra payments, which in Israel constitute such an important part of
an employee's income.

Throughout these months of turmoil, Rachel, with three small children to rear, had not taken a stand in the matter, and did not oppose my decision to let myself be eased out of the prestigious and well-paid job of editor of a daily newspaper. Nor did she urge me to accept or seek a new job with the government or the Histadrut, a possibility vaguely hinted at by the powers that be and their emissaries.

Reactions within the Arab sector were wary and generally noncommittal. Arab friends, who had a good idea as to what it was all about, commiserated, some no doubt secretly glad to see the hated establishment exposed, others taking care not to interfere in what they perceived as one of those "Jewish wars," still others failing to see what the fuss was about — after all, they figured, the whole business was no more than a sham, an Arabic-language daily allegedly addressed to an Arab readership being edited and run almost exclusively by Jews.

For public consumption — again in the Arab sector — Histadrut and government functionaries spread the word that I was to be moved to another prestigious position — namely, cultural attaché at the Israeli embassy in London.

Friends of ours at the U.S. embassy, for reasons best known to them, broached the subject with foreign-ministry officials, whose explanation was unequivocal — and very probably sincerely held — namely, that it was I who had chosen to quit the job at *Al-Yawm*. I say sincerely held because I myself have my doubts. After all, it was unheard of — impossible to believe — that in Israel a man in my position would agree to his ouster without the least hint of a fight.

I often wonder about the reason for this. Is it something to do with self-confidence and self-esteem and the lack of them? Rachel, my wife, seems to think so. One of the things she often says, sometimes apropos of nothing in particular, is that I always fail to value my real worth and therefore very often "sell short." This trait, she claims, is to blame for the aversion I usually have for real-life confrontations, as against "mere talk" — mere talk meant to include all those articles and reviews and books I write defending this or criticizing and assaulting that.

And Rachel is so often right and insightful that I often find myself in agreement with what she says, and I start counting the losses, especially those in a number of fateful cases in which this lack of self-confidence, along with my allegedly low self-esteem, now seems to me to have been at the root of the setbacks I had in my many confrontations with the system and with certain individuals. I am also reminded of what some psychologists have found — namely, that self-confidence is a distinct advantage in all human endeavors. According to these findings, self-confidence not only helps talented people fulfill and market their talents, but also helps people without talent, or without much talent, succeed beyond any reasonable expectation. These psychologists even claim that low self-confidence or self-esteem dooms many people, the talented and the untalented alike, to be less successful than they could be. In a strange sort of way, these findings tally nicely with the theory of the self-fulfilling prophecy, also known as the vicious circle.

LURIE TIGHTENS THE HOLD

As if this were not enough, another fight was brewing—with the *Jerusalem Post* this time. But first some background. Early in 1964, with the ethnic problem steadily deepening, I wrote Ted Lurie a letter announcing what I called the timely death of Amnon Bartur, the pen name under whose byline my weekly feature, "The Middle East Scene," had appeared for a number of years. I went on to explain how I reached my decision. "You may recall," I wrote, "that when we decided on 'Bartur,' it was because I was devoting the Marginal also to Arab affairs, and we thought two Arab columns by one writer would not look good. Now with my new Israeli preoccupations, this disadvantage disappears."

Lurie's response took me a little by surprise. "You may," he wrote, "be right in the arguments you advance for the demise of Bartur, or you may not; I haven't got time to go into it now because I am writing in great haste to say that we can't be faced with a *fait accompli* in this way, and so Bartur will still appear this week. As soon as you have time, I am prepared to discuss its future with you."

I continued to insist, and the decision was not all that unreasonable, so Lurie had no choice: the feature acquired a new heading, "In the Arab World."

Meanwhile, other difficulties cropped up, inevitably, it seems, and inexorably. Ten short months after making the decision to drop "Bartur," and after an absence of close to three months in London, I wrote Lurie this letter, dated December 24, 1964:

I have been thinking about the subject we discussed yesterday
in Jerusalem. I have come to the conclusion that send-me-one-
Marginal-Column-and-we-shall-see is just not good enough. My
feeling is that if you are not *keen* on the thing yourselves, I better

drop the whole thing. After all, both of us have been living, probably slightly more peacefully, during the past three months without
each other!

But even if you are what I call keen, three difficulties still present
themselves. The first is a question of principle. I do not agree that
a column ought in every case and in every detail to agree with the
policy of the paper in which it appears. A columnist is not an editorial
writer.

The second involves technique and presentation. You say that
everything connected with education should go to the education
page. Here too I disagree. A column is no less of an institution than a
page, and a columnist should be left to choose the subject for his own
column. Otherwise, economics should go to the economics page, arts
to the arts page, and so on. Which would be absurd . . .

Please think about the subject and let me know. But to avoid too
much discussion, I must add that it is a matter of take it or leave it, as
far as I am concerned.

Lurie's reply was prompt. He wrote in a letter dated December 28:

We accept your view that a column does not have to agree in each
case and in every detail with the policy of the paper and that the
columnist is not an editorial writer.

We do, however, differ from newspapers abroad that subscribe
to columnists as syndicated material and have no voice in directing
or planning what the columnists deal with or how (their only choice
being whether to print the column as supplied or not, and usually
they subscribe to two or three times as many as they can possibly
print). In our case, we must have the right to reserve some points
of policy . . . There may be many things wrong with education, and
any one is free to comment on them, but not to suggest a specific
prejudice and basic ill will.

Three weeks later, I sent in a weekly Marginal Column titled "Facing
Ourselves," in which I referred to certain pronouncements made by the
prime minister. It was intended for the issue dated January 12, 1965.

'Im ha-panim la-golah was the slogan under which the Twenty-Sixth
World Zionist Congress was held. Besides the disadvantages from which
all slogans usually suffer, this particular one had the added fault of being

virtually untranslatable. "Facing the Diaspora?" Perhaps. But what does it signify, precisely? I must confess that, hating slogans of all kinds anyway, I never gave the matter a second thought until I listened to Mr. Levi Eshkol addressing the World Conference of Jewish Journalists at the Holyland Hotel in Jerusalem last Wednesday. In the course of a lengthy impassioned appeal to Jewish journalists "to bring Israel to Diaspora Jewries," and ultimately to persuade them to come to Israel, the prime minister warned that otherwise in four years' time we may, heaven forbid, "find ourselves face-to-face with ourselves."

It was obvious from Mr. Eshkol's tone of voice that he considered this eventuality too terrible to contemplate, a calamity to be avoided at all costs. Come to think of it, however, one cannot help wondering. *'Im ha-panim la-golah*, it suddenly dawns on one, was not a mere slogan. It was an ingrained attitude, a way of life, and, worse still, a way of managing — or of avoiding managing — the affairs of this country. At the root of it rests the fantastic assumption that Israel is not, and cannot be, a normal country; that the Israelis are not, and never can be, a normal people in their own right, but rather a nucleus of a people the process of whose formation is practically endless; that instead of concentrating our efforts and our meagre resources on solving our own problems, we should squander them on a project the feasibility of which becomes daily more elusive.

This attitude is dangerous on more than one count. Among other things, it indicates a lack of confidence in ourselves, alternating with occasional doses of over-confidence. During a recent visit in England, I attended the annual conference of the Jewish National Fund. One of the speakers was Mr. Ya'acov Tsur, the JNF's chairman, who tried to show that Zionism was "a revolt against History," and boasted that it was "a revolt against Geography" as well. One sees the point — but the point can be stretched a little bit too far. There are facts which even Zionism cannot revolt against with advantage for very long. One of these is that the overwhelming majority of Diaspora Jews, both Zionists and non-Zionists, do not feel like packing up and coming to Israel, Mr. Eshkol's impassioned appeals notwithstanding.

Now, Zionism may be a revolt against History, Geography, and even Chemistry. But we cannot afford to ignore facts for long. After all, Israel is rather more than half-populated by people to whom Zionism — at least in this sense — is totally foreign. It may sound paradoxical, but the fact is that since 1948 at least, while the true Zionist's home has been in the Diaspora, the Jewish communities that came to Israel contained no organized Zionist movements. For all one knows, this may call for a new definition of

"Zionist" and "Zionism" — but, then, what's in a name? If Zionism does
not mean immigration, it must mean something quite different. It should
have become clear by now, however, that the Zionism of the organizations
represented at the recent World Zionist Congress does not mean immigration. It is useless, unseemly, and undignified to go on pretending that
this is not the case.

Above all, and worst of all, it tends to give us the illusion that we can in-
definitely avoid "finding ourselves face-to-face with ourselves." For this is
precisely what we ought to do and *need* to do — and the sooner the better.
We ought to sit up and take stock; how to produce the technicians and
professionals we need from amongst the human material we already have,
and not hope to get them ready-made from other Jewries; how to stop the
fearful process of Levantinisation which we have ourselves started by insisting on destroying the age-old cultures of our new immigrants; how to
deal with the growing political and moral pressures which we are facing
in the international sphere — and finally how to tackle the root of all these
pressures, the Arab refugee problem. These are weighty questions which
clamour for answers. We will have to provide these answers, even at the
cost of finding ourselves face-to-face with ourselves. In fact, if slogans in
general were not so hateful and meaningless, one would not hesitate to
coin one on the spot: *'Im ha-panim le-'atsmenu* — Facing Ourselves.

On the same day the column was to appear, Lurie
sent me a letter explaining why he decided against
publishing it. I give it here with my reply, dated January 16.

Dear Nissim:

Thanks for your column which I read last night with great interest —
and that's not a euphemism. Here are my comments:
  (a) I don't know what Eshkol said at that Journalists' Lunch but
if he said *hass vehalila* (God forbid), I should imagine he meant
heaven forbid there should be a catastrophe that would bring a kind
of catastrophic immigration from the West. Correct me if I'm wrong!
  (b) Your second paragraph is diametrically opposed to everything
we stand for, in other words, Zionism. Of course *we are* a "nucleus
of a people the process of whose formation is practically endless." It
is curious that this was almost the same way it was put in our leader
summing up the Zionist Congress the other day, when we wrote
that the building of a suitable new commonwealth hasn't been com-

pleted—"if such an idea can be completed." Whereas Lea and I are agreed that we like a fresh point of view, etc. etc., nevertheless as I said in my note, there's one place where we draw the line—where you *kofer ba'ikkar* [deny a basic principle of the (Jewish) faith].

(c) As for what you say about the "age-old cultures of our new immigrants" which we are insisting on destroying—this is an interesting subject. Perhaps you would like to write a column on what these age-old cultures are that should be preserved.

Dear Ted,

I finally got your letter of the 12th, which was mailed on the 14th and reached me yesterday. I will be as brief as possible:

(a) Eshkol said that if the present situation continues we will, in four years' time, find ourselves face-to-face with ourselves—"*panim el panim 'im 'atsmenu.*" He implied this would be a calamity. My point is that we better start today facing ourselves and our problems. *Hass vehalila* was not the operative phrase.

(b) By saying that what I wrote was diametrically opposed to everything the *Post* stands for, you put me in a fairly impossible position. In a closed institutionalized society governed by a closed institutionalized ideology, every dissenting view tends to seem *kefira b'ikkar* [a denial of a basic principle of the faith]. What the *Post* stands for today is the same as it stood for 30 years ago—and what its founders stood for 30 years before that. The world has undergone many changes in the meantime (even Communism is changing), and we will have to catch up. To give you one example: even the *Post* does not find it fit to cite the Balfour Declaration as a justification for setting up the State of Israel.

But why go so far? You say that my view is opposed to Zionism. What on earth is *that?* If we start looking at ourselves as a nation, it need not follow that we shut our doors to Jewish immigrants. It only means that we stop behaving like a bunch of goddamn idiots and wasting our time begging Diaspora Jews to come to Israel—to the partial neglect of our own problems and our own human material. Consider the idea of sending teachers to teach Americans, for instance. Few things in this whole wide world can sound more idiotic!

I like to think that these are not mere eccentricities. Even a die-hard Zionist like Ben-Gurion sometimes revolts against the present stagnation, and the state of mind of the younger generation is not unknown to you. If the *Post,* alongside the majority of the local papers, chooses to leave it for *Ha'olam Haze,* the *Times* of London, *Etgar,* and *Le Monde* to write about these things, it has every right to do so. But my feeling is that no good purpose would be served, not even what the *Post* stands for today. When I sent in my column I knew it was a borderline case; but I hoped that with resentment and ridicule of the Great Show so universal, the *Post* would take the plunge.

Finally, my claim that we have destroyed the age-old cultures of new immigrants was already propounded in a few columns, some of them printed, some rejected (as being *kefira b'ikkar!*). If I read you rightly, you seem to cast doubt as to whether there are such age-old cultures that should be preserved. Well, though they contain no philharmonic orchestras, they are there. They are the way these people live, *where* they live, the way they eat, sleep, and breed their children. You will say that these cannot be preserved. I agree. What I say is that their forceful, violent destruction can lead only to Levantinisation.

Where do we go from here?

MARGINAL COLUMN STOPPED

After this, things went downhill all the way. In response to one column, to appear on January 29, I got this short note — this time from the features editor, neither Lurie nor Lea Ben-Dor even bothering to dictate a comment. The heading I chose for the column was "Picking and Choosing," and I give it here following the features editor's rejection slip, which read: "You must have known that you were stepping on very delicate ground with the attached Marginal! Sorry, but I have to return it to you."

To have to choose between political parties is bad enough, one finds; but to be placed in a position where you have to choose between two leaders belonging to the same party seems all but intolerable. The fact remains, though, that in the present debate between David Ben-Gurion and Levi Eshkol, not only Mapai but the whole country seems to have accepted this position: every Israeli seems to have made up his or her mind for either the one or the other, or probably one ought to say *against* the one or the other. The rejection and acceptance are usually total. In recent weeks, for example, in the course of a conversation on, say, the 26th Zionist Congress, one often found oneself faced with some such remark: "But you are now talking exactly like Ben-Gurion! Do you mean to say that you accept his definition of Zionism and Zionist?"

Well, supposing one did: should this entail accepting *in toto* all the other facets of Ben-Gurion's position? Or take this business of setting up a judicial commission of enquiry into the Lavon Affair. Admiring Ben-Gurion's single-mindedness on this point and his insistence that justice and truth prevail, one cannot help wondering why opposition to an enquiry seems so universal. One simply refuses to believe that to conduct such an enquiry would bring woe and destruction upon the country as a whole, or that Israel can be really so busy with other matters as to be able to afford not to make an effort to establish the truth, the whole truth, on so serious a subject as the conduct of a group of men in whose hands it has placed its fortunes and its very life.

It is of course no use arguing that an enquiry of this kind would lead to other people demanding similar enquiries into similar "affairs" and security mishaps. In this connection, surprisingly little note has been taken of allegations made by some Ahdut Ha'avoda and Min Hayesod people that the 1954 blunder was not the only security mishap to occur up to that year; that a remarkably similar, almost identical one took place in 1951 in another Arab capital [Baghdad]; and that should Mapai and the Government approve of an enquiry into the Lavon Affair, Ahdut Ha'avoda would demand an enquiry into the 1951 affair, which occurred while Ben-Gurion himself was defence minister. It seems quite plain, however, that these allegations, rather than intimidating anyone, ought to make a thorough enquiry into the 1954 mishap even more vital and timely.

And yet—although one accepts Ben-Gurion's attitude to Zionism and would want to see a thorough enquiry conducted into the Lavon and all other such affairs, one would still not want to choose between him and Levi Eshkol—at any rate not in the totalistic fashion in which Israelis are now prone to do. There are many fields in which the time seems ripe, even overdue, for Israel to adopt new attitudes and try new approaches—and for all his past achievements, Ben-Gurion is not the best man to conduct or even set the tune to such new policies. In politics it is even less use to cry over spilt milk; yet one cannot help feeling that a lot of milk was spilt during the 15 years of Ben-Gurion's premiership, and that this was the case nowhere more than it was in our relations with the Arabs and the Russians. Though very little has been actually done in this direction, it has been a relief to note the change of tone prevailing since Ben-Gurion's resignation.

It is often argued that far from producing an improvement, the change of tone introduced by Levi Eshkol has all but misfired, with Arab hostility toward Israel markedly stiffening and Moscow's attitude not at all changed. This is a moot question, to which the best answer would probably be that these things take time—and rather more initiative than has so far been forthcoming. The injury inflicted on the Arabs by the loss of what they honestly consider part of their homeland will take a long time to heal. The most that any government in Israel can do in such a situation is to abstain from all acts or pronouncements likely to deepen the injury. This is plainly not what the Ben-Gurion administration tried to do; on the contrary, perhaps. And this is why it is that, though one would like to pick and choose between the various attitudes and positions of the two men, one finally decides that Levi Eshkol ought to be given more time.

After these incidents, I naturally stopped writing my weekly Marginal Column, and the feature was dropped altogether—all those who used to write it were either dead, retired, or just tired. However, on June 29, 1965, I sent this letter to Lurie. It speaks for itself.

Dear Ted,

Shortly after I came back from my trip abroad toward the end of last year, we had a meeting in which it was agreed that I resume my contributions. In your letter of December 28, 1964, you also "accepted [my] view that a column does not have to agree in each case and in every detail with the policy of the paper and that the columnist is not an editorial writer."

On this understanding I resumed sending you articles, but unluckily I found that two out of three (the total!) were rejected because they did not agree with the paper's policy. In several conversations which we had subsequently, we kept going round in circles and never managed to arrive at a mutually acceptable arrangement.

I am relating all this history because I think the time has come for me to know where I stand, precisely. On my part, I am willing to resume writing roughly two pieces a week on exactly the same old arrangement, keeping in mind the above quotation from your letter—but also admitting there are limits to what a newspaper can publish by way of opinions radically different from its own.

Now it remains for you to define your position—and an early reply will be much appreciated . . .

Lurie's response came only on July 15 — another indication of how drastically things had changed.

Dear Nissim:

I don't know why you say what you say in the last sentence of your letter about defining my position.

As I remember, we've had not one conversation but at least half a dozen about your contributions to the *Post*, and in each case I have told you, and repeatedly emphasized, that we were keenly interested in the kinds of columns that you had been writing about Arabs and Middle East affairs — cultural, political, sociological, etc. These are very important to us, and we would like you to resume.

You, for your part, said you were bored, stale, etc. and wanted to do other things which I was willing to give a try. Our real disagreement, if I remember correctly, was over an "Israeli" article in which you argued that if the majority at any time should wish to reject what is lumped together as "Zionism," then nobody had a right to object. This paper makes its basic stand on this "Zionism" and the need to instill it in people who do not share it.

Nissim, I think you have something to say, and I very often like the way you say it, as you know, but what it boils down to is that we can use a commentator on internal affairs only if his general attitudes fit into this framework in some way.

Clearly, my general attitudes did not "fit into this framework" in any way. Nor was I prepared to deny this. But it seems that Lurie still tried. At the Sheraton Hotel in Tel Aviv, far from our workplace, we had a long chat one day in August and agreed to put into writing whatever arrangement we reached. But Lurie's written confirmation never arrived, and in response to a telephone call I made to remind him, he came up with this highly original story in a letter dated August 13:

The delay in writing the note that you requested was due to the technical fault of my having taken the correspondence with me to Tel Aviv for that last meeting we had, at the Sheraton Hotel, so it has apparently been misplaced somewhere.

I can only repeat what I have said to you time and time again, namely, that we have always been interested in resuming your columns on Middle East and Arab affairs, which you interrupted entirely of your own accord, and therefore there is no question on our part of "refusing to return to the status quo ante," as you seem to suggest.

With this, my association with the *Post* all but ended. Following my leaving *Al Yawm,* Lurie called to apologize for the way the news was given in the paper — adding something about how distressed he felt that things were such that he had nothing to offer me!

On and off during the following years I continued to contribute to the book pages, and also an occasional Arab affairs piece for the Friday magazine — mainly just out of habit or for the sake of review copies of books I wanted to keep or simply for the few pennies that the *Post* paid for these contributions.

Over the course of the next four years, I had only one recorded argument with the editor on a point of policy. Ironically enough, this time around it was the *Post* that was to pose as a "defender" of the Palestinians! The following letter was dated March 24, 1970, and signed by Ted Lurie:

Dear Nissim,

I owe you an apology and an explanation. I am so far behind with my correspondence that I am only now replying to letters received in January, and that's my only excuse for not having got down to writing you a note a long time ago explaining why we didn't use your piece on the "arrested Palestinian society."

There's nothing wrong with the piece or its content except that we felt it would be against our interest to publish it. We are interested, as you know, in promoting understanding with the Palestinian Arabs, and both editors to whom I gave the piece to read expressed the same opinion — namely that it should not be published in the *JP*.

My reply came on March 30:

Dear Ted,

I find a good deal of irony in your letter — especially the implication that publishing an article of the kind I wrote would in some way offend the Palestinians, with whom you are interested in promoting understanding. In reply to this I can only recall what I wrote thirteen years ago in a Column One in the *Post* — namely that the Arabs do not want, nor need, patronizing; what they want, and need so badly, is self-knowledge on their own part and understanding on the part of others. We all want to promote understanding with the Palestinians; to my mind, patronizing them is not a way of attaining such understanding. We have all at one stage criticized the British — not only the British, but mainly them — for what we saw as their patronizing attitude to the Arabs. I hope we are not now putting ourselves in the same position.

But the regrettable thing about this is that it has served as an excuse for me to cancel the arrangement which we had reached after so many months — namely, to write for you the kind of articles which the *Post* now so obviously needs . . ."

In the meantime, relations with people who had always taken my side began to waver. As long as I had managed to know my limits — which in this particular case meant conducting the whole campaign as something in the nature of a family quarrel — it was okay with these liberal friends who saw themselves as being outside the establishment and who never failed to encourage me.

The trouble seemed to start when I began to socialize with members of the Arab minority with whom I had come in contact in the course of my work as editor of *Al Yawm*. Some of these not only were critical of the government, but also dared to question the very premises of the treatment they received as a minority. They included such outspoken — and boycotted and often harassed — journalists, writers, and political activists as poets Rashid Hussein and Mahmud Darwish; Knesset member Abdul ʿAziz al-Zuʿbi; *Haʾaretz* reporter Atallah Mansour, and others.

This proved to be too much even for persons whom we had considered close friends and had formerly invited for drinks of an evening — occasionally with Arab friends who were living in Tel Aviv, especially Rashid and his Jewish girlfriend, Anne, and Zuʿbi and his Jewish girlfriend and future wife, Rachel. Among our former frequent guests had been a number of Jewish friends with a special interest in, and some inside knowledge of, the problems of education. These had always raved about my columns on the subject and had often supplied bits of information about their own experiences in the field, each with his or her own axe to grind, as I later found out.

Shortly after I stopped writing my regular Marginal Column for the *Post,* one of these — Aliza Levenberg was her name — became so worked up — mainly, I think, about my closer association with Israeli Arabs — that she penned a long letter to the editor of the mass-circulation daily *Ma'ariv;* in it, she maligned me in no uncertain terms, though she refrained from naming names. Not that she had much reason to do this, since in the not-so-limited circle of readers to whom the letter was in reality addressed, there was not a shadow of a doubt concerning the identity of the person assaulted.

One fundamental trait of my character is that I never seem to give up on people, never get worked up enough to sever relations with people and put an end to a relationship. Accordingly I sat and wrote a brief note to Aliza and foolishly tried to appease her, correcting some of the distortions in her letter and defending my Arab friends whom she had maligned. The result was more than disappointing.

A DIALOGUE IN REHOVOT

Sometime in June 1966 I received a letter from the American Jewish Congress asking whether I could participate in their forthcoming fifth annual American-Israeli Dialogue. I had attended one session of the previous year's gathering, and since the invitation came at a time when I knew I was leaving my job at *Al Yawm* and heading for a period in which I wanted to make my views as widely publicized as possible, I decided to participate. As it happened, I almost literally walked out of the paper and into the dialogue.

The subject assigned to the participants that year was "Jewish Distinctiveness in Israel and America." However — as I was to learn later, after participating in three such dialogues — no matter the specific topic, the dialogue invariably turned into a heated debate between the Israeli and American sides, some of the former always managing to steer the discussion on to the question of why American Jews did not come to Israel to settle in great numbers, and the latter, thus put on the defensive, trying to explain to the Israelis that their presence in America might not be as bad for Israel as it appeared. Few American participants had the courage to give any kind of ideological justification for deciding to stay where they were.

In the 1966 dialogue, it was Eliezer Livneh who was the most outspoken and aggressive among the Israelis; he explained to me privately, when I remarked on his vehemence, that he wanted "to shake their self-confidence," that being the only way to shake "them." In the course of three days of listening to the wearyingly repetitive deliberations, accusations, and counteraccusations, I learned a good deal about American Jewry and met some of my best American Jewish friends and acquaintances, including the editor and managing editor of the quarterly *Judaism*, in which I subsequently published an essay on Israel's communal problem.

The dialogue took place at the Weizmann Institute in Rehovot on July 27–29. As always I took my participation very seriously indeed and spent a lot of time pondering and agonizing over how to deal with the specified topic. I went to Rehovot with a complete draft of my presentation, but in the course of the discussions — and especially in view of what some of my Israeli colleagues had to say there — I rewrote it. A shortened and perforce rather inadequate version was published in the *Congress Biweekly* of April 17, 1967. This was the first time I was to tackle, seriously and at length, some aspects of being Jewish, and especially of being a Middle Eastern Jew in Israel. Inevitably, too, since I had just been eased out of my job, and since my break with the establishment had a good deal to do with my attitudes toward certain aspects of the subject, my state of mind played a crucial role in the tone and direction of my paper.

In my opening paragraphs I objected to the gross generalizations I thought were implicit in the title of the dialogue. Israel, I explained, possessed not one but at least three Jewish identities — or distinctivenesses. These were the Eastern European Ashkenazi, the Middle Eastern Sephardi, and the Western European–North American cultures or identities. There were, I added, a number of other minor identities and cultures, but these I chose to call subcultures, among which I counted the Soviet-Jewish, the Sabra-Jewish, and the Zionist-Jewish. The Zionist-Jewish subidentity I claimed to be part of the Eastern European Ashkenazi culture; the Sabra-Jewish, part of the Middle Eastern Sephardi culture; and the Soviet-Jewish, increasingly, part of the Western European–North American.

The thrust of my argument was that far from the great gulf that some of the speakers thought was being created between American Jewry and Israel as a result of the influx of Middle Eastern and North African Jews into the country, there was in reality an affinity between the Western European–North American Jewish culture and that of the Oriental Jews. This, I said, stemmed mainly from the fact that the Jews of the West and those of the Middle East were the only Jewries that had had the experience of leading a full Jewish life without being cooped up in ghettos and shtetls — of living side by side with, and largely sharing the life of, the non-Jews among whom they dwelt.

As to the Eastern European Ashkenazi culture, I said that apart from a number of scattered Russian and American Jews now in their seventies or eighties, the only extant carriers of this culture were members of the ruling establishment in Israel. By a truly staggering feat of self-preservation, this particular section of a fast-disappearing generation of Russian-Polish Jews had managed not only to realize the Zionist ideal — at least the political part of it — but had also tried to mold the character of Israeli society and body politic in the image of its own static culture and worldview. The fear of "Levantinization," which some of the Israeli speakers sounded in their presentations, reflected this attempt at cultural hegemony.

I referred particularly to a passage in Eliezer Livneh's railings against American Jews for not immigrating to Israel. In that passage he said that "the veteran sections of the population" of Israel did not propose to absorb or "assimilate" newcomers from what he termed "the advanced countries of the Diaspora." Moreover, he assured his American listeners, those veteran sections of the population would themselves be willing to undergo "progressive change under the conscious pressure, influence and initiative of [those] newcomers." Shorn of its verbiage, I said, this could mean only one thing — namely, that, after eighty years of persistently forcing their cultural values and outlook on the various waves of immigrants, the last remnants of the Eastern European Ashkenazi leadership were now willing to loosen the reins a little — but only if their inheritors were newcomers from the so-called "advanced countries of the Diaspora."

Here I proposed to pass over what I considered the terrible implications of Livneh's words and tackle the question whether the Eastern European Ashkenazi establishment was at all capable of changing or mending its ways. This elite, I explained, during its short history in Palestine-Israel, had had five different encounters with five different cultural groups, and in none of these was it able or willing to establish a fruitful dialogue. It failed to establish a dialogue with the Jews who originally inhabited the land; it failed again with the Arabs who constituted the majority of the population; it also failed to find a common language with the German Jewish immigrants who came to Palestine in the early thirties; it failed yet again to establish meaningful contact with the masses of Jews who flooded the country in the late 1940s and early 1950s; and finally it failed to have a dialogue with its own sons and daughters, the native-born sabras. This showed, I said, that Mr. Livneh's disarming, if rather belated, offer could not be taken seriously. Far from being the generous gesture it purported to be, I explained, Livneh's proposition was either a threadbare maneuver or a sign of cultural impotence, and the experience of the past would prompt one to tell the Eastern European Zionist establishment: first put your own house in order!

Coming closer to the point of the dialogue, I maintained further that the point at issue was not one between Israelis and Americans, but rather between the Ashkenazi establishment and all the rest — the Oriental communities, the sabras, the Jewries of Western Europe and North America, and the Jews of the Soviet Union. "Some of you will be tempted to ask: 'What's left, then?' And my reply is that what is left is merely those whom Mr. Livneh, Mr. Israel Ben Meir and Mr. Israel Eldad represent. It is a small and diminishing group, representing roughly 15 percent of the population of Israel . . ."

Rejecting the distorted view of Judaism that this influential group had established, I went on to plead for "an act of restoration — the restoration to Judaism of its authentic, pre-Haskalah meaning and content." I explained further that I was not speaking of pristine Torah Judaism, but of postexilic Judaism as propounded by the great rabbis and scholars, from Hillel to Sa'adia Gaon, from Maimonides to Solomon Schechter — "a Judaism free from nationalism, territorialism, and racism." In a sense, I added, we ought to try to adopt a somewhat "primitive" notion of Judaism and divorce it completely from Zionism and all other forms of political activism. "This Judaism," I added, "will have to be recognized as the essentially Oriental religion it is and has always been. Mr. Livneh said rightly — though I am afraid for quite the wrong reasons — that Judaism had no affinity with Western civilization; if at all, he said, he finds an affinity with Buddhism rather than with Western Christianity. Dr. Zvi Kurzweil, on the other hand, argued that the affinity between Judaism and Western civilization was 'self-evident.' I find it strange that neither has taken the trouble to discover that if Judaism has affinity with any religious culture, then it is with none other than Islam and Muslim-Arab culture."

In my concluding remarks I said I agreed with Amnon Rubinstein and Mordechai Bar-On in feeling that we Israelis had no business preaching aliya to American Jews. I added that, unlike Livneh, Ben Meir, and Eldad, I did not think Judaism could be preserved only in Israel or that authentic Jewish life could not be led in the Diaspora. "Nor do I think that we Israelis should accept any obligation not to live the normal life of a small nation. It is not true — as Livneh woefully complains — that Israel as she is today can have no hope of surviving. It is, however, quite true that Israel will not remain for long as she is today. For Israel as she is run and as she is presented today has little to do with the real Israel. Being some sort of expert on Arab affairs, I am often asked: 'And when do you think the Arabs will make peace with Israel?' And my answer to this query is: 'When we Israelis make peace with Israel ourselves!' The frantic appeals that we heard today for what I would call 'an American rescue immigration in reverse' is only one symptom of the refusal on the part of the establishment to accept Israel—and it ought to be self-evident that no one will accept us unless we first accept ourselves."

One of the people who did not attend the Rehovot gathering but whose acquaintance I was to make thanks to the dialogue was Jacob Neusner, whose work I knew from American Jewish periodicals and who was the author of a detailed multivolume work on the history of the Babylonian Jews. One day in May 1967—shortly after a badly abridged version of my dialogue presentation was printed in the *Congress Biweekly*—I received a sort of fan letter, dated May 5, 1967, in which Neusner wrote that in a desert of cliches, slogans, and empty words, my remarks at the dialogue seemed to him "an oasis of pure water—good sense, freshness." He was struck, he said, by the soundness of my critique of "the Palestinian Ashkenazim," who had failed in five confrontations. "You could add to that," he added. "Our generation (3rd in the USA), they simply do not confront at all, any more than they do yours . . ." He also said he thought "that idiotic reply" of Livneh illustrated the rightness of my comments. He said also that he was sympathetic to my view of Judaism and my stress on the Sephardic way, which he thought was "most appropriate for the United States."

Needless to say, I was much encouraged, and replied promptly, expanding on my presentation and calling Livneh—among some other names—"Jewish unbeliever-turned-custodian-of-other-people's-Jewishness."

Neusner's reply came soon, but before I had time to reply, the situation on the Egyptian border became so unsettling that I was unable to concentrate sufficiently to write the kind of response I wanted to write. Following the resounding victory of the Six-Day War, which Neusner wrote that he had "not been too thrilled" by, our correspondence became regular. In one of his letters Neusner said that my English suggested to him that I was "a native-speaker." So how did I "learn so much Arabic as to be able to edit a newspaper?"

On the strength of something I said in the course of my presentation at the Rehovot dialogue, the late Rabbi Steven Schwarzschild, then editor of the quarterly *Judaism,* invited me to contribute a piece on what he called "the two Israels." It took me a mere fortnight to mail him the article, titled "The Two Israels: A Study of Europeocentrism." (The article is reprinted as Chapter 9 of this book.)

It was the start of a long and fruitful, if occasionally checkered, association. On receiving and reading my article, Schwarzschild wrote, in a letter dated December 24, 1966:

> It's high time that people in this country learn about the kind of thing that you are particularly concerned with — that the Israeli "intelligentsia" and the American-Jewish "intelligentsia" begin to speak with one another in a continuous and significant way — and you obviously know how to express yourself forcefully and in such a way that the various "establishments" will eventually have to begin to listen to us. This was my impression in reading your remarks at the so-called American-Israeli dialogue last summer — which I otherwise refused to publish — and therefore I asked that you be contacted — though I had seen other articles of yours in various places. In short, please be in touch.

Turning to some remark I made in my article, Schwarzschild commented that I was "underestimating the parallelism between the American Negro syndrome and that of 'the two Israels.' " The similarity, he wrote, "is even more frightening than you think, it seems to me." He also said that I was "still too indulgent with the East-European mentality. Why not go on the counter-attack? After all that, Jewishly-humanly, we have experienced and seen, still to be talking of the 'value' of Occidental civilization is surely some new height of historical sickness . . ."

Certain differences of opinion between Rabbi Schwarzschild and me started to crop up after the Six-Day War. In one of my letters I expressed disagreement with a disparaging reference he had made to dissidents like Jacob Petuchowski, Michael Selzer, Trude Weiss-Rosmarin. I wrote, in a letter dated October 3, 1967:

Dear Rabbi Schwarzschild,

> . . . Now that we are addressing each other with such candour, I think we are both entitled to insist on complete clarity of phrasing. What is the problem with which we are both so seriously concerned? You write: "There *must* be a way of tackling the problem — viz the rela-

tionships between the Jewish and Arab worlds, without insisting that one of the poles in the tensions, i.e., Israeli and Arab nationalisms, must be dissolved . . ." Yet the central point is precisely that the poles in this conflict are not, repeat not, *Israeli* and Arab nationalisms, but between so-called Jewish and so-called Arab ethnic nationalisms — between rabid pan-Jews and equally rabid pan-Arabs. As I made it clear in my article, I have no sympathy for either of these "pans" (though I am afraid the former has even less basis in history, logic or actuality than the latter). As a Jew, however, I feel I must first try to put my own house in order. Well, as an Israeli Jew I have nothing against Israeli nationalism and patriotism, but this should embrace *all* Israelis, Jews and non-Jews alike. I assure you, however, that such an *Israeli* Israel is anathema to the pan-Jews far more than it is for the pan-Arabs! In fact, I have a hunch that the latter would accept such an Israel *tomorrow,* whereas the former would fight to the death against it. Having grasped this, I feel convinced that work by people like us must start there. Of course, there are reasons why the pan-Jews constitute a menace — e.g., the position and fate of the Diaspora and of Judaism as a whole. However, since we are talking about the Arab-Jewish aspect it should be apparent that no resolution of this problem can ever be found in pan-Judaism. (Prof. Harel, formerly Harold, Fisch — who is on the *Tenuʿah lemaʿan Eretz Yisrael Hash-lemah* [the Movement for Greater Israel] — was asked recently about the movement. He said he had differences of opinion with the majority of its members: "What they consider final, I consider a means; in my eyes the *shlemut* of the borders is a means towards a more comprehensive completeness — *shlemut yoter makkifah.*" And so on and on. Do you envisage an end to this process?)

I am blessed if I know what to think about [the American Council for Judaism]. That you know them better I have not the least doubt. Still, the fact that "identification with them kills off any last chance of effectiveness in the Jewish community" proves, I am afraid, nothing against them. It only shows how wily their adversaries are and how perfect and certain are the workings of the self-fulfilling prophecy. A third way? Ah, I wish I knew how one can contemplate such a thing in the present circumstances.

| ℘RIDE OR SELF-EFFACEMENT:
ON REFUSING TO SAVE SKIN

*T*he last issue of *Al Yawm* was dated May 31, 1968.
The day after, the *Jerusalem Post* carried a long re-
port in which its reporter told the story of the Arabic daily, the first issue
of which had appeared on September 28, 1948, under the editorship of
Michael Assaf.

A turning point came in 1959, when the Histadrut became a partner in the
paper . . . There was also a new editor. Nissim Rejwan was a young journalist who had arrived with the immigration from Iraq. He had made a name
for himself as an observer of Arab affairs in his articles in the *Post*. On his
becoming editor, *Al Yawm* was enlarged. Mr. Rejwan tried to interest the
Arab intelligentsia in the paper and gave space to Arab writers, especially
on literary subjects. The circulation increased considerably.
     Mr. Rejwan remained editor for seven and a half years. It was not a com-
fortable time for him. He did not get on too well with the Histadrut. He
took an independent view, ignoring the intricate balance of forces in the
local political scene. Moreover, soon after he became editor, the Lavon Affair burst, and relations between the prime minister's office and the Histadrut reflected the tensions between Ben-Gurion and Lavon. The nominee
of the prime minister's office had to leave.

The *Post* reporter's account was of course incomplete. My "having to
leave" the paper came some five years after the Lavon affair ended with Ben
Gurion's victory, and the prime minister's office was an active, even the
main, factor. Besides, the paper under my editorship did not just enlarge
but became a morning daily.
     More to the point, I think, was the reporter's passing reference to my
having taken "an independent view." In those days and under those circumstances, taking an independent view was something unheard of, and
in my particular case especially, quite insufferable.

The formalities concerning my leaving *Al Yawm* took a very short time to complete, so much so that Eliahu, one of the few close friends who went on keeping in touch, likened it to "a beheading." A brief session with the arbiter, David Zakai, a retired Histadrut journalist, proved sufficient. Terms were so favorable to the employer that no one wanted to believe me when I explained them later: two and a half monthly salaries to be paid to me as compensation. Not only was Zakai influenced by his past employers; the Journalists Association itself had to reckon with a variety of trade union, as well as other, considerations. The result was that in the end I found myself all alone, only halfheartedly contending with those giants over things that I considered beneath my dignity. Francis (Amir) Ofner, a veteran journalist and admirer who had not even heard about the affair, later said to me, with obvious disapproval, that I had behaved "like a *grand seigneur.*"

Was it pride, sheer pride, that caused me to behave in ways that made it so easy for the powers that be to make such an easy job of it — even pretending, in some circles, that my ouster had been a voluntary step on my part? Disdain? Self-respect? A refusal to show one's hurt and a determination to go doggedly on when one is about to fall? For the fact is that my conduct in this sorry episode was seen as so shockingly fatalistic that none of those involved comprehended it, not even those who initiated the move. My refusal to "fight," to challenge the decision (a challenge, I should add, that would certainly have produced results), possibly had to do with what I see as two character traits of mine that at first sight seem contradictory but are, in reality, quite conceivable in unison. I am referring to pride and disdain on the one hand, and shyness, diffidence, and self-effacement on the other.

October 8, 1968
Dear Gad,

Together with your letter came another communication, a lengthy, heartening account from Rony Gabbay. Not from Victoria but from Perth. And in this lengthy and detailed communication a totally different doctrine about that land of milk and honey is propounded. Good for the kids, good for the parents, good for the Jews (especially if they are non-Europeans!). Away from the madding crowd, the tensions, the discriminations and the disabilities. In short, a whole doctrine of it, a whole way of life. And as a friend and relative and well-wisher and fellow sufferer and so on, I and Rachel are advised, urged, beseeched, cajoled and supplicated: Get the hell out and save your skin!

November 8, 1968
Dear Gad,

Last night I had a chat with a man called Juri, an economist, who told me a story of woe about how in 1951 he had tried to enlist at the Hebrew University to get his M.A. (he had a B.Sc. from Baghdad). He was first refused a form to fill out, then by a hundred and one devices they tried to prevent his enrollment — and finally, with an expectant wife in Pardesiyya, his working as a dishwasher in Jerusalem, and the refusal of the Agency to give him a hut in a *ma'bara* near Jerusalem, he had to give up! All of which reminded me of how some 200 students or would-be students from Iraq came to the university in 1950–51 and, with the exception of a few, *suffohem weihed weihed* ("got rid of them one after the other"). But you ought to know better about this aspect of life in the Promised Land! . . .

February 5, 1969
Dear Gad,

. . . Well, as you by now know I am what they call here a stubborn Jew! I just don't give up! I know I may do much better outside of this country, but I have two very good reasons not to take the plunge. First: What the hell! What sort of *solution* is this business of just picking up one's belongings and leaving? . . . But I shall be more candid now that I am going to tell you of the second good reason for my stubbornness. This can be summed up thus: There is no possible escape from The Problem. I think it would be fair to say that there are today in the world four kinds of Jews: Israeli Israelis; Diaspora Israelis; "Free World" Jews, for whom Israel is a permanent preoccupation, example, and ultimate shelter; and oppressed and persecuted Jews (in various degrees), for whom Israel is dream itself. On the margin, on the lunatic fringe, and in crankdom are those who oppose Israel actively — whether for religious reasons (Neturei Karta et al.) or for class reasons (the American Council for Judaism). Well — where is the least evil? Does it not in the end boil down to mere personal predilection? If a man like our "uncle" Aharon finds satisfaction in being a wholesale merchant in the East End, and if you, sir, can live a full life working in your own line—who would guarantee that X would be happy working in journalism in Australia, Canada, or England? Hell, if it has fallen to our lot to be of the so-called desert generation, why not be a desert generation in this particular strip of land? But as I said, it's really a matter of sheer personal temperament.

. . . But there is at least one bright side; I have been slowly changing, not my views, but certain emphases—and it makes a world of difference, as you know. For instance, though I still maintain that Israel should—and will eventually—"de-Zionize" and "de-Westernize," I now think that with the Arab stand being what it is, it would be just unfair and above all impractical to ask the Zionists to do anything. Why should they, when they have a perfect reason not to? So instead of "de-Zionizing for peace," I now would say "peace for de-Zionizing!" This, as you will have realized, has its own impact on my other hobbyhorse, the communal problem. To put it briefly, the Orientals, though certainly a factor in normalizing Israel and her place in the Middle East, cannot hope to be such a factor as long as the Arabs are a threat *or* are capable of being depicted as a threat. Internally, too, the whole issue may take on steadily less significance as the country continues to prepare for repulsing the enemy and defending herself against the mortal threat of destruction and genocide and all the rest. (In all this it is almost totally immaterial whether these threats, enemies, and other catastrophes are real or imaginary!)

*I*NDEX

CPSIA information can be obtained
at www.ICGtesting.com
Printed in the USA
BVOW08s0352301116
469252BV00001B/50/P